HIGH COURT CASE SUMMARIES

FEDERAL INCOME TAXATION

Keyed to Freeland's Casebook on Federal Income Taxation 16th Edition

WEST®

A Thomson Reuters business

Mat #41224672

© West, a Thomson business, 2005, 2007, 2010
© 2012 Thomson Reuters
    610 Opperman Drive
    St. Paul, MN 55123
    1–800–313–9378
Printed in the United States of America

ISBN: 978–0–314–27919–4

Table of Contents

Alphabetical Table of Cases

CHAPTER ONE

Orientation

Mayo Foundation for Medical Education and Research v. United States

Instant Facts: When the Treasury Department (D) changed its rule to specifically exclude medical residents from its definition of "students" earning income incidental to their education, such that residents and their employers became automatically subject to Social Security taxes, the Mayo Foundation (P) sued, arguing that the new regulation was invalid and that it was entitled to a refund of Social Security taxes paid.

Black Letter Rule: When Congress has not directly addressed an issue but has delegated rule-making authority to an agency, and the agency's interpretation is a reasonable construction of what Congress has said, the agency's rule will be upheld.

Mayo Foundation for Medical Education and Research v. United States

(Employer/Taxpayer) v. *(Government)*

562 U.S. ___, 131 S.Ct. 704 (2011)

CHEVRON ANALYSIS, NOT *NATIONAL MUFFLER*, APPLIES IN TAX CASES

■ **INSTANT FACTS** When the Treasury Department (D) changed its rule to specifically exclude medical residents from its definition of "students" earning income incidental to their education, such that residents and their employers became automatically subject to Social Security taxes, the Mayo Foundation (P) sued, arguing that the new regulation was invalid and that it was entitled to a refund of Social Security taxes paid.

■ **BLACK LETTER RULE** When Congress has not directly addressed an issue but has delegated rule-making authority to an agency, and the agency's interpretation is a reasonable construction of what Congress has said, the agency's rule will be upheld.

■ **PROCEDURAL BASIS**

Supreme Court review of the federal court of appeals' decision in favor of the Government, upholding the Treasury regulation.

■ **FACTS**

Social Security law provides that, although most employers and employees are required to pay Social Security taxes on the wages the employees earn, an exception exists for students performing work for their schools as an incident to their education. Determinations as to whether the exception applied were made on a case-by-case basis, but the Social Security Administration (SSA) had uniformly held that medical residents did not qualify for the exemption. In 1998, the Eight Circuit Court of Appeals held that the SSA had to apply the same case-by-case approach to medical residents as well as other student employees, and 7,000 claims for refunds of Social Security taxes followed. The Treasury Department (D) then adopted a new regulation interpreting the statute, stating that employment is only incidental to education (and thus exempt from Social Security taxes) when the educational aspect of the relationship between the employee and the educational institution is predominant. The Department (D) provided an example of the regulation's application, specifically noting that medical residents' employment for forty or more hours per week was not incidental to the educational aspect of the relationship with the medical school. The Mayo Foundation (P) brought suit, arguing that it was entitled to a refund of taxes paid in on its residents' wages and that the new regulation was invalid. The federal district court agreed with Mayo (P), and the Government (D) appealed. The court of appeals reversed, and the Supreme Court granted Mayo's (P) petition for certiorari.

■ **ISSUE**

Is the Treasury regulation providing that medical residents are not students earning income as an incident to their education, such that they are not exempt from Social Security taxes, valid?

■ **DECISION AND RATIONALE**

(Roberts, J.) Yes. When Congress has not directly addressed an issue but has delegated rule-making authority to an agency, and the agency's interpretation is a reasonable construction of what Congress has said, the agency's rule will be upheld. The first question, applying the *Chevron* analysis, is whether Congress has answered the specific question at issue, and here it has not. Mayo (P) argues that because the dictionary definition of "student" clearly encompasses residents, the statute is not ambiguous. But we believe that the statute remains ambiguous as applied to working professionals such as those at issue here. The plain text of the statute does not definitively clear up whether the exemption applies to medical residents.

Second, under *Chevron*, we must determine whether the agency's interpretation of the ambiguity is based on a permissible construction of the statute. Mayo (P) urges us to apply a *National Muffler* analysis, under which a court might view an agency's interpretation with skepticism based on the way the regulation evolved; here, for instance, the district court noted that the rule was promulgated only after an adverse judicial decision, which places it in a more questionable light. The *Chevron* approach, by contrast, does not turn on such considerations. We conclude that *Chevron* principles apply with full force in the tax context. *Chevron* deference is appropriate when Congress has delegated authority to an agency to promulgate rules with the force of law and the agency was exercising that authority when making the rule in question. The Treasury's full-time employee rule satisfies *Chevron*.

Mayo (P) agrees that the educational aspect of the employer-employee relationship must be predominant, but it argues that residents who work forty or more hours per week should not be automatically excluded from that category. We disagree. Regulations, like legislation, often require line-drawing. The Treasury Department's (D) full-time employee rule facilitates the administrability of the regulation and avoids litigation. We do not doubt that medical residents are engaged in educational pursuit, but the question of whether they are students for purposes of Social Security taxes is a different matter. Because it is one to which Congress has not directly spoken, and because the Treasury Department's (D) rule is a reasonable construction of what Congress has said, the judgment of the court of appeals is affirmed.

Analysis:

Per the IRS, medical residents, hospitals, and universities that filed refund claims for periods ending before April 1, 2005 qualified for the student exception, such that their claims were allowed. For all post-April 1, 2005 periods, however, medical residents are not eligible for the student exception under the full-time employee rule, even though the Supreme Court's decision in this case was not rendered until 2011. In other words, prior to publication by the IRS of the new rule and example, medical residents continued to benefit from the exemption, at least on a case-by-case basis. Note, though, that exemption isn't entirely beneficial. If students are subject to Social Security taxation, they are also entitled to benefits such as disability and survivor payments, so the Court's holding here is not entirely bad news for residents (though the employer hospitals may have a different take on it).

■ CASE VOCABULARY

CHEVRON DEFERENCE: A two-part test under which a court will uphold a federal agency's construction of a federal statute if (1) the statute is ambiguous or does not address the question at issue, and (2) the agency's interpretation of the statute is reasonable. If the court finds that the legislature's intent is clearly expressed in the statute, then that intent is upheld. The U.S. Supreme Court enunciated the rule in *Chevron U.S.A., Inc. v. Natural Res. Def. Council, Inc.*, 467 U.S. 837, 842–43, 104 S. Ct. 2778, 2781–82 (1984).

CHAPTER TWO

Gross Income: The Scope of Section 61

Cesarini v. U.S.

Instant Facts: Taxpayers sought to recover income tax payments made on $4,467.00 worth of treasure-trove.

Black Letter Rule: Treasure-trove is specifically includable as gross income.

Old Colony Trust v. Commissioner

Instant Facts: After an employer had paid his employee's tax liability, the government sought to include the amount paid by the employer as taxable income to the employee.

Black Letter Rule: The discharge by a third party of an obligation owed by the taxpayer is an economic benefit to the taxpayer, and is includable as gross income.

Commissioner v. Glenshaw Glass Co.

Instant Facts: Two companies sought to avoid the payment of taxes on punitive damages awarded in unrelated litigation.

Black Letter Rule: Punitive damages awards are taxable as gross income.

Charley v. Commissioner

Instant Facts: The IRS sought to tax the president of a corporation for travel credits he earned on business trips paid for by the corporation.

Black Letter Rule: Travel credits converted into cash in a personal travel account established by an employer constitute gross income to the employee.

Helvering v. Independent Life Insurance Co.

Instant Facts: The government sought to tax the owner of a building for the rental value of the portion of the building occupied by the owner.

Black Letter Rule: The rental value of a building used by the owner does not constitute income within the meaning of the Sixteenth Amendment.

Dean v. Commissioner

Instant Facts: The government sought to tax the sole shareholders in a closely-held corporation for the rental value of property that was held by the corporation, and in which the shareholders lived.

Black Letter Rule: The fair market value of residential property that is provided by an employer is to be included in gross income, even if the employer is the taxpayer's wholly-owned corporation.

Cesarini v. U.S.

(Taxpayer) v. *(Government)*

18 Ohio Misc. 1, 296 F.Supp. 3 (N.D. Ohio 1969), affirmed per curiam 428 F.2d 812 (6th Cir. 1970)

GROSS INCOME IS ALL–INCLUSIVE, SO EVERY EXCLUSION MUST BE SPECIFICALLY CONTAINED IN THE CODE

■ **INSTANT FACTS** Taxpayers sought to recover income tax payments made on $4,467.00 worth of found treasure.

■ **BLACK LETTER RULE** Treasure-trove is specifically includable as gross income.

■ **PROCEDURAL BASIS**

Action to recover income tax payments following the Internal Revenue Commissioner's rejection of the refund claim.

■ **FACTS**

In 1957, Mr. and Mrs. Cesarini (P) purchased a piano for approximately $15.00. In 1964, while cleaning out the piano, the Cesarinis (P) found $4,467.00 in old currency. The Cesarinis (P) exchanged the old currency for new, and reported the total amount on their tax return for 1964. They were forced to pay tax on the money totaling $836.51, which they subsequently asked be refunded. The Commissioner refused and this appeal followed.

■ **ISSUE**

Is treasure-trove includable as gross income?

■ **DECISION AND RATIONALE**

(Young, D.J.) Yes. Treasure-trove is specifically includable as gross income. Section 61(a) of the Internal Revenue Code, which defines gross income, is an all inclusive section. It provides in pertinent part: "Except as otherwise provided in this subtitle, gross income means all income from whatever source derived, including (but not limited to) the following items...." Subsections (1) through (15) go on to list several types of income that are includable as gross income. The Supreme Court has stated that Section 61's broad language was used by Congress to exert the full measure of its taxing power under the Sixteenth Amendment. In support of its position, the United States (D) relies on Revenue Ruling 61, 1953–1, which holds that treasure-trove is gross income. The Cesarinis (P) argue that this ruling does not apply for two reasons. The first reason is that subsequent to the ruling, Congress enacted a provision in the Code that includes the value of prizes and awards in gross income. From this, the Cesarinis (P) argue that since no such specific section was passed expressly taxing treasure-trove, it is therefore a nontaxable gift. This line of reasoning overlooks the fact that income form all sources is taxed unless the taxpayer can point to an express exemption. The second argument regarding the inapplicability of the revenue ruling must be dismissed because the Cesarinis (P) rely on a Tax Court case decided prior to the revenue ruling; a case which, in any event, did not address the issue before this court. We also note that, although not cited by the government (D), the Treasury's own regulations include treasure-trove within the definition of gross income. We must also reject the Cesarinis' (P) argument that if any tax was due, it was in 1957, when the piano was purchased, and that by 1964 the statute of limitations for collecting the tax had expired. To determine what year the tax was collectable, we must first determine when the money was reduced to undisputed possession. That determination requires us to refer to the law of Ohio, the state where the money was found. This court finds that, under Ohio law, the $4,467 was not reduced to actual possession until its actual discovery in 1964. Therefore, the United States (D) was not barred from collecting the $836.41 in tax during that year.

Analysis:

This case provides an excellent overview of the variety of interpretive materials—legislative, judicial, and administrative—used to decipher the meaning of the Code. The court here appropriately begins with the language of the statute, noting its broad scope, and goes on to examine Supreme Court decisions holding that the statute was intended to exert the full measure of the congressional taxing power. The court then uses administrative materials to address the specific issue with which it was faced—whether treasure-trove was taxable as gross income. Curiously absent from the government's (D) brief was a treasury regulation that held treasure-trove to be taxable as gross income. Finally the court moves on to interpret Ohio law in order to determine when the Cesarinis (P) became liable for the tax, holding that the treasure-trove became theirs only after it was found.

■ **CASE VOCABULARY**

TREASURE–TROVE: Treasure found.

Old Colony Trust v. Commissioner

(Not Stated) v. *(Internal Revenue Commissioner)*
279 U.S. 716, 49 S.Ct. 499 (1929)

AN ECONOMIC BENEFIT WHICH INCREASES THE WEALTH OF THE TAXPAYER IS GROSS INCOME TO THE TAXPAYER

■ **INSTANT FACTS** After an employer had paid his employee's tax liability, the government sought to include the amount paid by the employer as taxable income to the employee.

■ **BLACK LETTER RULE** The discharge by a third party of an obligation owed by the taxpayer is an economic benefit to the taxpayer, and is includable as gross income.

■ **PROCEDURAL BASIS**

Certification to the United States Supreme Court from the Circuit Court of Appeals for the First Circuit, which reviewed a decision of the United States Board of Tax Appeals.

■ **FACTS**

The American Woolen Company adopted a resolution whereby it was to pay the income tax liability of its senior officers. Pursuant to the resolution, the American Woolen Company paid to the government the tax liability of William Wood, the company president. In 1919 and 1920, the American Woolen Company paid $681,169.88 and $351,179.27, respectively. The Board of Tax Appeals held that the income taxes paid were additional income to Mr. Wood.

■ **ISSUE**

Does the payment by an employer of the income taxes assessable against the employee constitute additional taxable income to such employee?

■ **DECISION AND RATIONALE**

(Taft, C.J.) Yes. The discharge by a third party of an obligation owed by the taxpayer is an economic benefit to the taxpayer, and is includable as gross income. The payment of tax by an employer is in consideration of services rendered by the employee, and is gain derived by the employee from his labor. We do not think that, having induced a third person to pay his income tax, a taxpayer may avoid the payment of a corresponding tax. The record shows that the taxes were imposed upon Mr. Wood and that he performed his services under the express agreement that his income taxes would be paid by his employer. The taxes were paid for valuable consideration—the services rendered by Mr. Wood. Therefore, the payment was income to Mr. Wood. We cannot accept the argument that the payment was a gift. The payment for services, even though voluntary, was nevertheless compensation within the statute. It is also argued that if these payments constitute income to the employee, the employer will be called upon to pay the tax imposed upon this additional income, and that the payment of the additional tax will create further income which will in turn be subject to tax, with the result that there would be a tax upon a tax. But we cannot address this question because the Treasury has not attempted to collect further taxes.

Analysis:

A taxpayer need not directly receive money to realize an economic benefit. It is enough that a transaction has increased the wealth of the taxpayer. One of the most common examples is the discharge of a debt. The court here held the $680,000 payment for taxes was income to Mr. Wood because Wood was made wealthier by that amount. The court's rejection of the argument that the payment was a gift serves as an example of the skepticism with which courts view "gifts" in the employer-employee relationship. The suspicion here is all the more appropriate since it is very likely that American Woolen Co. promulgated the policy to make its executives richer. The taxes paid by the company were nothing more than compensation income. Today, § 61(a)(12) expressly provides that the discharge of a debt is gross income.

Commissioner v. Glenshaw Glass Co.

(Internal Revenue Commissioner) v. *(Taxpayer)*

348 U.S. 426, 75 S.Ct. 473 (1955)

GROSS INCOME IS AN ACCESSION TO WEALTH, CLEARLY REALIZED, AND OVER WHICH THE TAXPAYER HAS COMPLETE DOMINION

■ **INSTANT FACTS** Two companies sought to avoid the payment of taxes on punitive damage awards in unrelated litigation.

■ **BLACK LETTER RULE** Punitive damage awards are taxable as gross income.

■ **PROCEDURAL BASIS**

Certiorari to the United States Supreme Court, from the Court of Appeals decision to affirm the Tax Court's separate rulings that punitive damages are not taxable.

■ **FACTS**

Glenshaw Glass Co. (Glenshaw) (P) and William Goldman Theatres, Inc. (Goldman) (P) were involved in unrelated antitrust litigation. As part of a settlement, Glenshaw (P) received $800,000, of which $324,529.94 represented punitive damages. Glenshaw (P) did not report the latter amount as income. In its antitrust suit, Goldman (P) was awarded treble damages amounting to $375,000. As did Glenshaw (P), Goldman (P) failed to report the punitive amount—$250,000—as taxable income. The Internal Revenue Commissioner sought to recover the deficiencies, but both the Tax Court and the Court of Appeals found for the taxpayers.

■ **ISSUE**

Are punitive damages gross income under the Internal Revenue Code?

■ **DECISION AND RATIONALE**

(Warren, C.J.) Yes. Punitive damages are includable as gross income. In pertinent part, the Internal Revenue Code defines gross income as "gains or profits and income derived from any source whatever." We have previously held that this language was intended to exert Congress' full taxing power. Consequently, this Court has given the phrase liberal construction in order to recognize Congress' intent to tax all gains unless specifically exempted. Here we have instances of undeniable accessions to wealth, clearly realized, and over which the taxpayers have complete dominion. The fact that payments were extracted from wrongdoers does not detract from their character as taxable income. Moreover, it would be anomalous to permit compensatory damages to be taxed, while holding that punitive damages are not taxable. We find no evidence of an intent on the part of Congress to exempt these payments. We also reject the argument that re-enactment of the statute without change since the Board Tax of Appeals held punitive damages nontaxable indicated congressional satisfaction with that holding. We have no indication that the Board's decision was before Congress. Furthermore, immediately after that holding, the Commissioner published his nonacquiescence, maintaining the position that punitive damages are taxable. Thus, it cannot be said that Congress intended to codify the holding of Board of Tax Appeals.

Analysis:

In holding that punitive damages are gross income, the Supreme Court affirms the presumption that all gains are taxable, unless they are specifically exempted. This case is oft-cited for the definition of gross income that it provides, a definition that has become standard. According to the Court, gross income is an "accession to wealth, clearly realized, and over which the taxpayer has complete dominion." The test is purposefully broad in order to fulfill what the Court deems to be Congress's intent—to exert the full measure of its constitutional taxing power.

Charley v. Commissioner

(Taxpayer) v. *(Internal Revenue Commissioner)*

91 F.3d 72 (9th Cir. 1996)

ECONOMIC BENEFITS ARE GROSS INCOME, REGARDLESS OF THEIR SOURCE

■ **INSTANT FACTS** The IRS sought to tax the president of a corporation for travel credits he earned on business trips paid for by the corporation.

■ **BLACK LETTER RULE** Travel credits converted into cash in a personal travel account established by an employer constitute gross income to the employee.

■ PROCEDURAL BASIS

Appeal to the Ninth Circuit challenging the finding of the Tax Court that travel credits constituted gross income.

■ FACTS

Dr. Philip Charley (P) was the president and, together with his wife, majority owner of Truesdail Laboratories (Truesdail). When Dr. Charley (P) chose to travel by air on business trips, Truesdail would bill the client for round-trip first class travel. But Dr. Charley (P) would purchase a coach ticket for the trip, instructing the travel agent to charge him the first-class price. Dr. Charley (P) would then use his frequent flier miles, which were earned in connection with his business travel for Truesdail, to upgrade from coach to first-class. Finally, Dr. Charley (P) would instruct the travel agent to credit is personal travel account for the difference between the coach ticket and the first-class ticket. During 1988, Dr. Charley (P) received $3,149.93 in his personal travel account from this scheme.

■ ISSUE

Do travel credits converted to cash in a personal travel account established by an employer constitute gross income to the employee for federal income tax purposes?

■ DECISION AND RATIONALE

(O'Scannlain, Cir. J.) Yes. Travel credits converted into cash in a personal travel account established by an employer constitute gross income to the employee. In *Commissioner v. Glenshaw Glass Co.* [holding that punitive damages are gross income under the Internal Revenue Code], the Supreme Court defined gross income as an accession to wealth, clearly realized, and over which the taxpayer has complete dominion. The tax court found that Dr. Charley (P) could either use the credits or redeem them for cash. The tax court also found that Dr. Charley (P) was wealthier after the transaction. We disagree with Dr. Charley (P) that no taxable event occurred. We do not reach the issue, as Dr. Charley (P) would have us, of whether frequent flyer miles constitute gross income. Rather, this case can be analyzed in one of two ways. The travel credits that were converted to cash can be characterized as additional compensation equal to the difference between the first-class rate and the coach rate. In the alternative, if it is assumed that the frequent flyer miles were not given to Dr. Charley (P), then the transaction can be viewed as dealing in property, expressly taxable under IRC § 61(a)(3). The gain from the disposition of property is equal to the difference between "amount realized" (i.e., the sum of any money received plus the fair market value of other property received) and the property's adjusted basis. Because Dr. Charley (P) received the miles at no cost, he had a zero basis in them. He then exchanged these miles for cash, resulting in a gain also equal to the difference between the first-class rate and the rate for flying coach. We therefore hold the travel credits to be taxable income under the facts of this case.

Analysis:

This case is somewhat anomalous with respect to the taxability of frequent flyer miles earned from business trips. It is an issue that Congress and the IRS have struggled with. There should be little doubt that frequent flyer miles earned on business trips paid for by an employer constitute gross income, but the problem comes with their valuation. Technically, the fair market value of flyer miles at the time of redemption is the "amount realized," whether characterized as a dealing in property or compensation income. However, the nature of plane tickets makes it difficult to determine the fair market value because the same ticket can wildly vary in price. The IRS therefore refrains from taxing these miles, unless they are traded in for cash, a point at which valuation becomes very easy. Had Dr. Charley (P) not cashed in his miles, he may not have been taxed on their use. Notice the similarities between this case and *Old Colony Trust v. Commissioner*, in which the Court held that the payment of taxes by an employer on his employee's behalf also constituted gross income to the employee. In both cases, the employee was given a "perk" that resulted in the realization of gross income.

■ **CASE VOCABULARY**

BASIS: The acquisition cost of any property.

Helvering v. Independent Life Insurance Co.

(*Internal Revenue Commissioner*) v. (*Taxpayer*)

292 U.S. 371 (1934)

PERSONAL IMPUTED INCOME IS NOT GROSS INCOME

■ **INSTANT FACTS** The government sought to tax the owner of a building for the rental value of the portion of the building occupied by the owner.

■ **BLACK LETTER RULE** The rental value of a building used by the owner does not constitute income within the meaning of the Sixteenth Amendment.

■ PROCEDURAL BASIS

Certiorari to the United States Supreme Court from the Court of Appeals, which affirmed the decision the Board of Tax Appeals.

■ FACTS

Independent Life Insurance Co. (Independent) (P) owned a building in which it occupied a space for which it did not charge itself rent. The government then sought to tax Independent (P) for the fair rental value of the portion of the building which it occupied.

■ ISSUE

Must a taxpayer include in gross income the rental value of a building owned and occupied by the taxpayer.

■ DECISION AND RATIONALE

(Butler, J.) No. The rental value of the building used by the owner does not constitute income within the meaning of the Sixteenth Amendment. Moreover, if the statute lays taxes on the part of the building occupied by the owner or upon the rental value of that space, it cannot be sustained, for that would be to lay a direct tax requiring apportionment.

Analysis:

This case provides an introduction to imputed income, which has been defined as a flow of satisfactions from durable goods owned and used by the taxpayer or from goods and services arising out of the personal exertions of the taxpayer on his own behalf. In other words, it's the value of one's own services or goods that are used to benefit oneself. For example, if an attorney represents himself in a case, he has realized a benefit equal to the value of his legal services. This benefit is *imputed income.* In this case, the imputed income was the rental value of the building owned and occupied by the taxpayer. The Supreme Court holds that this is not "income" within the meaning of the Sixteenth Amendment, and not taxable by Congress. Be wary of always categorizing imputed income as non-taxable, however. Even benefits that are not tangible can lead to taxable income if the benefit results in a financial gain for the taxpayer. Here, there was no tangible benefit to the company because it owned the building and there was no requirement that it receive rent for that building.

Dean v. Commissioner

(Taxpayer) v. *(Internal Revenue Commissioner)*
187 F.2d 1019 (3d Cir. 1951)

FINANCIAL BENEFITS RECEIVED FROM ONE'S OWN CORPORATION ARE NOT IMPUTED INCOME AND ARE, THEREFORE, TAXABLE

■ **INSTANT FACTS** The government sought to tax the sole shareholders in a closely-held corporation for the rental value of property that was held by the corporation, and in which the shareholders lived.

■ **BLACK LETTER RULE** The fair market value of residential property that is provided by an employer is to be included in gross income, even if the employer is the taxpayer's wholly-owned corporation.

■ **PROCEDURAL BASIS**

Appeal to the Third Circuit from a Tax Court decision holding the fair market rental value of their home owned by taxpayers' wholly-owned corporation was to be included as gross income.

■ **FACTS**

Mr. and Mrs. Dean (P) were the owners of Nemours Corporation. In 1931, a bank insisted that Mrs. Nemours (P) transfer the family home to the corporation. After the transfer, Mr. and Mrs. Nemours (P) continued to occupy the property as a residence.

■ **ISSUE**

May a taxpayer be taxed on the rental value of property held in the name of a corporation of which the taxpayer is the sole shareholder?

■ **DECISION AND RATIONALE**

(Goodrich, Cir. J.) Yes. The fair market value of residential property that is provided by an employer is to be included as gross income, even if the employer is the taxpayer's wholly-owned corporation. It was the taxpayer's legal obligation to provide a family home and if he did it by the occupancy of a property which was held in the name of a corporation of which he was president, we think it fair that the fair value of that occupancy was income to him. The fact that the corporation was a mere shell does not matter; it was a separate entity.

Analysis:

Here, the value of the residence in which the taxpayers lived is taxable because, but for the company providing the home, the taxpayers would have had to pay for a home. Thus, by receiving the value of a home (i.e., by not having to pay for housing), the taxpayers received a benefit of having extra money. Unlike in *Helvering*, where there was no actual benefit realized because the company was not otherwise required to pay rent, there was an actual benefit here. In essence, while the taxpayers in *Helvering* were not paying rent, it was because they themselves owned the building, not because their employer had provided them space. The distinction is critical because in the first case, where the taxpayers owned and occupied the building, there was no tax liability, but in the second, where the taxpayers occupied the building but did not own it, there was. The distinction seems to be stretched in this case, because

---

the taxpayers were the sole owners of the entity that owned the home. The court gave this little consideration, however, finding that since the entity is a separate being under the law, it would be treated as such for tax purposes as well.

CHAPTER THREE

Exclusion of Gifts and Inheritances

Commissioner v. Duberstein

Instant Facts: The Commissioner asked the United States Supreme Court to consider two cases which had reached different outcomes in different circuits. In Duberstein, the taxpayer had received a car from a business associate after providing useful information, and in Stanton, the taxpayer had received a $20,000 gratuity from his employer upon his resignation.

Black Letter Rule: A transfer is a gift, excludable from income under section 102(a) [General income does not include the value of property acquired by gift, bequest, devise or inheritance.] if it proceeds from a detached and disinterested generosity motivated by affection, respect, charity or similar feeling. Whether a transfer meets this standard is a matter of fact to be determined by the district court.

Lyeth v. Hoey

Instant Facts: The IRS treated the amount received by Lyeth (P) from a settlement of the contest of his grandmother's will as income rather than an excludable inheritance, and required him to pay taxes on it. Lyeth sued for a refund.

Black Letter Rule: Property received by an heir under a settlement agreement ending the contest of a will is received as a result of the heir's rights as an heir and is thus an inheritance which is excluded from gross income.

Wolder v. Commissioner

Instant Facts: Wolder (P) entered into an agreement to provide Mrs. Boyce with legal services for life if she would leave him some stock in her will. The IRS claimed this was taxable income.

Black Letter Rule: Payment for services is income as provided under Section 61(a) Int.Rev.Code, even if it is made through a bequest in a will.

Commissioner v. Duberstein

(IRS) v. *(Taxpayer)*

363 U.S. 278, 80 S.Ct. 1190 (1960)

SUPREME COURT REFUSES TO ESTABLISH A NEW TEST OF WHAT CONSTITUTES A GIFT FOR TAX PURPOSES

■ **INSTANT FACTS** The Commissioner asked the United States Supreme Court to consider two cases which had reached different outcomes in different circuits. In Duberstein, the taxpayer had received a car from a business associate after providing useful information, and in Stanton, the taxpayer had received a $20,000 gratuity from his employer upon his resignation.

■ **BLACK LETTER RULE** A transfer is a gift, excludable from income under section 102(a) [General income does not include the value of property acquired by gift, bequest, devise or inheritance.] If it proceeds from a detached and disinterested generosity motivated by affection, respect, charity or similar feeling. Whether a transfer meets this standard is a matter of fact to be determined by the district court.

■ **PROCEDURAL BASIS**

Appeal to the United States Supreme Court of two separate and apparently contradictory opinions issued by the Second and Sixth Circuits.

■ **FACTS**

Commissioner v. Duberstein: Duberstein (D) was president of Duberstein Iron & Metal. He did business in that capacity with Berman, who was president of Mohawk Metal Corp. Berman asked Duberstein (D) for the names of potential customers. Duberstein (D) provided this information. Most of their transactions were carried out over the phone, though Duberstein (D) did state that he knew Berman personally. Berman found Duberstein's (D) information so useful that he wished to give him a gift. Berman called Duberstein (D) to inform him that he was giving him a brand new Cadillac. [This was back in 1951, when Cadillacs were still cool.] Duberstein (D) stated that that was not necessary, but Berman insisted. Duberstein (D) had not requested such a gift, and already had two cars of his own. Berman deducted the cost of the car as a business expense. Duberstein (D) acknowledged that he did not believe that Berman would have given him the car if he had not provided Berman with the helpful information. Duberstein (D) did not report the car as income, arguing it was a gift. The Commissioner (P) asserted a deficiency, arguing the car was not a gift, but rather remuneration for services rendered, and won in district court. The Court of Appeals for the Sixth Circuit reversed and found that the car was a gift. The Commissioner (P) then sought cert before the United States Supreme Court. *Stanton v. United States*: By 1942, Stanton (P) had worked for Trinity Church for ten years. He was comptroller of the Church Corporation and president of Trinity Operating Company, the company that managed the church's extensive real estate holdings. He resigned on November 30, 1942 to form his own business. At that time his annual salary was $22,500. The Trinity Operating Company board of directors voted to grant him a gratuity of $20,000 to be paid in ten monthly installments of $2,000. The board explained this action as arising from their great personal fondness for Stanton (P) and in recognition of his having done a good job in a very difficult time. However, there was also some indication of possible friction between Stanton (P) and the board. The board had decided to fire the company's treasurer and Stanton (P) had attempted to intervene on his behalf. The board fired the treasurer anyway and resented Stanton's (P) interference. The treasurer was given a six-month settlement, which was similar to what

Stanton received, but without the word gratuity. Stanton's (P) secretary was also given a gratuity when she resigned at the same time as Stanton (P). Stanton (P) did not include the gratuity in his income. The Commissioner (D) asserted a delinquency. Stanton (P) paid the delinquency and then sued for a refund. Stanton (P) won in district court, where a bare finding was made that the gratuity was a gift. This was overturned by the Court of Appeals for the Second Circuit. Stanton (P) petitioned for cert. before the Supreme Court. The Commissioner (D) acquiesced in order to get a resolution to the apparent disparity between the Sixth and Second Circuits. It was the Commissioner's assertion in these two cases that the Supreme Court should adopt a new test to define a gift for these purposes. The Commissioner suggested several elements to this test. First, payments from an employer to an employee, even when wholly voluntary, ought to be taxable. Second, the concept of a gift is inconsistent with anything the donor exempts as a business expense. Third, that a gift must have a "personal" element. And finally, that a corporation can't properly make a gift of its assets.

■ ISSUE

Is a gift for purposes of *Section 102(a) Int.Rev.Code* properly defined as a transfer that proceeds from a detached and disinterested generosity motivated by affection, respect, admiration, charity or other similar feeling?

■ DECISION AND RATIONALE

(Brennan, J.) Yes. We do not believe that a new test is necessary. The principles governing the determination of what is a gift in this circumstance are necessarily general. The specifics have been sufficiently spelled out by prior opinions of this Court. In these prior opinions several requirements have been established. First a gift can not be a transfer that is required under any moral or legal obligation. It can not be a transfer that is based on the anticipation of future economic benefit. It can not be a transfer made in exchange for services rendered, even if the donor receives no economic benefit. For a transfer to be a gift it must proceed from a detached and disinterested generosity. A gift should result from feelings of affection, respect, admiration, charity or similar emotions. Thus, the most important test of whether a transfer is a gift is the underlying intention of the donor. The test proposed by the Commissioner would extend the limitations on the meaning of gift far beyond what is justified by the statute or the case law. It is true that it is likely that most transfers from employer to employee are not gifts. The fact that the donor deducts a gift as a business expense is relevant to determining the donor's intentions, as is the personal contact between the parties, and the status of the donor as a corporation. But these are factual questions to be considered in the context of the entire transaction. We do not want to create a situation where a court which is supposed to be deciding if a transfer was a gift instead becomes a trial of the appropriateness of the donor's business deductions, or a matter of fiduciary or corporate law. The tax tribunals are busy enough without having to decide whether a corporation should legally have made a transfer that could be considered a gift. Whether a transfer is a gift is closely tied to the specific circumstances. It is a non-technical decision with which the trier of fact is likely to have personal experience. Therefore primary weight must be given to the conclusions of the trier of fact. Those who feel that this is too messy or leads to too much litigation must apply to Congress for greater specificity within the statute. Because this is a question of fact appellate review will be quite limited. If the trier of facts in the case is a jury the judgment must stand unless it is found that reasonable men could not differ on the issue. And if the trier of fact is a judge then the appellate court must find the judgment "clearly erroneous". Based on this we find that the Court of Appeals for the Sixth Circuit was incorrect in reversing the original finding in *Duberstein*, and that the car was not a gift as it was transferred in recognition of services rendered and in the hope that future services would follow. In *Stanton* we are in disagreement. We do not feel that the judgment of the Court of Appeals for the Second Circuit can stand. However, the findings of the District Court were so sparse that they gave no insight as to the court's concepts of the determining facts and legal standard. Thus we vacate the judgment of the Court of Appeals and the case is remanded to the District Court for further findings not inconsistent with this opinion.

■ CONCURRENCE AND DISSENT

(Frankfurter, J.) The only addition made by this case to previous decisions on this subject is the direction that it is the trier of fact's job to search among the competing motives found in each case to discover the intent that was at the root of the transfer. If they are to do this we should not create new phrases which lower courts will inevitably spend a great deal of energy interpreting. I am particularly concerned about the direction by the Court that lower courts should rely upon their "experience with human affairs" or their understanding of "the mainsprings of human conduct." The experience and understanding of human conduct vary greatly from one person to another. Thus relying on these will lead to a great diversity in the administration of the tax laws. And I believe that the tax law should be as uniform as possible in a country such as ours. I agree with the judgment in *Duberstein.* But I would have upheld the Appellate Court in *Stanton.*

Analysis:

The term "gift" is not defined in § 102(a). This section simply states: Gross income shall not include the value of property acquired by gift, bequest, devise, or inheritance. Under common law, a gift is any voluntary transfer of property to another made freely without obligation or consideration. Thus we end up with a definition of gift that leaves the courts with the problem of determining the intent of the donor. Deciding a person's intent is a subjective thing, and leads to disparate judgments. The test proposed here by the Commissioner would have cleared up the disparities, but the Supreme Court feels that it would go too far. What the Court is basically doing here is refusing to legislate from the bench, and referring the problem to Congress if it needs to be fixed. Interestingly, Congress did eventually take up at least part of this issue. The result is found in § 102(c), which specifically requires any transfer from an employer to an employee to be included in gross income. Therefore, under current law *Stanton* would have had to include the gratuity he received in his gross income.

■ CASE VOCABULARY

"CLEARLY ERRONEOUS": The standard applied when an Appellate Court reviews the findings of a judge. A finding can be clearly erroneous even if supported by some evidence when the Appellate Court after reviewing all of the evidence has a definite and firm conviction that a mistake has been made.

GRATUITOUS: Freely given without consideration.

SHIBBOLETH: A saying particular to a group of people, something that definitively identifies a group.

TRANSFER: To convey or pass over possession or control from one to another. Gifts, a sale, a transfer of title, are all examples of possible ways a transfer can take place.

Lyeth v. Hoey

(Heir) v. *(Tax Collector)*

305 U.S. 188, 59 S.Ct. 155 (1938)

PROPERTY RECEIVED BY AN HEIR FROM SETTLEMENT OF A WILL CONTEST IS STILL AN INHERITANCE

■ **INSTANT FACTS** The IRS treated the amount received by Lyeth (P) from a settlement of the contest of his grandmother's will as income rather than an excludable inheritance, and required him to pay taxes on it. Lyeth sued for a refund.

■ **BLACK LETTER RULE** Property received by an heir under a settlement agreement ending the contest of a will is received as a result of the heir's rights as an heir and is thus an inheritance which is excluded from gross income.

■ **PROCEDURAL BASIS**

Appeal to the Supreme Court of the United States of the overturning of the District Courts summary judgment in Lyeth's (P) favor by the Circuit Court of Appeals.

■ **FACTS**

Mary B. Longyear (Longyear) died in 1931. Her heirs under Massachusetts's law were her four surviving children and two grandsons by her deceased daughter. Under her will she left these heirs only small legacies. The remained of her $3,000,000 estate was left to a trust, the purpose of which was to provide income for the preservation of the papers of Mary Baker Eddy the founder of the Christian Scientists. The heirs objected to this will claiming that there was a lack of testamentary capacity that there had been undue influence in its creation. [Personally, if I had a grandmother who could leave me $3,000,000 I would spend some time with her so I, hopefully, wouldn't have these kinds of issues.] The probate court held a hearing on the matter and decided there was enough basis to the heirs' claim to order issues framed for a jury trial. At this point the heirs and the legatees reached a settlement agreement. Under this agreement the will would be admitted to probate, and the pecuniary bequests to individuals would be honored, but the residual bequest would be disregarded with the residual after the pecuniary bequests being divided between the heirs and the trust. This was approved by the probate court and a decree was entered on April 26, 1932. As a result of the agreement Lyeth (P), who was one of Longyear's two grandsons, received property worth $141,484.03 in July of 1933. The Commissioner of Internal Revenue treated the whole amount as income received in 1933, and assessed a tax of $56,389.65. Lyeth (P) paid this amount and then sued for a refund. The District Court entered a summary judgment in his favor, but this was overturned by the Court of Appeals.

■ **ISSUE**

Should the property received by an heir as the result of a settlement to the contest of a will be considered an inheritance, which is excluded from gross income by statute?

■ **DECISION AND RATIONALE**

(Hughes, J.) Yes. State law differs from state to state on the question of whether property received under the settlement of a contested will can be considered to have been inherited. In Massachusetts an amount received from the parts of a will left unmodified by the settlement are considered to have been inherited, but those parts received through the modifications imposed under the settlement are considered in the same light as property received under the terms of a contract. In coming to the

---

conclusion that they did in this case the Appellate Court followed Massachusetts's law. This was a mistake. While state law determines who is an heir, and how the rights of an heir may be vindicated, the definition of an inheritance for purposes of applying a federal tax statute is not a local matter. Congress intended that there should be a uniform application of a nationwide scheme of taxation. We further believe that Congress intended the word "inheritance" in this statute to have a broad meaning. (In the case the justice refers to Section 22(b)(3) of the *Revenue Act of 1932*; the current enactment of this provision is found in *Section 102(a) Int.Rev.Code*. It states: Gross income does not include the value of property acquired by gift, bequest, devise or inheritance.) This intention is apparent in the way Congress substituted the word "inheritance" for the earlier term "descent" out of a desire to more fully include both real and personal property. Congress' intent to exempt inheritances broadly can also be seen in the fact that while Congress has now imposed a tax on the whole of estates they have shown no intention to tax this money again once it is distributed. There is no question that Lyeth (P) was an heir under Massachusetts law. This status is what gave him standing to contest the will, and thus it is through this status that he recovered under the settlement. If instead of settling, the contest had gone forward and he had been granted a judgment for part of the estate, that would clearly be an inheritance. It is the same under a settlement. He was an heir in fact. What he was entitled to as a result of being an heir was a matter of his grandmother's will and its validity. But the money he did receive was an inheritance. The judgment of the Circuit Court of Appeals is reversed and that of the District Court is affirmed.

Analysis:

In this case, as in *Duberstein*, the Court declines to place limitations on the exclusions found in 102(a) that are not clearly required by the statute. Just as the word "gift" is not defined in § 102(a), neither is the word "inheritance." This omission has existed since the Income Tax of 1913. Therefore, Congress had ample opportunity to define and limit these terms if it chose. What this case established is that inheritance is defined broadly. The result is that money received in settlement of a will contest is considered an inheritance, and in fact so are virtually all transfers of property made with donative intent in the devolution of a decedent's estate.

■ CASE VOCABULARY

HEIR: A person who under law will inherit from an estate if there is no valid will.

LEGATEE: A person who takes property under the terms of a will.

PECUNIARY BEQUESTS: A gift of money through a will.

RESIDUARY BEQUEST: The gift through a will of all of the remaining estate not already disposed of under the will.

Wolder v. Commissioner

(Lawyer) v. *(IRS)*

493 F.2d 608 (2d Cir. 1974)

MONEY EARNED BY PROVIDING SERVICES IS INCOME AND NOT AN INHERITANCE EVEN WHEN PAID THROUGH A WILL

■ **INSTANT FACTS** Wolder (P) entered into an agreement to provide Mrs. Boyce with legal services for life if she would leave him some stock in her will. The IRS claimed this was taxable income.

■ **BLACK LETTER RULE** Payment for services is income as provided under *Section 61(a) Int.Rev. Code*, even if it is made through a bequest in a will.

■ **PROCEDURAL BASIS**

Appeal to the United States Court of Appeals, Second Circuit, of a ruling in Tax Court.

■ **FACTS**

In 1947 Margaret K Boyce (Boyce) entered into an agreement with Victor R. Wolder (Wolder) (P) which included mutual promises. Wolder (P) promised to provide Boyce with legal services for as long as she lived without charging her. Boyce promised to leave Wolder (P) her stock in White Laboratories Inc. or such other securities as might go to her in the event of a merger or consolidation of White Laboratories. White Laboratories merged with Schering Corp., and so what was actually left to Wolder (P) was 750 shares in Schering and $15,845.00. When Boyce died her residuary legatees challenged the bequest to Wolder (P). [Amazing how much time people spend challenging wills, isn't it?] The New York court found that Wolder (P) had provided the services and that he was entitled to the bequest. The Commissioner of Internal Revenue sought to tax the property Wolder (P) had received as income. Wolder (P) objected claiming that the property was an inheritance excluded from income under *Section 102(a) Int.Rev.Code*. The Tax Court found the property to be taxable income. Wolder (P) appealed.

■ **ISSUE**

Is a bequest made under an agreement to provide payment for the provision of services excluded from gross income as an inheritance under the terms of Section 102(a)?

■ **DECISION AND RATIONALE**

(Oakes, J.) No. Wolder (P) relies on Section 102(a) Int.Rev.Code which does provide that "Gross income does not include the value of property acquired by gift, bequest, devise, or inheritance." And he relies on the holding in *United States v. Merriam* [cash bequest to executors in lieu of compensation were an inheritance and not income as they were simply bequests conditioned on assuming the role of executor, and not payment for services]. We do not believe that the decision in *Merriam* really stands up to analysis in this day and age when we look to substance and not to form. More importantly *Merriam* is not applicable to the facts of this case. Here there is not question that the parties contracted for services which were rendered and that therefore the provision of Boyce's will were in satisfaction of that contract. In Commissioner v. Duberstein, the Supreme Court held that the true test of whether something was a gift under Section 102(a) is whether the transfer is a bona fide gift and not a form of compensation. This is determined by an examination of the intent of the donor as it applies to the reason for the transfer.

Applying that test here it is clear that the intent or reason for the bequest was to pay for the legal services provided. If Boyce had not included the bequest in her will as promised Wolder (P) could have sued for its payment under their agreement, and if he had done so the proceeds of that suit would have been included in his income. Section 61(a) specifically provides that "Except as otherwise provided in this subtitle, gross income means all income from whatever source derived including" ... "(1) Compensation for services, including fees, commissions and similar items ..." Further we do not feel that the fact that under New York law this transfer is considered to be an inheritance is relevant here. Matters of the federal tax code can't be determined by New York state law.

Analysis:

One of the keys to this decision is stated by the court early on: "we look to substance and not to form." The only justification for arguing that the bequest to Wolder (P) in this case should be excluded from income is that it came to him through a will. This is a matter of form. The obvious intent behind and reason for the bequest was to pay Wolder (P) for services. This is the substance of the matter, despite the form in which the transfer was made. This is true for the other transfers excluded under § 102(a). A gift, given as compensation for past services or in anticipation of possible future services, is not excluded from income because in substance it is compensation and it is only in form that it is a gift.

■ CASE VOCABULARY

IN LIEU OF: A term used to indicate the substitution of one thing for another, basically meaning: instead of. It specifically excludes the meaning: in addition to.

TESTAMENTARY TRANSFERS: To change the ownership of property from one person to another through the instrument of a will.

CHAPTER FOUR

Employee Benefits

Herbert G. Hatt

Instant Facts: The majority shareholder and manager of a funeral home sought to exclude from gross income the rental value of his residence, which was provided by the corporation.

Black Letter Rule: The fact that a taxpayer is a shareholder in a closely held corporation does not alone disqualify him from excluding lodging benefits furnished for the convenience of the corporation.

Herbert G. Hatt

(Taxpayer)

28 T.C.M. 1194 (1969), affirmed per curiam 457 F.2d 499 (7th Cir. 1972)

CLOSE SCRUTINY IS REQUIRED OF EXCLUSIONS FOR LODGING GIVEN IN CLOSELY HELD CORPORATIONS

■ **INSTANT FACTS** The majority shareholder and manager of a funeral home sought to exclude from gross income the rental value of his residence, which was provided by the corporation.

■ **BLACK LETTER RULE** The fact that a taxpayer is a shareholder in a closely held corporation does not alone disqualify him from excluding lodging benefits furnished for the convenience of the corporation.

■ **PROCEDURAL BASIS**

Not provided.

■ **FACTS**

Herbert Hatt (P) was the majority shareholder, president, and general manager of a funeral home business in Evansville, Indiana. The funeral home contained both, an apartment in which Hatt (P) and his wife resided from 1957 to 1962, and a dormitory to house an ambulance crew. The business phone rang in Hatt's (P) apartment, and he often met customers in the apartment after regular business hours. Moreover, the custom in Evansville was to have a funeral home employee to deal with customers live on the premises. Although corporate income tax returns were filed, Hatt (P) did not file a personal income tax return from 1957 to 1960, inclusive.

■ **ISSUE**

Is the majority shareholder of a corporation disqualified from excluding the value of lodging provided to him for the convenience of the corporation?

■ **DECISION AND RATIONALE**

No. The fact that a taxpayer is a shareholder in a closely held corporation does not alone disqualify him from excluding lodging benefits furnished for the convenience of the corporation. Section 119(a) of the Internal Revenue Code provides: "There shall be excluded from gross income of an employee the value of any meal or lodging furnished to him, his spouse, or any of his dependents by or on behalf of his employer for the convenience of the employer." For the employee to be eligible for exclusion, subsection (a)(2) requires that the "employee be required to accept the lodging on the business premises of his employer as a condition of his employment." Hence, the statute requires that the lodging be: (1) on the business premises; (2) a condition of employment; and (3) for the convenience of the employer. The government contends that the last two conditions are not met. To meet the "condition of employment" requirement the employee must be required to accept the lodging in order to enable him to properly perform the duties of his employment. The test is basically the same for the "convenience of the employer" requirement. We believe this test has been met here. The funeral business is such that it requires 24 hour service. Customers expect for someone to be available at all times. The custom in the Evansville (P) area bears this out. Every funeral home in the area had a designated employee live on the premises. The facts show that Hatt (P) often conducted business in the apartment after regular business hours. While the ambulance crew could have taken calls, they were not authorized to handle business matters. We think that Hatt (P) has made the requisite showing for the claimed exclusion under § 119.

Analysis:

The IRS closely scrutinizes § 119 exclusions in the context of closely held corporations. In providing for the exclusion under § 119, Congress realized that some employment benefits are provided for the benefit of the employer, and not as additional compensation to the employee. In this case, the government argued that because the employee had full control over the terms of the employment and could decide what was and was not convenient for the employer, the lodging was neither a prerequisite for employment nor was it for the convenience of the employer. The court rejects the government's argument and adopts an objective test. The court looked at the purported business reasons for furnishing the lodging, focusing on the facts that someone had to be present at all times, that Hatt (P) was on call twenty-four hours a day, and that the lodging was an industry standard. Note, however, that the court's holding hinges on the fact that the business was a corporation. Had this been a sole proprietorship, Hatt (P) would have lost the exclusion because a person cannot be his own employee.

CHAPTER FIVE

Awards

Allen J. McDonell

Instant Facts: A taxpayer sought a tax refund, claiming the erroneous inclusion as gross income of an amount attributable to an employer-provided trip.

Black Letter Rule: The fact that an employer chooses which employees will be sent on a business trip by way of a drawing does not make the trip a taxable prize or award.

Allen J. McDonell

(Taxpayer)
26 T.C.M. 115 (1967)

SOME "AWARDS" OR "PRIZES" RECEIVED IN AN EMPLOYMENT CONTEXT MAY ESCAPE SECTION 74

■ **INSTANT FACTS** A taxpayer sought a tax refund, claiming the erroneous inclusion as gross income of an amount attributable to an employer-provided trip.

■ **BLACK LETTER RULE** The fact that an employer chooses which employees will be sent on a business trip by way of a drawing does not make the trip a taxable prize or award.

■ **PROCEDURAL BASIS**

Action for a refund in United States Tax Court.

■ **FACTS**

Mr. and Mrs. McDonell (P) sought a refund for taxes paid on $600, which they claim they erroneously included as gross income. Mr. McDonell (P) was employed by the Dairy Equipment Co. (DECO) as a home office salesman. In 1959, DECO initiated an incentive sales contest for its distributors and territorial salesman. The contest winners and their wives received a trip to Hawaii. Although the contest was not open to home office salesmen, DECO implemented a policy whereby one home office salesman for every three contest winners would be sent along to make sure the contest winners enjoyed themselves and, more importantly, to guide discussions relating to DECO's business and to enhance the DECO's image. The home office salesmen were chosen by way of a random drawing in order to avoid discontent and dissatisfaction. Those chosen were expected to go, and were told that the trip should not be considered vacation and that they were expected to participate in all planned activities and not go off alone. Because the company believed that it would be impossible for stag salesmen to host a trip for couples, DECO also sent the home salesmen's wives. Mr. McDonell (P) was chosen as one of four home office salesmen to go. The McDonells (P) included in their tax return the estimated cost to DECO attributable to Mrs. McDonell's (P) presence on the trip. The government determined a deficiency based on the entire cost of the trip.

■ **ISSUE**

Are the expenses paid for by an employer for a business-related trip includible as gross income to the employee because the employer chooses the employee by way of a random drawing?

■ **DECISION AND RATIONALE**

(Tannenwald, J.) No. The fact that an employer chooses which employees will be sent on a business trip by way of a drawing does not make the trip a taxable prize or award. The method of selection in this case was founded on a sound business reason—to avoid discontent. The fact that the trip was also a vacation for contest winners also does not make the trip a vacation for the McDonells (P). There was a duty to go, which carried with it an obligation to perform services for the employer. Moreover, the fact that the McDonells (P) enjoyed the trip is immaterial. We must also note that the McDonells did not go swimming or shopping, two activities for which Hawaii is famous. There is no indication that the trip was received as disguised remuneration to Mr. McDonell (so the trip was not taxable).

Analysis:

Section 74 of the Internal Revenue Code provides that "gross income includes amounts received as prizes and awards." The section covers virtually every type of monetary prize or award, with exceptions for scholarships, employee achievement awards that are minor, and certain prizes that are transferred to charities. Once again, this case illustrates the "substance over form" rationale that is so prevalent in income tax law. The factors this court found particularly relevant were that (1) the McDonells' (P) presence on the trip was for the benefit of DECO; (2) the McDonnells (P) were all but required to go; (3) DECO had an adequate reason for using a drawing as a method of choosing those employees who would attend; and (4) the McDonells did not get to do what they wanted on the trip. The court found that all the circumstances indicated there really was no prize or award, but that the trip was business related.

CHAPTER SIX

Gain From Dealings in Property

Philadelphia Park Amusement Co. v. U.S.

Instant Facts: A taxpayer sued to recover overpaid income taxes, claiming that it was entitled to depreciate the cost of a franchise, obtained through the exchange of a bridge, using the undepreciated cost of the bridge as the basis for the franchise.

Black Letter Rule: The cost basis of the property received in a taxable exchange is the fair market value of the property received in the exchange.

Taft v. Bowers

Instant Facts: A donee of stock sought to recover income taxes paid on the amount the stock appreciated while in the hands of the donor.

Black Letter Rule: The Constitution does not prevent Congress from treating as taxable income to the recipient of a gift the increase in the value of the gift while it is owned by the donor.

Farid–Es–Sultaneh v. Commissioner

Instant Facts: A taxpayer sought to have her basis in corporate stock determined by the value of the shares when she acquired them, because she claimed the stock was acquired by purchase, in exchange for the release of marital rights.

Black Letter Rule: A transfer which should be classed as a gift under the gift tax law is not necessarily to be treated as a gift, income-tax-wise.

International Freighting Corporation, Inc. v. Commissioner

Instant Facts: After a company gave to certain employees bonuses consisting of corporate stock that had appreciated in the hands of the company, the government sought to tax the company for a gain equal to the amount the stock had appreciated.

Black Letter Rule: When a taxpayer disposes of property in exchange for services, there is an "amount realized" equal to the fair market value of the services.

Crane v. Commissioner

Instant Facts: The owner of an apartment building, having a fair market value equal to the mortgage on the building, sold the building for $3000, subject to the mortgage, and reported a taxable gain of $1,250 under the theory that the "property" she acquired and transferred was merely her equity in the apartment building.

Black Letter Rule: A taxpayer who sells property encumbered by a nonrecourse mortgage must include the unpaid balance of the mortgage in the computation of the amount realized on the sale.

Commissioner v. Tufts

Instant Facts: A partnership reported a loss on the sale of property encumbered by a nonrecourse mortgage equal to the excess of the balance on the mortgage over the fair market value of the property, an amount of $55,740.

Black Letter Rule: When a party transfers property encumbered by a nonrecourse mortgage with an unpaid balance that exceeds the fair market value of the property, the transferor has realized an amount equal to the unpaid mortgage balance.

Philadelphia Park Amusement Co. v. U.S.

(Taxpayer) v. *(Government)*

130 Ct.Cl. 166, 126 F.Supp. 184 (Ct. Cl. 1954)

THE COST BASIS OF PROPERTY ACQUIRED IN A BARTER TRANSACTION IS ITS FAIR MARKET VALUE WHEN RECEIVED

■ **INSTANT FACTS** A taxpayer sued to recover overpaid income taxes, claiming that it was entitled to depreciate the cost of a franchise, obtained through the exchange of a bridge, using the undepreciated cost of the bridge as the basis for the franchise.

■ **BLACK LETTER RULE** The cost basis of the property received in a taxable exchange is the fair market value of the property received in the exchange.

■ **PROCEDURAL BASIS**

Action by taxpayer to recover overpaid income taxes.

■ **FACTS**

In 1889, the Philadelphia Park Amusement Co. ("Company") (P) was granted a 50–year franchise to operate a passenger railway. In 1934, in exchange for a ten-year extension on the franchise, the Company (P) deeded over to the city a bridge it had built at a cost of $381,000. The Company (P) eventually abandoned the franchise and later asserted depreciation deductions and a loss upon abandonment. The Company (P) sought to use the cost of the bridge as its cost basis in the franchise.

■ **ISSUE**

Is the cost basis of property acquired in a taxable exchange the fair market value of the property given in the exchange?

■ **DECISION AND RATIONALE**

(Laramore, J.) No. The cost basis of the property received in a taxable exchange is the fair market value of the property received in the exchange. Section 1012 of the Internal Revenue Code provides that "the basis of property shall be the cost of such property." To maintain harmony with the fundamental purpose of this section, it is necessary to consider the fair market value of the property received in a taxable exchange as the cost basis to the taxpayer. Otherwise, the taxpayer would receive a stepped-up basis if the property received has a fair market value less than that of the property given up, but would be double-taxed if the fair market value of the property received is more than that of the property given up. Therefore, the cost basis of the 10–year extension was its fair market value at the time of the exchange. We need not decide whether the cost of the franchise at the time of the exchange was its fair market value, or that of the bridge, because in a arms length transaction the properties are equal in fact or presumed to be equal. If the fair market value of the franchise cannot be determined, the fair market value of the bridge should be established, and that will be presumed to be the value of the franchise. The Company (P) claims that neither value can be ascertained. In that case, the Company (P) would be entitled to carry over the undepreciated cost of the bridge as the cost basis of the franchise. But we believe that the value of either the bridge or the franchise can be ascertained with a reasonable degree of accuracy. We, therefore, conclude that the 1934 exchange was a taxable exchange and that the taxpayer is entitled to use as the cost basis of the 10–year extension franchise its fair market value at the time of the exchange. Remanded.

Analysis:

The Company (P) in this case built a bridge for $381,000. Years later, it exchanged that bridge for a 10–year extension on a franchise. This is a taxable exchange, a situation no different than if the Company (P) had paid cash for the franchise extension. At this point the Company would be taxed on any gain equal to the difference between the value of the franchise and the adjusted basis in the bridge, $381,000 less adjustments. But that was not the issue here. Instead the question presented was how to determine the Company's (P) basis in the franchise, after the exchange. Section 1012 provides that in a cash transaction, the basis of property received is the amount of cash given. Logic would dictate that, in a barter transaction, the value of the property given should be the basis in the property received, right? Wrong. The court holds the basis in property acquired in such an exchange is the value of the property *received*. Further complicating this case was the fact that the fair market value of the franchise—the property received—was difficult to ascertain. To deal with this problem the court holds that, if the value of what is received in an arm's length barter transaction cannot be determined, it is assumed that the value of what was received is equal to the value of what was given up. In this case the value of the bridge was used to determine the value of the franchise, which in turn was used to determine the basis in the franchise. The court goes on to hold that if neither property can be valued, there is a de facto nonrecognition transaction where both parties keep the basis they had in the property they gave up. This really amounts to a deferral, where any gain will be taxed once the property is exchanged for cash or something that can be valued.

Taft v. Bowers

(Taxpayer) v. *(Collector of Internal Revenue)*

278 U.S. 470, 49 S.Ct. 199 (1929)

THE BASIS IN PROPERTY ACQUIRED BY GIFT IS THE SAME AS ITS BASIS IN THE HANDS OF A DONOR

■ **INSTANT FACTS** A donee of stock sought to recover income taxes paid on the amount the stock appreciated while in the hands of the donor.

■ **BLACK LETTER RULE** The Constitution does not prevent Congress from treating as taxable income to the recipient of a gift the increase in the value of the gift while it is owned by the donor.

■ **PROCEDURAL BASIS**

Appeal to the United State Supreme Court, challenging the decision of the Court of Appeals to reverse the district court's finding that the government could not tax the appreciation in stock received by gift while the stock was owned by the donor.

■ **FACTS**

During the calendar years 1921 and 1922 the father of Elizabeth C. Taft (P) gave her shares of Nash Motors Company stock, then more valuable than when acquired by him. She sold them in 1923 for more than their market value when the gift was made. The United States demanded an income tax imposed upon the difference between the cost to Taft's (P) father and the price received after the sale by Taft (P). Taft (P) paid the tax exacted and sued to recover the portion imposed on the advance in value while her father owned the stock. Taft (P) argued that only the appreciation during her ownership could be regarded as income, and any appreciation occurring before her ownership of the stock is not income within the meaning of the Sixteenth Amendment. The District Court agreed, and the Court of Appeals reversed.

■ **ISSUE**

Does the Sixteenth Amendment prohibit Congress from exacting a tax upon the appreciation in the value of property received by a donee occurring prior to the gift?

■ **DECISION AND RATIONALE**

(McReynolds, J.) No. The Constitution does not prevent Congress from treating as taxable income to the recipient of a gift the increase in the value of the gift while it is owned by the donor. The mandate of § 1015 of the Internal Revenue Code is clear. The statute provides that "if property was acquired by gift . . . , the basis shall be the same as it would be in the hands of the donor or the last preceding owner by whom it was not acquired by gift, except that if such basis is greater than the fair market value of the property at the time of the gift, then for the purpose of determining loss, the basis shall be such fair market value." Congress' intent was to require Ms. Taft (P) to pay the tax. The only question is whether Congress had the power to do so. The Sixteenth Amendment provides: "Congress shall have power to lay and collect taxes on incomes from whatever source derived, without apportionment among the several States, and without regard to any census or enumeration." The Amendment does not define income, but it is settled that Congress cannot define as income something which prior to the Amendment's enactment was not regarded as income. This Court has defined income as "the gain derived from capital, from labor, or from both combined, provided it includes profit gained through a sale or conversion of capital assets." If Taft's (P) father had sold the stock at market value he would have realized income taxable under the Sixteenth Amendment. We do not think that he could deprive the government of its share simply by making a gift. The stock represented only a single investment of capital—that made by Taft's (P) father. When through sale the increase in capital was separated from the investment, it became taxable income under the Sixteenth Amendment. The statute has deprived Taft (P) of no right, nor has it subjected her to any hardship. To accept Taft's (P) view would defeat Congress' intent to take part of all gain derived from capital investments. To prevent that result, Congress had the power to require donees to accept the position of the donor in respect to the property received. Affirmed.

Analysis:

Section 1015 creates a carryover basis for donees. Under § 1012, basis is usually determined by referring to the cost of acquiring the property. But a cost basis cannot be used where property is acquired by gift because the donee's basis would be zero. A zero basis to the donee would mean that he would be taxed on the entire amount realized upon disposition of the property, a result that is contrary to the exclusion of gifts from gross income as provided in § 1012. The Court's holding here is consistent with both § 1012 and § 1015. Any appreciation that occurs in the hands of the donor does not affect the basis in the property. Suppose that Taft's (P) father had given her stock valued at $800, which he purchased for $1000. If, after further depreciation, Taft (P) sold the stock for $500, one would think that she had realized a loss of $500, equal to the difference between the amount realized and the carryover basis. But § 1015 prohibits taxpayers from transferring losses. Under the statute, if the donor transfers depreciated property, the donee takes a basis equal to the fair market value of the property at the time of the exchange. Only the loss attributable to the time the property was held by the donee will be recognized.

Farid–Es–Sultaneh v. Commissioner

(Taxpayer) v. *(Commissioner of Internal Revenue)*

160 F.2d 812 (2d Cir. 1947)

TO DETERMINE WHETHER A GIFT HAS BEEN MADE UNDER THE TAX CODE COURTS WILL LOOK TO THE SUBSTANCE OF THE TRANSACTION AND NOT ITS FORM

■ **INSTANT FACTS** A taxpayer sought to have her basis in corporate stock determined by the value of the shares when she acquired them, because she claimed the stock was acquired by purchase, in exchange for the release of marital rights.

■ **BLACK LETTER RULE** A transfer that should be classified as a gift under the gift tax laws is not necessarily treated as a gift for income tax purposes.

■ **PROCEDURAL BASIS**

Appeal to the Second Circuit challenging the decision of the Tax Court, which held that shares acquired pursuant to an antenuptial agreement were a gift, carrying with it the basis of the transferor.

■ **FACTS**

In 1923, Ms. Farid–Es–Sultaneh (P) received 700 of the shares from Mr. Kresge, with whom she was contemplating marriage, to protect her in the event he should die prior to the marriage. At the time the shares were worth $315. Mr. Kresge subsequently gave Ms. Farid–Es–Sultaneh (P) an additional 1800 shares, worth $330 each, for the same purpose. Mr. Kresge's basis in the stock was 16per share. Prior to their marriage, the two entered into an antenuptial agreement whereby Ms. Farid–Es–Sultaneh (P) agreed to release all dower and marital rights, including the right to her support, in exchange for those shares already received. The couple married and then divorced. Ms. Farid–Es–Sultaneh (P) received no alimony, even though Mr. Kresge was worth about $375,000,000. Ms. Farid–Es–Sultaneh (P) sold 12,000 shares of the S.S. Kresge Company at varying prices, for a sum total of $230,802.36. The Commissioner determined a deficiency on the ground that the stock was acquired by gift, and thus the basis in the hands of Mr. Kresge carried over to her.

■ **ISSUE**

Is property received pursuant to an agreement releasing marital rights a gift for income tax purposes?

■ **DECISION AND RATIONALE**

(Chase, Cir. J.) No. The Supreme Court has held that property transferred in trust for the benefit of a prospective wife pursuant to an ante-nuptial agreement is a gift under the gift tax laws, but a transfer which should be classified as a gift under the gift tax laws is not necessarily to be treated as a gift for income tax purposes. We find nothing requiring that a transfer, taxable as a gift under the gift tax, is to be accorded the same treatment under the income tax law. Congress has enacted a statute providing that the release of marital rights should not be treated as consideration under the estate tax law. This provision has also been held applicable to the gift tax law. In our opinion, however, income tax provisions are not to be construed as though they were in pari materia with either the estate tax law or the gift tax law. It is up to Congress to determine the legal effect a transfer made for consideration should have. We believe that the consideration given by Ms. Farid–Es–Sultaneh (P) is fair consideration. Although the transfers made before the ante-nuptial agreement were called a "gift" by the agreement, they were contingent upon the death of Mr. Kresge, an event which never occurred. Consequently, it seems no gift was made prior to the ante-nuptial agreement. Ms. Farid–Es–Sultaneh's (P) inchoate interest in the property of her affianced husband greatly exceeded the value of the stock. It was fair consideration under the ordinary legal concept of that term. The shares were held by way of purchase. Reversed.

Analysis:

This case illustrates that federal tax law often carries with it its own "common law." For example, there is really no doubt that release of marital rights is adequate consideration under state law. But the court's discussion here illustrates that common legal terms often carry a special definition under federal income tax law, in order to fulfill Congress's intent. Notice also the application of *Philadelphia Park Amusement Co. v. U.S.* Ms. Farid–Es–Sultaneh (P) gave up marital rights worth millions in exchange for several hundred shares of stock. Consequently, under *Philadelphia Park* the basis in the shares was the value of the shares at the time they were received, and not the value of the marital rights given up.

International Freighting Corporation, Inc. v. Commissioner

(Taxpayer) v. *(Commissioner of Internal Revenue)*

135 F.2d 310 (2d Cir. 1943)

THE TRANSFER OF APPRECIATED PROPERTY IN SATISFACTION OF A LEGAL OBLIGATION EFFECTS A TAXABLE GAIN EQUAL TO THE DIFFERENCE BETWEEN THE AMOUNT REALIZED AND THE ADJUSTED BASIS IN THE TRANSFERRED PROPERTY

■ **INSTANT FACTS** After a company gave to certain employees bonuses consisting of corporate stock that had appreciated in the hands of the company, the government sought to tax the company for a gain equal to the amount the stock had appreciated.

■ **BLACK LETTER RULE** When a taxpayer disposes of property in exchange for services, there is an "amount realized" equal to the fair market value of the services.

■ **PROCEDURAL BASIS**

Appeal to the Second Circuit challenging the decision of the Tax Court, which held taxpayer realized a gain when it transferred appreciated property to its employees as a bonus.

■ **FACTS**

International Freighting Corporation (IFC) (P), a subsidiary of the duPont Company, initiated a bonus plan under which it granted eligible employees 150 shares of duPont's common stock. In 1936, IFC (P) gave stock bonuses with a market value of $24,858.75, but which cost IFC only $16,153.36. IFC took a deduction of $24,858.75, as compensation paid to employees. In a notice of deficiency the Commissioner (D) reduced the deduction to $16,153.36. The Tax Court held that IFC was entitled to a deduction totaling, $24,858.75, but that IFC (P) realized an offsetting gain of $8,705.39 by paying the bonus in stock which had cost the taxpayer $8,705.39 less than its market value when it was transferred. IFC appealed.

■ **ISSUE**

If an employer transfers appreciated stock to its employees, does the employer realize a gain equal to the amount the stock appreciated while owned by the employer?

■ **DECISION AND RATIONALE**

(Frank, Cir. J.) Yes. When a taxpayer disposes of property in exchange for services, there is an "amount realized" equal to the fair market value of the services. So when IFC (P) gave stock with a fair market value greater than its basis to its employees, the company realized a gain in the amount of the difference between the basis of the stock and its fair market value when transferred. We first note that the delivery of the shares was not a gift because (1) a corporation cannot make gifts, (2) the value of the shares could not be deducted as an expense, and (3) the employees would not have been obliged, as they were, to pay income tax on the value of the stock. The delivery of the shares constituted a disposition of property for a valid consideration. We must assume that the consideration received by IFC (P)—the employees' services—was at least equal to the value of the shares. Because the transaction was a disposition of property for a valid consideration equal at least to the market value of the shares when delivered, there was a taxable gain equal to the difference between the cost of the shares and that market value. Section 1001(a) of the Internal Revenue Code provides that the "gain from the sale or other disposition of property shall be the excess of the amount realized therefrom over the adjusted basis provided in section 1011." Subsection (b) goes on to define the amount realized as "the sum of any money received plus the fair market value of the property (other than money) received." Of course, where there is a disposition of stock for services, no "property" or "money" is received by the person disposing of the stock. But, in similar circumstances, it has been held that "money's worth" is received, such receipt coming within § 1001(b). Affirmed.

Analysis:

This case is really about defining the term "amount realized," as used in § 1001(b). Section 1001(b) speaks in terms of only "money" and "property" received in calculating the amount realized. Consequently, IFC (P) argued that there was no amount realized because it received only services, which are neither "money" nor "property." The court rejected this view. It held that when services are received in a taxable exchange, the amount realized is the fair market value of the services received. But since the value of the employees' services could not be independently ascertained, the court used the rationale of *Philadelphia Park Amusement Co. v. U.S.* and held that, in a stock bonus plan, the value of the services received is equal to the fair market value of the stock given to the employees. This gave IFC (P) an amount realized of $24,858.75. The question then became: what was the gain realized by IFC (P)? Under § 1001(a) a gain realized is the difference between the amount realized and the basis in the property that is given up, i.e., the fair market value of the employees' services minus the cost of duPont stock to IFC (P). Thus, IFC (P) realized a gain of $8,705.39, determined by the difference between $24,858.75 and $16,153.36, i.e., the value of the employees' services as determined under *Philadelphia Park* less IFC's (P) cost basis in the stock. The "big picture" lesson here is that the transfer of appreciated property in satisfaction of a legal obligation effects a taxable gain equal to the difference between the amount realized and the adjusted basis in the transferred property.

Crane v. Commissioner

(Taxpayer) v. *(Commissioner of Internal Revenue)*

331 U.S. 1, 67 S.Ct. 1047 (1947)

THE AMOUNT OF A NONRECOURSE MORTGAGE THAT IS ASSUMED IN THE DISPOSITION OF PROPERTY MUST BE INCLUDED IN BOTH THE SELLER'S *AMOUNT REALIZED* AND IN THE BASIS OF THE TRANSFEREE, WHETHER A PURCHASER, DEVISEE, OR OTHER TAKER

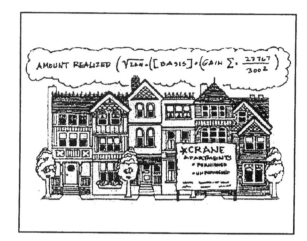

■ **INSTANT FACTS** The owner of an apartment building, having a fair market value equal to the mortgage on the building, sold the building for $3000, subject to the mortgage, and reported a taxable gain of $1,250 under the theory that the "property" she acquired and transferred was merely her equity in the apartment building.

■ **BLACK LETTER RULE** A taxpayer who sells property encumbered by a nonrecourse mortgage must include the unpaid balance of the mortgage in the computation of the amount realized on the sale.

■ **PROCEDURAL BASIS**

Appeal to the United States Supreme Court, challenging the Court of Appeals' decision to reverse the holding of the Tax Court, which expunged the deficiency determined by the Commissioner.

■ **FACTS**

Mrs. Crane (P) was the beneficiary of her husband's will, which devised to her an apartment building encumbered by a mortgage equal to the property's fair market value. For the next six years, Mrs. Crane (P) managed the property—collecting the rents, making repairs, paying taxes, and remitting the excess income to the mortgagee. During this time Mrs. Crane (P) took annual deductions for depreciation of the property totaling $28,045.10. Mrs. Crane (P) eventually sold the property, subject to the mortgage, for $3,000 cash, incurring $500 in expenses. Mrs. Crane (P) reported a taxable gain of $1,250, which was 50% of the cash received less expenses. Her theory was that the "property" she acquired in 1932 was only the equity, or the excess in the value of the apartment building and lot over the amount of the mortgage. The equity having a fair market value of zero at the time of the devise, Mrs. Crane (P) argued she took a carry-over basis of zero, and that after realizing a net amount of $2,500 upon the sale of the "equity" she needed to report only 50%, as allowed by the Revenue Act. The Commissioner (D), however, determined that there was taxable gain of $23,767.03. His theory was that Mrs. Crane (P) acquired and sold the physical property, or the owner's rights with respect thereto. The original basis was $262,042.50, the building's appraised value at the time it was acquired by Mrs. Crane (P). But according to the Commissioner (D), the basis at the time of the sale was $233,997.40, an amount representing the original basis less the depreciation taken on the building. Subtracting the adjusted from the balance on the mortgage plus $2,500, gave Mrs. Crane (P) a taxable gain of $23,767.03.

■ **ISSUE**

May a gain be computed on the sale of property encumbered by a mortgage by using an equity basis and an amount realized that does not include the amount of the mortgage?

■ **DECISION AND RATIONALE**

(Vinson, C.J.) No. The gain on a sale of property that is encumbered by a mortgage should be computed by using the basis in the property, undiminished by the mortgages thereon, and an amount realized that includes the amount of any debt that is assumed by the purchaser. Section 1001(a) of the

Internal Revenue Code defines the gain "from the sale or other disposition of property" as "the excess of the amount realized therefrom over the adjusted basis provided in Section 1011." Sub-section (b) goes on to define the *amount realized* "from the sale or other disposition of property" as "the sum of any money received plus the fair market value of the property (other than money) received." Under sections 1011 and 1016 the adjusted basis is the cost basis in the property less any deduction taken for "exhaustion, wear and tear, obsolescence, amortization, and depletion...." The basis in property acquired from a decedent is defined by section 1014, which provides that "the basis of property in the hands of a person acquiring the property from a decedent" is "the fair market value of the property at the date of the decedent's death." Accordingly, our first step is to determine the basis in the property, as acquired from a decedent. For several reasons we disagree with Mrs. Crane's (P) argument that "property," as used in § 1014, means "equity." First, the dictionary defines property as the physical thing subject to ownership or the aggregate of the owner's rights with respect to such thing; equity is not given as a synonym. Second, the Treasury Department's regulations with respect to estate taxes require that a decedent's property be valued without reference to liens. Third, Congress has used the word "equity" when it has intended to do so. Finally, construing the word "property" to mean "equity" would have unreasonable consequences on the taking of deductions for depreciation and on the collateral adjustments. If the mortgagor's equity were the basis he would be allowed deductions for depreciation that represented only a fraction of the actual physical exhaustion. Furthermore, the basis would have to be recomputed every time the mortgagor made a payment on the loan, creating a tremendous accounting burden for all parties. We thus conclude that the property basis under § 1014 is the fair market value of the property, undiminished by mortgages thereon, giving Mrs. Crane (P) a basis of $262,042.50. The second step is to determine Mrs. Crane's (P) adjusted basis in the property, after subtracting depreciation deductions that were taken. Section 1011 requires the basis to be adjusted to include the allowable deductions for depreciation, here totaling $28,045.10. Our final step is to determine the "amount realized" on the sale. As noted above, § 1001(b) defines amount realized as the sum of any money plus the value of property received. We cannot accept Mrs. Crane's (P) position that she realized an amount of only $2,500 ($3,000 less expenses of $500), for that would mean she sold the property at one percent of its fair market value. We believe that a mortgagor who sells property subject to the mortgage and for additional consideration, realizes a benefit in the amount of the mortgage plus the boot. It matters not that the mortgagor is not personally liable on the debt, for our cases have held that there need not be an actual receipt by the seller himself of "money" or "other property." We, therefore, conclude that the Commissioner was correct in determining that there was an amount realized of $257,500.00 on the sale of this property. Affirmed.

■ DISSENT

(Jackson, J.) I believe that the finding of the Tax Court should not be disturbed. The Tax Court concluded that Mrs. Crane (P) acquired only an equity worth nothing. The arguments which support the theory that Mrs. Crane (P) acquired the whole property and became liable for the whole debt are proper, but are not so conclusive that it was not within the province of the Tax Court to concluded otherwise. Mrs. Crane (P) received no financial benefit from the assumption of the mortgage because she was never personally liable upon it. I would reverse the Court of Appeals and sustain the decision of the Tax Court.

Analysis:

The Court holds here that the amount of a nonrecourse liability incurred on the acquisition of property is included in the basis. In other words, if one takes property that is subject to a nonrecourse mortgage by sale, devise, or gift, that person has a basis in the property equal to the balance on the mortgage plus any other money or property that he gave in order to obtain the property. In so holding, the Court rejects the proposition that, *under the Tax Code*, a sale of property can mean only the transfer of a mortgagor's equity. So when Mrs. Crane (P) was bequeathed the apartment building encumbered by a mortgage, she received a carryover basis equal to the mortgage and any equity. After deciding what Mrs. Crane's (P) basis was, the Court had to determine the adjusted basis for ascertaining losses and gains. A taxpayer is allowed to take a deduction for the depreciation in the value of property held for income. However, this "benefit" to the taxpayer must be offset by some detriment. That detriment is a reduction in the basis of the property equal to the amount of the allowable deductions. Consequently, after Mrs. Crane (P) had taken deductions totaling $28,045.10, her basis in the apartment building was reduced by that same amount. In the second part of the opinion, the court holds that the assumption of a nonrecourse debt by a purchaser in a sale of property is to be included in the amount realized. So when Mrs. Crane (P) transferred the property, subject to the mortgage, for $3000, she realized an amount equal to the $3,000 (less expenses) plus the amount of the debt assumed. Now we are ready to compute Mrs. Crane's (P) gain from the sale of the property. Section § 1001 provides that the gain is equal to the excess of the *amount realized* ($255,000 + $3000 cash − $500 in expenses) over the *adjusted basis* ($262,042.50 − $28,045.10). This gave Mrs. Crane (P) a gain of $23,502.60.

■ **CASE VOCABULARY**

MORTGAGOR: The party who grants the lien to secure the mortgage; the debtor.

NONRECOURSE LIABILITY: A debt upon which the debtor is not personally liable.

Commissioner v. Tufts

(Commissioner of Internal Revenue) v. *(Taxpayer)*

461 U.S. 300, 103 S.Ct. 1826 (1983)

FOR DETERMINING THE GAIN REALIZED FROM DEALINGS IN PROPERTY, NONRECOURSE DEBTS WILL BE TREATED AS TRUE DEBTS FOR TAX PURPOSES

■ **INSTANT FACTS** A partnership reported a loss on the sale of property encumbered by a nonrecourse mortgage equal to the excess of the balance on the mortgage over the fair market value of the property, an amount of $55,740.

■ **BLACK LETTER RULE** When a party transfers property encumbered by a nonrecourse mortgage with an unpaid balance that exceeds the fair market value of the property, the transferor has realized an amount equal to the unpaid mortgage balance.

■ **PROCEDURAL BASIS**

Appeal to the United States Supreme Court, challenging the Court of Appeals' reversal of the Tax Court's decision to uphold the deficiencies against the taxpayers.

■ **FACTS**

Mr. Tufts (P) was the member of a general partnership formed in 1970 for the purpose of constructing an apartment complex. The partnership took out a $1,851,500 nonrecourse mortgage loan. The partnership's claimed adjusted basis in the property in 1972 was $1,455,740. The partnership became unable to make the payments due on the mortgage. Each partner sold his interest to a third party, who assumed the mortgage. The fair market value of the property on the date of transfer did not exceed $1,400,000. Each partner reported the sale on his income tax return and indicated a loss to the partnership of $55,740. The Commissioner (D) determined that the sale resulted in a partnership gain of approximately $400,000 based on the theory that the partnership had realized the full amount of the nonrecourse debt. The United States Tax Court agreed with the Commissioner (D), but the Court of Appeals reversed.

■ **ISSUE**

If the unpaid amount of a nonrecourse mortgage exceeds the fair market value of property sold, does the seller realize an amount equal to the unpaid mortgage balance?

■ **DECISION AND RATIONALE**

(Blackmun, J.) Yes. When a party transfers property encumbered by a nonrecourse mortgage with an unpaid balance that exceeds the fair market value of the property, the transferor has realized an amount equal to the unpaid mortgage balance. In *Crane v. Commissioner* this Court held that a taxpayer who sells property encumbered by a nonrecourse mortgage must include the unpaid balance of the mortgage in the computation of the amount realized on the sale. But the Court expressly withheld a determination of whether that rule would apply where the fair market value of the property transferred was less than the balance on the unpaid mortgage. We read *Crane* as an approval of the Commissioner's (D) decision to treat nonrecourse mortgages in this context as a true loan, and not merely resting on the theory of economic benefit. Because no difference between recourse and nonrecourse obligations is recognized in calculating basis, *Crane* teaches that the Commissioner (D) may ignore the nonrecourse nature of the obligation in determining the amount realized upon disposition of the property. This treatment balances the fact that the mortgagor may exclude the amount of the loan from gross income. A contrary rule would give the mortgagor untaxed income at the time the loan is extended, in addition to giving him an increase in the basis of the property. Moreover, this treatment avoids the situation where the taxpayer may claim a loss that he has not suffered, as was done here. In this case it was the bank who was at risk when the market value of the property fell below the unpaid balance on the mortgage. The partners lost nothing, yet they reported a tax loss of over $55,000. We, therefore hold that the Commissioner (D) properly required the partners to include among the assets realized the outstanding amount of the obligation. Reversed.

■ CONCURRENCE

(O'Connor, J.) I concur with the Court. Were we writing on a clean slate except for the *Crane* decision, I would take a different approach. Instead of treating a nonrecourse debt as a true loan, I would bifurcate the transaction and treat the acquisition and sale of the property separate from the arrangement and retirement of the loan. The first part of the analysis would give the taxpayer a basis in the property equal to the purchase price or the fair market value of the property on the date of acquisition. Upon disposition of the property the taxpayer would realize a gain or loss that is dependent on the fate of the property. In the separate borrowing transaction the taxpayer received cash from the mortgagee, at which time he need not recognize income. If he later surrenders the property when it is worth less than the unpaid balance on the loan, we have the classic situation of cancellation of indebtedness, requiring the taxpayer to recognize income in the amount of the difference between the proceeds of the loan and the value of the property. The reason we should treat the two aspects of the transaction separately is that different forms of income carry with them different tax consequences. The logic of this approach notwithstanding, I do not agree it should be adopted judicially in light of *Crane* and countless lower court cases that have applied the rule announced by the Court today.

Analysis:

This case addresses the issue the Court left open in *Crane*: whether the rule adopted in that case applies when the fair market value of the property sold is less than the unpaid balance on a mortgage secured by the transferred property. The Court here holds that it does. In the Court's view, *Crane* established the proposition that nonrecourse mortgages should be treated as true loans for tax purposes. The court reasons that treating a nonrecourse loan any differently would give the taxpayer untaxed income upon receiving the loan proceeds and would give the taxpayer an increased basis. The policy behind the court's holding is sound, but not grounded in "real-world" economics. Justice O'Connor's concurring opinion suggests treating the transaction in two parts: a loan, and a disposition of property. This treatment makes sense, but unfortunately it was not adopted, probably because the Court felt bound to follow *Crane*. What is the purchaser's basis when he takes property encumbered by a mortgage that exceeds the fair market value of the property? The circuits that have faced this issue are split, with one holding that the fair market value of the property is the basis, and another holding these transactions to be a "sham," resulting in a zero basis to the purchaser.

CHAPTER EIGHT

Discharge of Indebtedness

U.S. v. Kirby Lumber Co.

Instant Facts: After a company had purchased, for less than par value, bonds which it had issued at par value, the government sought to tax the difference as gross income.

Black Letter Rule: If a corporation purchases and retires any bonds at a price less than the issuing price or face value, the excess of the issuing price or face value over the purchase price is a gain or income for the taxable year.

Zarin v. Commissioner

Instant Facts: A taxpayer owed to a casino nearly $3.5 million, a debt that was unenforceable under state law, but which he settled for $500,000; the government sought to tax the difference as income from the discharge of indebtedness.

Black Letter Rule: An unenforceable obligation is not "indebtedness" within the meaning of the Code.

U.S. v. Kirby Lumber Co.

(*Government*) v. (*Taxpayer*)
284 U.S. 1, 52 S.Ct. 4 (1931)

TAXABLE INCOME IS REALIZED WHEN A LEGAL OBLIGATION IS SETTLED FOR LESS THAN THE TOTAL AMOUNT OF THE OBLIGATION

■ **INSTANT FACTS** After a company had purchased, for less than par value, bonds which it had issued at par value, the government sought to tax the difference as gross income.

■ **BLACK LETTER RULE** If a corporation purchases and retires any bonds at a price less than the issuing price or face value, the excess of the issuing price or face value over the purchase price is a gain or income for the taxable year.

■ PROCEDURAL BASIS

Not provided.

■ FACTS

The Kirby Lumber Company (P) issued its own bonds for $12,126,800, for which it received their par value. Later that year it purchased some of those bonds in the open market for less than par value, the difference in price being $137,521.30. The government (D) sought to tax this difference as income to Kirby (P).

■ ISSUE

Does a company realize income if it purchases and retires bonds at less than face value?

■ DECISION AND RATIONALE

(Holmes, J.) Yes. If a corporation purchases and retires any bonds at a price less than the issuing price or face value, the excess of the issuing price or face value over the purchase price is a gain or income for the taxable year. Section 61 of the Internal Revenue Code provides that gross income "means all income from whatever source derived." If these words are taken in their popular meaning, Kirby (P) had realized an accession to income. Reversed.

Analysis:

This case established the rule that a discharge of indebtedness is gross income within the meaning of the Code. The rationale behind the case is simple. When Kirby (P) issued bonds, it essentially took out a loan. The company received and used funds, but realized no income because there was a legal obligation to repay the bondholders. When Kirby (P) purchased the bonds for less than face value, they essentially paid off a loan for less than the loan amount. Thus, Kirby realized income on the difference. This case was decided under the catch-all provision of § 61(a), but sub-section (a)(12) now codifies the rule and expressly provides that gross income includes the discharge of indebtedness. There are, however, several exceptions to the inclusion of *Kirby*-type income: 1) When the discharge occurs in bankruptcy; 2) when the discharge occurs while the taxpayer is insolvent, but only to the extent of the insolvency; 3) when the discharge is of a qualified farm debt; 4) when the debt relates to business property; 5) when the debt arises out of a purchase directly from the creditor, i.e., purchase-money debts; and 6) when the discharge is a "gift" under § 102.

■ CASE VOCABULARY

CORPORATE BONDS: Written instruments, usually negotiable, that evidence a company's promise to pay a fixed amount at a future time, usually with intermittent interest payments.

Zarin v. Commissioner

(Taxpayer) v. *(Internal Revenue Commissioner)*
916 F.2d 110 (3d Cir. 1990)

THE SETTLEMENT FOR LESS THAN FACE VALUE OF A DEBT DISPUTED IN GOOD FAITH IS NOT GROSS INCOME TO THE OBLIGOR

■ **INSTANT FACTS** A taxpayer owed to a casino nearly $3.5 million, a debt that was unenforceable under state law, but which he settled for $500,000; the government sought to tax the difference as income from the discharge of indebtedness.

■ **BLACK LETTER RULE** An unenforceable obligation is not "indebtedness" within the meaning of the Code.

■ PROCEDURAL BASIS

Appeal to the Third Circuit, reversing the decision of the Tax Court, which held that the taxpayer recognized income from the discharge of indebtedness resulting from his gambling activities.

■ FACTS

David Zarin (P) incurred a gambling debt of $3,435,000 owed to Resorts International Hotel (Resorts). Resorts facilitated Zarin's (P) gambling activities by offering him a credit line in June 1978. As a result of its investigation, the State of New Jersey issued an order making further extensions of credit to Zarin (P) illegal. Nevertheless, Resorts continued to grant Zarin (P) credit through two procedures later found to be illegal. Zarin (P) began to lose, and became heavily indebted to Resorts. Although Zarin (P) indicated he would pay the obligations, Resorts filed an action in state court. Zarin (P) denied liability on the ground that the debt was unenforceable under New Jersey gaming regulations. The parties settled out of court for $500,000. The Commissioner determined deficiencies in Zarin's federal income taxes, arguing that Zarin recognized $2,935,000 of income from the discharge of indebtedness on the ground that Zarin owed $3,435,000 but paid only $500,000. The Tax Court agreed, and held for the Commissioner.

■ ISSUE

Does a taxpayer recognize income from the discharge of indebtedness when he settles an unenforceable debt for less than the contested amount?

■ DECISION AND RATIONALE

(Cowen, Cir. J.) No. Gross income does not include the settlement of an unenforceable obligation for less than the total amount of the obligation. The Commissioner's (D) position is flawed for two reasons. Section 61(a)(12) expressly includes in the definition of gross income any "income from the discharge of indebtedness." Section 108(d)(1) defines the term indebtedness. That section provides that indebtedness means any indebtedness "(A) for which the taxpayer is liable, or (B) subject to which the taxpayer holds property." Neither of these definitions is applicable here. Under New Jersey law, it is clear that the debt owed to Resorts was unenforceable. Therefore, it was not a debt for which Zarin (P) was liable. Furthermore, Zarin did not have a debt subject to which he held property. The debt arose out of his acquisition of gambling chips. These chips were not property because Zarin (P) could do nothing more with the chips than gamble and purchase services at the casino. They had no other economic benefit. Instead, the chips are best characterized as an accounting mechanism. New Jersey law supports this view, for it provides that gambling chips are merely the evidence of indebtedness. Thus, the chips were not property within the meaning of Section 108(d)(1). The second reason why the Commissioner's position is flawed is that we believe the transaction should be viewed as a disputed debt or contested liability, rather than as a canceled debt,. Under the contested liability doctrine, if a taxpayer, in good faith, disputes the amount of a debt, a subsequent settlement of the dispute is treated as the actual amount of the debt for tax purposes. The excess of the original debt over the settled amount is ignored for tax purposes. We adopt this view. We also reject the Commissioner's argument that the contested liability doctrine does not apply here. Its is true that the contested liability doctrine applies only when the debt is for an amount which cannot be determined, i.e., an unliquidated debt. We believe, however, that Zarin's (P) debt was unliquidated. The settlement itself shows that the parties attached a value to the debt that was lower than face value. In other words, the parties agreed that Zarin's (P) acquisition of the chips was worth less than $3.4 million, but failed to agree on the exact amount. The transaction between Zarin (P) and resorts can best be characterized as a disputed debt. Zarin (P) owed an unenforceable debt of $3,435,000 to Resorts. After disputing this obligation, the parties settled for $500,000. That settlement fixed the amount of the loss and the amount of the debt for tax purposes. Since Zarin (P) paid the $500,000, he has no adverse tax consequences. Reversed.

■ DISSENT

(Stapleton, Cir. J.) I respectfully dissent. The *only* reason Zarin (P) did not have to report the $3.4 million credit advancement as gross income was that he had an offsetting obligation to pay. When Resorts released Zarin (P) of his obligation he recognized gross income under *United States v. Kirby Lumber Co.* [Supreme Court holds that the discharge of indebtedness is gross income]. This case should turn on the treatment the debt is given by the parties. For present purposes, it will suffice to say that where something that would otherwise be includable in gross income is received on credit in a purchase money transaction, there should be no recognition of gross income where the debtor continued to recognize an obligation to repay. But once the debtor no longer recognizes the obligation, he has recognized gross income.

Analysis:

The discharge of a legally unenforceable debt is not gross income. There are many questions posed by the court's holding. First, if it is well settled that income from illegal gains is gross income, why should Zarin (P) be untaxed on an economic benefit simply because state law provides that he need not repay his obligation? The court holds that under the definition provided in § 108, Zarin's (P) debt is not "indebtedness" within the meaning of the Code. The problem with relying on § 108 is that the definition provided therein expressly applies only to that section. But the court here was ascertaining the definition of "indebtedness" within the meaning of § 61. The court also bases its decision on the contested liability doctrine. Under its own terms, the doctrine is only applicable when the amount of the liability cannot be ascertained. The court strains to apply the doctrine, holding that the settlement was proof that the parties attached a different value to the debt, thus the actual value could not be determined. Notice that the court could have relied on § 108(e)(5), which provides that a debt discharged by a creditor who was also the seller of property, i.e., a purchase-money creditor, will be treated as a reduction in price.

CHAPTER NINE

Damages and Related Receipts

Raytheon Production Corporation v. Commissioner

Instant Facts: A government sought to tax as gross income damages a company received in settlement of an antitrust suit settlement.

Black Letter Rule: Compensation for the loss of good will in excess of its cost is gross income.

Raytheon Production Corporation v. Commissioner

(*Taxpayer*) v. (*Commissioner of Internal Revenue*)

144 F.2d 110 (1st Cir. 1944)

DAMAGES ARE TAXABLE IF THEY ARE IN LIEU OF TAXABLE INCOME

■ **INSTANT FACTS** A government sought to tax as gross income damages a company received in settlement of an antitrust suit settlement.

■ **BLACK LETTER RULE** Compensation for the loss of good will in excess of its cost is gross income.

■ **PROCEDURAL BASIS**

Not provided.

■ **FACTS**

Raytheon Production Corporation (Raytheon) (P) filed an antitrust suit against R.C.A., alleging that the latter destroyed Raytheon's (P) vacuum tube business. The suit was settled, with Raytheon (P) receiving damages.

■ **ISSUE**

Are settlement damages required to be included in a taxpayer's gross income?

■ **DECISION AND RATIONALE**

(Mahoney, Cir. J.) Yes. Damages which represent a reimbursement for lost profits are income. The reason being that since the profits would be taxable income, the proceeds of litigation which are their substitute are also taxable. The test is not whether the action is one in tort or contract, but rather the question is: In lieu of what were the damages awarded? Raytheon (P) alleges that the damages received were as compensation for the destruction of goodwill, an asset. Where the suit is for injury to goodwill, the recovery represents a return of capital, generally not taxable. However, goodwill, like any asset, has a cost to the owner. If Raytheon's (P) recovery was in excess of its cost of establishing goodwill, the company essentially realized a gain made over its basis in the goodwill. Compensation for the loss of good will in excess of its cost is gross income. [Moral of this case—the IRS wants to collect every penny it can.]

Analysis:

Although some types of litigation damages are expressly covered by the Code, others have been ignored by Congress, leaving it to the court to decide which are includable as gross income. The court in this case establishes a simple rule: damages are taxable if they are in lieu of something that is also taxable. The court here was faced with whether the recovery represented lost profits to Raytheon (P), or compensation for loss of goodwill and damage to business. The court found it was the latter, and held that recovery for loss of goodwill is only taxable to the extent that the recovery exceeds the basis in the goodwill. However, recoveries for damage to goodwill are usually taxable in their entirety, unless the company was purchased as a going concern. This case provides us with a two-part analysis for determining whether and to what extent damages are taxable. First it is necessary to determine what type of damages are being recovered. The Code expressly addresses some types of damages

---

(punitive, physical injury, etc.). If the type of damages recovered is not addressed by the Code, it becomes necessary to determine what the recovery is attributable to. If attributable to lost or damaged property, a gain or loss may be realized; if lost profits are being recovered, the entire amount is taxable.

■ **CASE VOCABULARY**

GOOD WILL: An intangible asset of a business, representing its reputation, client or customer base, and other items important for its appraisal.

CHAPTER TEN

Separation and Divorce

Young v. Commissioner

Instant Facts: John and Louise (P) entered into a property settlement agreement pursuant to their divorce and then into a second agreement to settle Louise's (P) claim against John (P) when he defaulted on the first; pursuant to the second agreement, John (P) agreed to transfer valuable property to Louise (P), which she then sold to a third party. The tax court held that John's (P) transfer to Louise (P) was not a taxable event but that Louise's (P) sale to the third party was, and both Louise (P) and the Commissioner appealed.

Black Letter Rule: A transfer of property is "incident to a divorce," and is thus a nontaxable event, if it is related to the cessation of the marriage.

Young v. Commissioner

(Divorced Couple) v. *(IRS Commissioner)*

240 F.3d 369 (4th Cir. 2001)

EFFECTUATING PROPERTY SETTLEMENT AGREEMENTS DOES NOT GIVE RISE TO TAXABLE EVENTS

■ **INSTANT FACTS** John and Louise (P) entered into a property settlement agreement pursuant to their divorce and then into a second agreement to settle Louise's (P) claim against John (P) when he defaulted on the first; pursuant to the second agreement, John (P) agreed to transfer valuable property to Louise (P), which she then sold to a third party. The tax court held that John's (P) transfer to Louise (P) was not a taxable event but that Louise's (P) sale to the third party was, and both Louise (P) and the Commissioner appealed.

■ **BLACK LETTER RULE** A transfer of property is "incident to a divorce," and is thus a nontaxable event, if it is related to the cessation of the marriage.

■ **PROCEDURAL BASIS**

Federal appellate court review of a tax court ruling.

■ **FACTS**

Louise and John Young (P) married in 1969 and divorced in 1988. Pursuant to a settlement agreement executed a year later, John (P) delivered to Louise (P) a promissory note, payable in installments and secured by 71 acres of property that he had received as part of the same settlement. In 1990 John (P) defaulted on his obligation, and Louise (P) brought a collection action. The court ordered judgment in her favor, but before execution of the judgment, the couple entered into a second settlement agreement, pursuant to which John (P) promised to transfer to Louise (P), in full settlement of his obligation, 59 acres of land consisting of 42.3 of the 71 acres that were the subject of the first settlement agreement, plus some adjoining property. John (P) retained an option to repurchase the property, which option he sold to a third party who exercised the option and bought the land from Louise (P) for $2.2 million. Neither John (P) nor Louise (P) claimed any capital gains from the sale or transfer of this property on their federal income tax returns, and the Commissioner asserted deficiencies against both of them. After a trial of the consolidated cases, the tax court ruled that John (P) experienced no capital gain pursuant to 26 U.S.C. § 1041, which provides that no gain or loss is recognized on a transfer of property to a former spouse if the transfer is incident to the divorce. However, the court held that Louise (P) took John's (P) basis in the property and realized a taxable gain upon its sale to a third party, so she and her current husband owed the IRS over $400,000. Louise (P) and her husband appealed, as did the Commissioner.

■ **ISSUE**

Did the transfer of land from the husband to his former wife constitute a transfer "incident to" the couple's 1988 divorce for purposes of the nonrecognition rules?

■ **DECISION AND RATIONALE**

(Motz, J.) Yes. A transfer of property is "incident to a divorce," and is thus a nontaxable event, if it is related to the cessation of the marriage. The Treasury regulations extend a safe harbor to transfers

---

made within six years of divorce, if they are made pursuant to a divorce or separation instrument. A property transfer not made pursuant to a divorce instrument is presumed to be unrelated to the cessation of the marriage, but this presumption can be rebutted by showing that the transfer was made to effect the division of property owned by the former spouses at the time the marriage ended. The tax court ruled that the transfer in this case was related to the marriage and that thus neither party experienced a gain upon the initial transfer, but that Louise (P) took John's (P) basis in the property and did indeed then experience a gain upon her sale to the third party. Louise (P) actually argues that the initial transfer was not incident to the divorce, and that John (P) bears the tax burden, because she was a judgment creditor when she entered into the second settlement agreement. But the only relevant status here is spouse or former spouse—beyond that, Louise's (P) status makes no difference. The sole reason for the second settlement agreement was to resolve the disputes that arose from the Youngs' (P) divorce and subsequent property settlement. Had the transfer occurred at the time of the divorce, there would be no question that the transaction fell under 26 U.S.C. § 1041, so it should not matter that it happened later. Congress has chosen to defer, but not eliminate, the recognition of gain or loss on interspousal property transfers until the property is conveyed to a third party outside the single economic unit that a married (or formerly married) couple is thought to be. Thus, no taxable event occurred here until Louise (P) chose to sell the property to a third party. Affirmed.

Analysis:

This case demonstrates that, generally speaking, no gain or loss is recognized on a transfer of property from one spouse to a former spouse, if the transfer is incident to the couple's divorce. A transfer of property is "incident to the divorce" if it occurs within one year after the date the marriage ceases, or is related to the cessation of the marriage. A transfer of property is "related to the cessation of the marriage" if the transfer is made under a divorce or separation instrument and occurs within six years after the date the marriage ends. As the opinion notes, there is a rebuttable presumption that any transfer not made under a divorce or separation instrument, and any transfer occurring more than six years after the marriage ends, is *not* related to the cessation of the marriage.

■ CASE VOCABULARY

BASIS: The value assigned to a taxpayer's investment in property and used primarily for computing gain or loss from a transfer of the property. When the assigned value represents the cost of acquiring the property, it is also called *cost basis*.

NONRECOGNITION RULE: A statutory rule that allows all or part of a realized gain or loss not to be recognized for tax purposes. Generally, this type of provision only postpones the recognition of the gain or loss.

CHAPTER TWELVE

Assignment of Income

Lucas v. Earl

Instant Facts: After a husband and wife entered into a valid contract stating that all earnings acquired by either party were to be received and held in joint tenancy, the government sought to tax the husband for the whole of his earnings, rather than tax each party for one-half of the total.

Black Letter Rule: Income tax cannot be avoided by anticipatory arrangements and contracts devised to prevent salary from vesting in the person who earned it.

Commissioner v. Giannini

Instant Facts: The government sought to tax the Director and President of a corporation on money that he refused as income, but was later donated on his behalf.

Black Letter Rule: A taxpayer who makes an unqualified refusal to accept compensation, without a direction of its disposition, does not realize taxable income.

Helvering v. Horst

Instant Facts: After the owner of negotiable bonds gave to his son negotiable interest coupons detached from the bonds shortly before their due date, the government sought to tax the father for the interest payments.

Black Letter Rule: An assignment of the right to receive income from property is an economic benefit to the owner of the property, and is income realized and taxable to the owner of property.

Blair v. Commissioner

Instant Facts: The government sought to tax the owner of an income interest in a trust for life on portions of all his future income that were assigned to his children.

Black Letter Rule: The assignee of an unconditional assignment of a beneficial interest in a trust is taxable upon the income he receives as owner of the beneficial interest.

Estate of Stranahan v. Commissioner

Instant Facts: In order to increase his personal income so that he could take advantage of interest deductions, a father sold stock dividends to his son; and the government sought to impose upon the father the tax for the dividends.

Black Letter Rule: Tax avoidance motives alone will not serve to obviate the tax benefits of a transaction.

Susie Salvatore

Instant Facts: After the sale of certain property had been agreed upon, its owner conveyed one-half interest in the property to her children, giving them each a 1/10 share in the sale; but the government sought to tax the mother on the entire proceeds from the sale.

Black Letter Rule: A taxpayer may not avoid taxation by making an anticipatory assignment of property for which a sale has been negotiated and agreed.

Lucas v. Earl

(Commissioner of Internal Revenue) v. *(Taxpayer)*
281 U.S. 111, 50 S.Ct. 241 (1930)

A TAXPAYER CANNOT ESCAPE TAXATION BY ASSIGNING OR GIVING AWAY INCOME THAT HAS BEEN EARNED OR WILL BE EARNED BY THE TAXPAYER

■ **INSTANT FACTS** After a husband and wife entered into a valid contract stating that all earnings acquired by either party were to be received and held in joint tenancy, the government sought to tax the husband for the whole of his earnings, rather than tax each party for one-half of the total.

■ **BLACK LETTER RULE** Income tax cannot be avoided by anticipatory arrangements and contracts devised to prevent salary from vesting in the person who earned it.

■ PROCEDURAL BASIS

Appeal to the United States Supreme Court, challenging the decision of the Court of Appeals to reverse the Board of Tax Appeals' finding that a taxpayer was liable for taxes on money he earned, but which he assigned to his wife.

■ FACTS

Mr. Earl (P) and wife entered into a contract providing, essentially, that all property acquired and income earned by either party was to be "received, taken, and owned" by both of them as joint tenants. The contract was valid under the law of California. The Commissioner of Internal Revenue sought to impose a tax upon the husband for the whole of his earnings, the contract notwithstanding.

■ ISSUE

May a husband avoid a tax on his salary by assigning a portion thereof to his spouse?

■ DECISION AND RATIONALE

(Holmes, J.) No. Income tax cannot be avoided by anticipatory arrangements and contracts devised to prevent salary from vesting in the person who earned it. The Revenue Act of 1918 imposes a tax upon the net income of every individual including "income derived from salaries, wages, or compensation for personal services . . . of whatever kind and in whatever form paid." Mr. Earl (P) argues that the statute only taxed income received beneficially, and that his salary became joint property on the very instant it was received. We reject this view. Mr. Earl (P) was the only party to the contracts by which the salary and fees were earned, and it cannot be said that the last step in the performance of those contracts could be taken by anyone but himself. We believe the statute does not permit Earl (P) to avoid a tax on income through assignments and contracts by which the fruits are attributed to a different tree from that on which they grew. Reversed.

Analysis:

Taxpayers often attempt to assign income to family members who are in a lower tax-bracket, lowering the total tax liability. Both the I.R.S. and Congress have frowned upon theses efforts, as did the Court here. In reaching its decision, the Court focuses on four factors: (1) Mr. Earl (P) earned the money and alone had the right to receive it; (2) the money was paid out on Mr. Earl's (P) behalf, and he had the power to direct it; (3) Mr. Earl (P) was the person who earned the salary; and (4) Mr. Earl (P) directed the disposition of the money. Thus, the income was taxable as attributable to him. But this opinion goes beyond just the facts. Not only is it the seminal case in the assignment of income area, this case introduces a metaphor that has become fundamental in understanding assignment of income cases. Justice Holmes wrote that Mr. Earl (P) could not avoid a tax on income through assignments and contracts by which "the fruits are attributed to a different tree from that on which they grew." In Justice Holmes view, Mr. Earl (P) was the "tree" and his income was the "fruit," which could not be assigned to another "tree," i.e., his wife.

Commissioner v. Giannini

(*Commissioner of Internal Revenue*) v. (*Taxpayer*)

129 F.2d 638 (9th Cir. 1942)

A TAXPAYER HAS NOT REALIZED INCOME IF HE IS OFFERED COMPENSATION WHICH HE NEITHER RECEIVES NOR DIRECTS ITS DISPOSITION

■ **INSTANT FACTS** The government sought to tax the Director and President of a corporation on money that he refused as income, but was later donated on his behalf.

■ **BLACK LETTER RULE** A taxpayer who makes an unqualified refusal to accept compensation, without a direction of its disposition, does not realize taxable income.

PROCEDURAL BASIS

Appeal to the Ninth Circuit challenging the decision of the Board of Tax Appeals, which held that the taxpayer owed no tax on money he refused to take as income.

FACTS

A.P. Giannini (P) served as President and Director of Bancitaly Corporation, and from 1919 to 1925 he received no compensation for these services. In 1927, the corporation's board of directors resolved to compensate Giannini (P) at the rate of 5% of net profits each year, with a guaranteed minimum of $100,000 per year. Consequently, the Board credited Giannini's (P) withdrawal account and debited its own salary account $445,704.20, the equivalent of 5% of the corporations net profits for the first half of 1927. Shortly thereafter, Giannini (P) informed the board that he would not accept any further compensation for the year 1927, suggesting that the corporation should do something worthwhile with the money. The board found the refusal definite and absolute. Giannini (P) did not receive any further compensation for 1927. In early 1928, the Board of Directors resolved to donate to the University of California $1,357,607.40, an amount representing 5% of the net profits for 1927 less the $445,704.20 already received by Giannini (P). The donation was made in Giannini's (P) name. The Commissioner (D) found deficiencies for Giannini (P) and his wife totaling $260,746.21. He argued that Giannini's (P) waiver of compensation for his services with the suggestion that it be applied to a useful purpose amounted to a realization of income. The Gianninis (P) filed separate appeals.

ISSUE

Does a taxpayer realize income if he makes an unqualified refusal to take compensation that is offered to him?

DECISION AND RATIONALE

(Stephens, Cir. J.) No. A taxpayer who makes an unqualified refusal to accept compensation, without a direction of its disposition, does not realize taxable income. A taxpayer realizes income when he directs its disposition. The Commissioner (D) argues that the Supreme Court has held that any disposition of a contractual right to receive compensation, whether it be by waiver, transfer, assignment, or other means, amounts to a realization of taxable income. We believe the Commissioner has misread the Supreme Court's decisions regarding the assignment of income. Those cases all focused on the taxpayer's dominance and control over the disputed income. In the instant case, the Board of Tax Appeal found that the taxpayer did not receive the money and did not direct its disposition. All the arrangements regarding the donation were made by the corporation, with Giannini (P) acting only as an officer thereof. Under these circumstances we cannot say that the money was beneficially received by Giannini (P) and therefore subject to taxation. Affirmed.

Analysis:

To be effective, a renunciation of income must be unqualified. In other words, the person to whom the compensation is owed cannot direct its disposition in any manner. In addition, a renunciation must occur prior to the performance of the services. Renunciation of income comes up more often than you might think. For instance, often when personal representatives administer an estate, they will waive their right to compensation for their services. The IRS initially sought to tax the personal representatives for the salary they could have earned, but in Revenue Ruling 66–167, it was determined that so long as the waiver occurs prior to the performance of any service, the amount of compensation waived is not includable in gross income, nor is it a gift to the estate.

Helvering v. Horst

(Commissioner of Internal Revenue) v. *(Taxpayer)*

311 U.S. 112, 61 S.Ct. 144 (1940)

A TAXPAYER MAY NOT AVOID TAXATION BY ASSIGNING INCOME DERIVED FROM PROPERTY, UNLESS THE PROPERTY IS ALSO ASSIGNED

■ **INSTANT FACTS** After the owner of negotiable bonds gave to his son negotiable interest coupons detached from the bonds shortly before their due date, the government sought to tax the father for the interest payments.

■ **BLACK LETTER RULE** An assignment of the right to receive income from property is an economic benefit to the owner of the property, and is income realized and taxable to the owner of property.

■ **PROCEDURAL BASIS**

Appeal to the United States Supreme Court, challenging the decision of the Court of Appeals, which reversed the order of the Board of Tax Appeals sustaining the tax on the donor of the interest coupons.

■ **FACTS**

Mr. Horst (P), the owner of negotiable bonds, detached and gave to his son the interest coupons from the bonds. The Commissioner (P) ruled that the interest payments were taxable to Mr. Horst (P) as donor. The Board of Tax Appeals agreed, but the Court of Appeals reversed.

■ **ISSUE**

Is the owner of interest bearing property liable for interest paid on the property if those payments are assigned to a third party?

■ **DECISION AND RATIONALE**

(Stone, J.) Yes. An assignment of the right to receive income from property is an economic benefit to the owner of the property, and is income realized and taxable to the owner of property. The disposition of income to procure its payment to another is the enjoyment, and hence the realization, of the income by he who disposes of it. The holder of a coupon bond is the owner of two independent rights. One is the right to demand and receive at maturity the principal amount. The other is the right to receive interim interest payments. A taxpayer need not directly receive income in order to have realized it. Income may be realized if its disposition is controlled by the person who has the right to receive it. The rationale is that the assignor has diverted the payment from himself to others as the means of satisfying his wants. In other words, he has enjoyed the fruits of his labor or investment, just as one who uses the income to purchase goods. Mr. Horst (P) precluded any possibility of collecting the interest payments when he gave the coupons to his son. But this disposition of his right to receive income is, nonetheless, enjoyment of the income, no different than had he used the coupons to purchase goods, pay debts, or donated them to charity. Reversed.

Analysis:

An assignment of income from property is invalid as a means to avoid taxes on that property unless the property itself is also assigned. The fruit-tree metaphor used in *Lucas v. Earl* is useful in analyzing this case. There are two relevant aspects of property for tax purposes: (1) the property itself (the tree), and (2) the income produced or derived from the property (the fruit). In this case, the negotiable bonds represented the tree, while the interest coupons represented the fruit. It was the latter that was held not to be assignable for tax purposes. In the Court's view, assigning the income from property is no different than assigning salary. Mr. Horst (P) "used" the interest to make a gift. He derived money's worth from the disposition of the coupons. The only other method of receiving this benefit would have been to give his son money, which obviously would have been taxable.

Blair v. Commissioner

(Taxpayer) v. *(Commissioner of Internal Revenue)*
300 U.S. 5, 57 S.Ct. 330 (1937)

A TAXPAYER MAY SUCCESSFULLY ASSIGN INCOME FROM PROPERTY IF THE TAXPAYER DOES NOT OWN THE PROPERTY FROM WHICH THE INCOME IS DERIVED

■ **INSTANT FACTS** The government sought to tax the owner of an income interest in a trust for life on portions of all his future income that were assigned to his children.

■ **BLACK LETTER RULE** The assignee of an unconditional assignment of a beneficial interest in a trust is taxable upon the income he receives as owner of the beneficial interest.

■ **PROCEDURAL BASIS**

Appeal to the United States Supreme Court, challenging the judgment of the Circuit Court of Appeals reversing the decision of the Board of Tax Appeals.

■ **FACTS**

Mr. Blair (P) was the owner of an income interest in a trust for life. He assigned a portion of all of his future income from the trust to his children. The Supreme Court concluded the assignment was valid under state law.

■ **ISSUE**

Is the assignor of an income interest in a trust taxable upon the income paid to the assignees?

■ **DECISION AND RATIONALE**

(Hughes, C.J.) No. The assignee of an unconditional assignment of a beneficial interest in a trust is taxable upon the income he receives as owner of the beneficial interest. Unlike our cases dealing with the assignment of income earned by the assignor, this case concerns a tax upon income as to which the tax liability attaches to ownership. It is true that the beneficiary of the trust is liable for the tax upon the income distributable to the beneficiary. But this does not preclude a valid assignment of the beneficial interest. The one who receives the income as the owner of the beneficial interest is to pay the tax. If there has been a valid, unconditional assignment of the beneficial interest, the assignee becomes the beneficiary. The assignee is then taxable for the income he receives. It matters not in this case that Mr. Blair (P) assigned only the "right to receive income." Mr. Blair (P) owned only a right to receive income from the trust, and a portion of that right is exactly what he assigned. Because the assignments were valid, the assignees became the owners of the specified beneficial interest in the income. The assignees, not Mr. Blair (P), were taxable on the income received from the trust.

Analysis:

This case demonstrates the difficulty in employing the fruit-tree metaphor in every case. In this case, the proceeds from the trust would normally be considered the fruit, while the trust would be the tree. In such a situation the interest in the trust would be unassignable. However, in this case the interest in the trust becomes the underlying property—the tree—in Mr. Blair's (P) hands because that is all he owns and has control over. So when Mr. Blair (P) assigned a portion of his interest in the trust, he assigned a portion of *his* tree, which just happened to be the fruit of another tree. The key here is that the only thing Mr. Blair (P) had the right to control was the income he was to receive from the trust. Thus, he was able to avoid having to pay taxes on that income by assigning it to someone else before he earned it. In this sense, the assignment of a future right to income is akin to the waiver or renouncement of compensation that we saw in *Commissioner v. Giannini.*

Estate of Stranahan v. Commissioner

(Taxpayer) v. *(Commissioner of Internal Revenue)*

472 F.2d 867 (6th Cir. 1973)

FUTURE INCOME FROM PROPERTY MAY BE ASSIGNED FOR VALID CONSIDERATION IN AN ARM'S LENGTH TRANSACTION

■ **INSTANT FACTS** In order to increase his personal income so that he could take advantage of interest deductions, a father sold stock dividends to his son; and the government sought to impose upon the father the tax for the dividends.

■ **BLACK LETTER RULE** Tax avoidance motives alone will not serve to obviate the tax benefits of a transaction.

■ **PROCEDURAL BASIS**

Appeal to the Sixth Circuit, challenging the decision of the Tax Court denying an estate's petition for a redetermination of a deficiency in the decedent's income tax.

■ **FACTS**

Frank D. Stranahan (P) entered into an agreement with the Internal Revenue Service (IRS) under which he owed the IRS $754,815.72 in interest due to deficiencies in federal income, estate and gift taxes. Stranahan (P) paid the total in 1964. Stranahan's (P) income, however, was not large enough to absorb the interest deduction for which he was eligible. In order to take advantage of the full deduction allowed, Stranahan (P) decided to accelerate his income for 1964 by assigning to his son anticipated stock dividends worth $122,820 in exchange for a $115,000 check. The Tax Court concluded that the assignment was in reality a loan masquerading as a sale, lacking any business purpose; and therefore held that Stranahan (P) realized income when the dividend was declared paid.

■ **ISSUE**

May a taxpayer sell income from property for valid consideration in order to minimize tax liability?

■ **DECISION AND RATIONALE**

(Peck, Cir. J.) Yes. Tax avoidance motives alone will not serve to obviate the tax benefits of a transaction. Mr. Stranahan's estate (P) concedes that the sole purpose of the sale was to take advantage of the interest deduction. The tax consequences of the sale are determined by the transaction's substance, rather than its form. But it appears that both the form and the substance of the present transaction were an assignment of future income for valid consideration. The son paid consideration for future income. The fact that the assignment was intra-family does not nullify the transaction, but does subject it to scrutiny. It is true that a taxpayer may not escape taxation by legally assigning or giving away a portion of the income derived from income producing property. Here, however, the acceleration of income was not designed to avoid or escape recognition of the dividends but rather to reduce taxation by fully utilizing an available deduction. Further, the fact that the transaction was for good and valid consideration, and not merely gratuitous, distinguishes this case from others in the assignment of income area. The "tree-fruit" metaphor relied upon by the Tax Court is inapplicable because its genesis lies in a gratuitous transaction, while the instant situation concerns a transaction for valid consideration. The fact that the risk of not receiving the dividends was remote does

---

not matter, for risks did in fact exist. We conclude that the transaction was economically realistic, with substance, and therefore should be recognized for tax purposes.

Analysis:

The court here rejects the use of the tree-fruit metaphor when the fruit is sold. The court also rejects the idea that *Lucas, Horst* and other assignment-of-income cases stand for the proposition that income may not be assigned in any manner in order to lower one's tax liability. Instead, the court reads these cases as holding only that income cannot be assigned gratuitously to avoid its recognition by the assignor. In the court's view, when an assignment of income is accompanied by valid consideration in an arm's length transaction, it will be held valid for tax purposes. In reaching its holding, the court discusses two recurring themes in tax law. The first is that a transaction's tax consequences will be determined by the substance of the transaction, not its form. The second principle applied by the court is that intra-family transactions are heavily scrutinized. In scrutinizing the assignment, the court noted that its sole purpose was to reduce Mr. Stranahan's (P) tax liability, but that this fact alone did not vitiate the transaction.

Susie Salvatore

(Taxpayer)

29 T.C.M. 89 (1970)

THE SUBSTANCE OF A TRANSACTION DETERMINES WHETHER THERE HAS BEEN A SALE OF PROPERTY OR MERELY AN ASSIGNMENT OF INCOME FROM PROPERTY

■ **INSTANT FACTS** After the sale of certain property had been agreed upon, its owner conveyed one-half interest in the property to her children, giving them each a 1/10 share in the sale; but the government sought to tax the mother on the entire proceeds from the sale.

■ **BLACK LETTER RULE** A taxpayer may not avoid taxation by making an anticipatory assignment of property for which a sale has been negotiated and agreed.

■ **PROCEDURAL BASIS**

Action by a taxpayer for a redetermination of her tax liability.

■ **FACTS**

Susie Salvatore (P), the mother of five children, was the sole owner of a gas station devised to her by her late husband. Mrs. Salvatore's (P) children ran the station, with her receiving $100 per week of the income therefrom. The family eventually decided to sell the station. The family agreed that the proceeds from the sale would first be used to satisfy outstanding liabilities, $100,000 of the remaining amount to be given to Mrs. Salvatore (P), with the balance being divided amongst the children. Mrs. Salvatore (P) eventually accepted an offer from Texaco for $295,000. After Texaco made a down payment of $29,500. Mrs. Salvatore (P) executed a warranty deed conveying an undivided one-half interest in the property to her five children. Mrs. Salvatore (P) filed a gift tax return, reporting a gift made to each of her children of a 1/10 interest in the property. After the sale was completed and the liabilities paid off, Mrs. Salvatore (P) received $118,542, one-half the balance, with the rest being distributed to the children after the gift tax was paid. Mrs. Salvatore (P) reported total gains of $115,728. In a notice of deficiency, the Commissioner determined that Mrs. Salvatore (P) owed $238,856.

■ **ISSUE**

Is a taxpayer liable on the entire gain realized from the sale of property, even if a portion of the property was assigned by gift prior to the sale?

■ **DECISION AND RATIONALE**

(Featherston, J.) Yes. A taxpayer may not avoid taxation by making an anticipatory assignment of property for which a sale has been negotiated and agreed. The Supreme Court has held that a sale by one person cannot be transformed for tax purposes into a sale by another by using the latter as a conduit through which to pass title. The evidence shows that Mrs. Salvatore (P) owned the service station prior to entering into the sale agreement with Texaco. The subsequent conveyance, unsupported by consideration, of an undivided one-half interest in the property to her children was merely an intermediary step in the transfer of title to Texaco. The children were merely "a conduit through which to pass title." Although the form of the transaction was that of a gift prior to the transfer of title, in substance the transaction was an anticipatory assignment of one-half of the income from the sale. This conclusion is confirmed by the fact that Mrs. Salvatore's (P) share from the sale depended on the amount the sale netted. Therefore, all the gain from the sale was taxable to Mrs. Salvatore (P).

Analysis:

A gratuitous assignment of property, the sale of which has been arranged, will likely be deemed a sham transaction and an invalid assignment of income. The transaction in this case was couched as a gift, but here it is a clear case of assignment of income. To reach this conclusion the court invokes the substance over form rationale, so prevalent in tax cases. Notice that unlike the previous case, in which the court held the taxpayer had no tax liability for assigned income, here there was no valid consideration for the assignment. When looking at the form of a transaction, and when scrutinizing an intra-family transaction especially, consideration is a key element. If missing, it is likely that the sale will be deemed a sham for purposes of avoiding tax liability. Also, note that the problem here is one of timing: the assignment occurred after the decision to sell had been made and an agreement to sell negotiated. Finally, you should also keep in mind that the fact that the transaction is between a taxpayer and a charitable organization will not lessen the scrutiny applied, as can be seen in Revenue Ruling 69–120, which provides that a taxpayer that sold a life insurance contract and an annuity contract to a charitable organization realized gross income when the contracts were surrendered for cash value by the organization.

CHAPTER THIRTEEN

Income Producing Entities

Corliss v. Bowers

Instant Facts: A taxpayer, who had established a trust for the benefit of his wife, brought a constitutional challenge against provisions of the Revenue Act of 1924 that taxed a grantor of a trust on trust income if the grantor retained a reversionary interest in the corpus of the trust.

Black Letter Rule: The constitution does not prohibit Congress from treating the grantor of a revocable trust as owner of the trust, who is taxable on its income.

Helvering v. Clifford

Instant Facts: After a taxpayer, for the benefit of his wife, set up a trust over which he exercised unfettered discretion as trustee, the government sought to tax the husband on the income produced by the trust on the theory that under the catch-all definition of gross income he was the owner of the trust.

Black Letter Rule: The facts and circumstances attendant on the creation and operation of a trust determine whether a taxpayer is the owner of the corpus of a trust, and therefore taxable on its income.

Commissioner v. Culbertson

Instant Facts: The government sought to tax a rancher on the entire income generated by a partnership between he and his four sons.

Black Letter Rule: The question of whether a real partnership has been formed within the meaning of the federal tax laws depends on the bona fide intent of the parties to join together as partners.

Overton v. Commissioner

Instant Facts: The owners of a corporation were held liable for taxes on the theory that dividends received by their wives on stock registered in the wives' names were income to the husbands for tax purposes.

Black Letter Rule: Stock dividends which are payable to shareholders cannot be assigned to third parties through the creation of different classes of stock.

Johnson v. Commissioner

Instant Facts: Although a basketball player formed a corporation to which he assigned his income in exchange for a monthly salary, the government sought to tax the player on the whole of the income, not just the monthly salary.

Black Letter Rule: In order for a personal service corporation to be considered the controller of income, the service performer must be an employee of the corporation whom the corporation has the right to direct and control in some meaningful sense, and there must exist between the corporation and the entity using the services a contract recognizing the corporation's controlling position.

Borge v. Commissioner

Instant Facts: An entertainer sought to offset losses he incurred in a poultry business against profits he earned as an entertainer by assigning both to a wholly owned corporation, and contracting for a minimal salary.

Black Letter Rule: A single wholly owned corporation may be compromised of two separate organizations, trades or businesses within the meaning of the Code for purposes of reallocating income between organizations, trades or businesses controlled by the individual.

Corliss v. Bowers

(Taxpayer) v. *(Collector of Internal Revenue)*
281 U.S. 376, 50 S.Ct. 336 (1930)

THE GRANTOR OF A TRUST WHO RETAINS CONTROL OVER THE TRUST MAY BE TAXED ON TRUST INCOME

■ **INSTANT FACTS** A taxpayer, who had established a trust for the benefit of his wife, brought a constitutional challenge against provisions of the Revenue Act of 1924 that taxed a grantor of a trust on trust income if the grantor retained a reversionary interest in the corpus of the trust.

■ **BLACK LETTER RULE** The constitution does not prohibit Congress from treating the grantor of a revocable trust as owner of the trust, who is taxable on its income.

■ PROCEDURAL BASIS

Appeal to the United States Supreme Court from the decision of the Court of Appeals upholding the District Court's dismissal of a suit to recover income tax paid.

■ FACTS

Mr. Corliss (P) set up a trust giving his wife a life estate in its income, and the remainder to his children. Mr. Corliss (P) retained the right to abolish or change the trust in any manner at his will. In 1924, the trust paid its income over to Mrs. Corliss (P), but the government taxed Mr. Corliss (P) on the income. Mr. Corliss (P) sought to recover the income tax he paid attributable to the trust income on the grounds that the statute permitting the income to be attributed to him was unconstitutional. The District Court dismissed the complaint and the Court of Appeals affirmed.

■ ISSUE

May Congress constitutionally attribute income from a trust to its grantor who retains control over the trust?

■ DECISION AND RATIONALE

(Holmes, J.) Yes. The constitution does not prohibit Congress from treating the grantor of a revocable trust as owner of the trust. The Revenue Act of 1924 provides that "when the grantor of a trust has, at any time during the taxable year ... the power to revest in himself title to any part of the corpus of the trust then the income of such part of the trust for such taxable year shall be included in computing the net income of the grantor." The statute clearly purports to tax Mr. Corliss (P). It is true that the trustee held legal title to the income, while Mrs. Corliss held an equitable interest in the trust income. But the federal tax laws are not as concerned with issues of title as they are with dominion over the property taxed. Mr. Corliss clearly held the power to stop payment of the income. If income is subject to a man's unfettered command, it may be taxed to him whether he chooses to enjoy it or not. Affirmed.

Analysis:

Taxpayers often attempted to assign income to family members by using a trust in which the grantor retained a substantial interest. Congress took note, and enacted provisions that curbed this abuse. Today, §§ 676 and 677 attribute income to the grantor of a trust, if the grantor retains the power to

---

revoke the trust or if the income could be used for his benefit. Either of these provisions would have made the income distributed to Mrs. Corliss taxable to Mr. Corliss (P). This case specifically upholds Congress's power to attribute income from a trust to its grantor. In the Court's view, the fact that Mr. Corliss (P) retained the power to abolish the trust, although he had no legal title, was enough for Congress to constitutionally attribute the income to Mr. Corliss.

■ CASE VOCABULARY

ADVERSE PARTY: Any person having a substantial beneficial interest in the trust which would be adversely affected by the exercise or nonexercise of the power which he possesses respecting the trust.

Helvering v. Clifford

(Commissioner of Internal Revenue) v. *(Taxpayer)*

309 U.S. 331, 60 S.Ct. 554 (1940)

GROSS INCOME INCLUDES INCOME FROM A TRUST OVER WHICH THE TAXPAYER HAS A SUFFICIENT INTEREST IN THE CORPUS

■ **INSTANT FACTS** After a taxpayer, for the benefit of his wife, set up a trust over which he exercised unfettered discretion as trustee, the government sought to tax the husband on the income produced by the trust on the theory that under the catch-all definition of gross income he was the owner of the trust.

■ **BLACK LETTER RULE** The facts and circumstances attendant on the creation and operation of a trust determine whether a taxpayer is the owner of the corpus of a trust, and therefore taxable on its income.

■ FACTS

Mr. Clifford (P) made himself trustee of securities which he owned. The net income from the trust was to be paid to his wife. The trust was for a term of five years, but would terminate if either spouse died. Upon termination, the corpus of the trust was to go to Mr. Clifford (P), while all income from the trust was to be treated as property of his wife. Under the terms of the trust, Mr. Clifford (P) retained full discretion with respect to the amount of income the trust was to pay to his wife. Mr. Clifford (P) also had the power to exercise the voting power incident to the stock, alienate the stock, invest the income from the trust, and collect the income. Neither the corpus of the trust, nor its income, were liable for the wife's debts. Furthermore, the wife had no power to transfer, encumber, or anticipate any interest in the trust or any income therefrom prior to its disbursement. Upon transfer of the stock, Mr. Clifford (P) paid a gift tax. In 1934, all the income from the trust was paid to Mrs. Clifford, who included it in her tax return. The Commissioner, however, determined a deficiency in Mr. Clifford's (P) tax return on the theory that the trust income was taxable to him. The Board of Tax Appeals agreed, but the Circuit Court of Appeals reversed.

■ ISSUE

May a taxpayer, after having established a trust, be treated as the owner of the corpus, who is taxable on its income?

■ DECISION AND RATIONALE

(Holmes, J.) Yes. The facts and circumstances attendant on the creation and operation of a trust determine whether an individual is the owner of the corpus of a trust, and therefore taxable on its income. Section 61(a) of the Internal Revenue Code defines gross income as "all income from whatever source derived." The broad language indicates the intent on the part of Congress to exercise the full measure of its taxing power. The separation of one economic unit into two or more by use of state legal devices are not conclusive under Section 61(a). In this case, the short duration of the trust, the fact that Mr. Corliss' wife was the beneficiary, and the retention of control over the corpus by Mr. Corliss (P) all lead to the conclusion that he continued to be the owner under Section 61(a). In substance, his control of the corpus was virtually the same before and after the creation of the trust. Mr. Corliss (P) was, in no realistic manner, any "poorer" after the trust had been created. Where the head of a household has income that exceeds his needs, it likely makes little difference to him where the portion of that income is routed. In such a circumstance, the decisive factor may be his retention of control over the principal.

This notwithstanding, our point is that no one fact is normally decisive. Rather, all the considerations and circumstances of the kind we have mentioned are appropriate foundations for findings on this issue. We would also add that although § 676 of the Code provides the specific treatment to be accorded to revocable trusts, that section cannot be interpreted to imply that the grantor of short-term trusts may not be deemed its owner under the catch-all provision of § 61(a). If anything, § 676 has merely provided a rule of thumb to be applied in a certain set of cases. Reversed.

■ DISSENT

(Roberts, J.) The Court's decision disregards the fundamental principle that legislation is not the function of the judiciary but of Congress.

Analysis:

Although this case was decided under the Revenue Act of 1934, the import of its holding is that a taxpayer who retains a sufficient interest in the corpus of a trust may be deemed its owner under what is now § 61(a). The 1934 Act provided no guidance for short-term trusts, which were often used to assign income. The government thus sought "judicial legislation" under the guise of § 61 in order to close off the loophole. The court, however, set up no bright-line rule to determine when an interest is "sufficient" to ascribe ownership of the trust to the grantor. Instead, it called for a factual inquiry focusing on such factors as the duration of the trust, the retention of control over the corpus, and the family relationships involved. The ad hoc nature of this inquiry made the application of the Code in this area uncertain, a result that always undermines the voluntary nature of the federal income tax. To address this problem Congress enacted several provisions dealing with grantor trusts. Section 673 provides the treatment to be accorded to trusts when the grantor has a reversionary interest. Section 674 taxes a grantor on income produced by a trust in which he or a nonadverse party has the power to decide who will receive the corpus of the trust. Section 675 governs those trusts in which the grantor or a nonadverse party holds significant administrative power over the corpus. Section 677 taxes a grantor on trust income that supports the grantor's spouse, or benefits the grantor. And § 678 taxes a third party (not the grantor) who has the power to keep the income or the corpus for his own benefit.

■ CASE VOCABULARY

NONADVERSE PARTY: Any person who does not have a substantial benefit in the trust which would be adversely affected by the exercise or nonexercise of the power which the adverse party possesses respecting the trust.

Commissioner v. Culbertson

(Commissioner of Internal Revenue) v. (Taxpayer)
337 U.S. 733, 69 S.Ct. 1210 (1949)

THE BONA FIDE INTENT OF THE PARTIES DETERMINES WHETHER A FAMILY PARTNERSHIP HAS BEEN VALIDLY FORMED FOR TAX PURPOSES

■ **INSTANT FACTS** The government sought to tax a rancher on the entire income generated by a partnership between him and his four sons.

■ **BLACK LETTER RULE** The question of whether a real partnership has been formed within the meaning of the federal tax laws depends on the bona fide intent of the parties to join together as partners.

■ **PROCEDURAL BASIS**

Appeal to the United State Supreme Court, challenging the decision of the Court of Appeals to reverse the Tax Court's holding that the contribution of vital services or original capital are necessary for inclusion in a partnership under the tax laws.

■ **FACTS**

W.O. Culbertson (P) formed a partnership with his four sons to conduct the family ranching operation. In doing so, Mr. Culbertson (P) sold an undivided one-half interest in the ranch to his sons. But the sons contributed no capital to the partnership. The sales price was instead paid by gifts from Mr. Culbertson (P) and the operating proceeds from the ranch. The eldest son served as foreman of the ranch for a brief period, before entering the army. The second son never performed any services for the newly formed partnership. The two youngest sons attended school and worked on the ranch during the summer only. A partnership return was filed for 1940 and 1941 indicating a division of income amongst each partner. The Commissioner (D) held that the entire income from the partnership was to be taxed to Mr. Culbertson (P). Tax Court agreed, holding that a partnership for tax purposes was not formed because the sons contributed neither vital services nor their own capital to the partnership. The Court of Appeals reversed on the theory that the intent to provide vital services and capital in the future was enough to form a partnership under the tax laws.

■ **ISSUE**

Under the federal tax laws, does the formation of a partnership require that each partner contribute vital services or original capital?

■ **DECISION AND RATIONALE**

(Vinson, C.J.) No. The question of whether a partnership has been formed within the meaning of the federal tax laws depends on the bona fide intent of the parties to join together as partners. The Court of Appeals was of the opinion that a family partnership entered into without tax avoidance motives should be given recognition for tax purposes if formed with an intent that the partners contribute capital or services at sometime in the future. This reasoning must be rejected because it runs counter to the demands of *I.R.C. § 701* ("A partnership as such shall not be subject to the income tax. . . . Persons carrying on business as partners shall be liable for income tax only in their separate or individual capacity.") and *I.R.C. § 61(a)(1)* (gross income includes income derived from compensation for services), which require that he who presently earns the income through his own labor and skill and the utilization of his own capital be taxed thereon. We have made clear that participation in the business by the partners during the taxing year is important. However, the question is not whether the services or capital contributed by a partner are of sufficient importance to meet some objective standard, but whether, considering all the facts, that parties in good faith and acting with a business purpose intended to join together in the present conduct of the enterprise. It is unquestionable that the lack of any contribution by partners of "vital services" or "original capital" places a heavy burden on the partner to prove a bona fide intent to join together. But those factors are not determinative of the issue, neither in conjunction or individually. It is up to the partnership to determine which services are to be contributed presently by each of the partners. The sole task for the Tax Court is to determine the partners' true intent. As to the present case, we make no intimation as to whether capital or services were contributed by the partners. The case is to be remanded for a decision consistent with this opinion. Reversed and remanded.

Analysis:

The bona fide intent test requires an inquiry into factors such as the partnership agreement, the conduct of the partners, the testimony of uninterested parties, the relationship between the partners, their capital contributions, and the control over the income. Although the approach used in this case is still valid, Congress has provided several safe-harbors, which preclude an attack on family partnerships. Section 704(e)(1) recognizes a partner if he owns a capital interest in a partnership in which capital is a material income-producing factor, even if the interest was acquired by gift. Section 704(e)(2) recognizes a partnership interest created by gift, except to the extent that (1) the income is determined without allowance of reasonable compensation to the donor for services provided by him and (2) the share of the income attributable to donated capital is proportionately greater than the share of the donor attributable to his capital. Section 704(e)(3) treats an intrafamily purchase as a gift from the seller, and the fair market value of the interest is treated as donated capital.

Overton v. Commissioner

(Taxpayer) v. *(Commissioner of Internal Revenue)*
162 F.2d 155 (2d Cir. 1947)

THE SUBSTANCE OF CORPORATE DIVIDENDS PAID DETERMINES WHETHER CORPORATE INCOME HAS BEEN INVALIDLY ASSIGNED FOR TAX PURPOSES

■ **INSTANT FACTS** The owners of a corporation were held liable for taxes on the theory that dividends received by their wives on stock registered in the wives' names were income to the husbands for tax purposes.

■ **BLACK LETTER RULE** Stock dividends which are payable to shareholders cannot be assigned to third parties through the creation of different classes of stock.

■ **PROCEDURAL BASIS**

Appeal to the Second Circuit, challenging the Tax Court's holding that dividends paid to the wives of stockholders were income to the husbands.

■ **FACTS**

Mr. Overton (P) and Mr. Oliphant (P) were shareholders in Castle & Overton, Inc., a New York corporation. The corporate certificate was amended to change the outstanding 1,000 shares of common stock into 2,000 shares divided into two classes of stock. The old stock was exchanged for 1,000 shares of Class A stock, and the shareholders gave to their wives 1,000 shares of Class B stock. The holders of Class B stock had virtually no corporate voting rights, were restricted in their ability to alienate the stock, and limited to realizing a value of only $1 per share upon liquidation. In fact, the only substantive right Class B stockholders had was to receive 80% of all dividends announced over $10. Over a five year period, Class B stock earned dividends of $150.40 per share, while Class A stock earned $77.60 per share.

■ **ISSUE**

May dividends paid to a class of stockholders be treated as income to other shareholders?

■ **DECISION AND RATIONALE**

(Swan, Cir. J.) Yes. Stock dividends which are payable to shareholders cannot be assigned to third parties through the creation of different classes of stock. We agree with the Tax Court that the arrangement, though made in the form of a gift of stock, was in reality an assignment of part of the taxpayer's future dividends. Since Class B stock represented only $1,000 of the corporate assets, it is clear that the property which earned the dividends paid to Class B shareholders was the property represented by the Class A stock held by the husbands. Had the husbands transferred some of their original stock, they could have lessened the income tax on the family group. But they would have been liable for substantial gift tax. When the husbands made gifts of Class B stock, they gave their wives nothing more than the right to future earnings flowing from the property owned by their husbands. We have previously held that anticipatory assignments of income are ineffective tax-wise.

Analysis:

The corporate form can be used to assign income, such as by the payment of dividends by smaller, closely held corporations. This case does little more than apply the assignment of income doctrine announced in *Lucas v. Earl* to the context of dividend payments. The shareholder husbands in this case, instead of using a contract vesting income in their wives, used dividend payments to accomplish the same end. Under the substance over form rationale, the payments were invalid assignments of income. The dividends were an anticipatory arrangement to prevent income from vesting in the husbands, violating the rule of *Lucas.*

Johnson v. Commissioner

(*Taxpayer*) v. (*Commissioner of Internal Revenue*)

78 T.C. 882 (1982)

THE OWNER OF A PERSONAL SERVICE CORPORATION MAY BE TAXED ON THE ENTIRE INCOME EARNED BY THE CORPORATION

■ **INSTANT FACTS** Although a basketball player formed a corporation to which he assigned his income in exchange for a monthly salary, the government sought to tax the player on the whole of the income, not just the monthly salary.

■ **BLACK LETTER RULE** In order for a personal service corporation to be considered the controller of income, the service performer must be an employee of the corporation whom the corporation has the right to direct and control in some meaningful sense, and there must exist between the corporation and the entity using the services a contract recognizing the corporation's controlling position.

■ **PROCEDURAL BASIS**

Not provided.

■ **FACTS**

Charles Johnson (P), a basketball player, formed a personal service corporation as a financial planning device. Because the team Johnson played for, the Warriors, refused to enter into a player-contract with a corporation, Johnson (P) negotiated and signed contracts with the team, and then assigned his contractual rights to the corporation, which would pay him a monthly salary. The Warriors did agree to make payments directly to the corporation.

■ **ISSUE**

Are amounts paid to a personal service corporation pursuant to a contract between the service performer employee and the service user/purchaser taxable to the corporation?

■ **DECISION AND RATIONALE**

No. In order for a personal service corporation to be considered the controller of income, the service performer must be an employee of the corporation whom the corporation has the right to direct and control in some meaningful sense, and there must exist between the corporation and the entity using the services a contract recognizing the corporation's controlling position. The Supreme Court has held that income must be taxed on the person who earns it. But since corporate earnings are often attributable to the personal services of their employees, a simplistic application of this rule would lead to the non-recognition of corporations as taxable entities. In this case, Mr. Johnson (P) had a contract with the corporation, giving the latter control over Mr. Johnson's (P) services. Thus, the first element of our test is satisfied. However, we find the second element lacking. The crucial factor is that there was no contract or agreement between the corporation and the Warriors. Indeed, the Warriors expressly refused to enter into a contract with the corporation. Thus the existing employment relationships were between Mr. Johnson (P) and his corporation, and between Mr. Johnson (P) and the Warriors. The assignment of earnings to the corporation does not transfer the tax consequences, it merely demonstrates Mr. Johnson's (P) control over the income. This control is sufficient to make those amounts income to Mr. Johnson (P) under *I.R.C. § 61(a)(1)* (Gross income includes income derived from the compensation for services).

Analysis:

The IRS has long sought to attack the use of incorporation as a method of assigning income. Congress has provided some guidance in the area. Section 482 permits the Treasury to "distribute, apportion, or allocate gross income, deductions, credits, or allowances" between or among corporations, businesses, and entities that are controlled by the same interests. But § 482 is often inapplicable in the area of "personal service corporations"—those whose function is to exploit a single employee's services—because § 482 requires that there be two or more business entities. Here the assignment occurred between only Mr. Johnson (P), the person, and his wholly owned corporation. Therefore, the government had to rest its case on the extensive reach of § 61(a) and the assignment of income doctrine established thereunder. As the court noted, a mechanical application of *Lucas v. Earl* would all but eliminate the recognition of many corporations as taxable entities. A more precise test was necessary. Consequently, the court holds that for an individual and his wholly owned corporation to fall outside the reach of § 61(a) and *Lucas*, two requirements need to be met. First, the service-providing employee must actually be an employee that the corporation can control in a meaningful sense. Second, the corporation must have a contract with the entity that is using the services of the employee. This requirement was obviously not met in this case because the Warriors refused to contract with a corporation for its players' services. Mr. Johnson (P) was therefore taxable on the entire income earned from the Warriors.

Borge v. Commissioner

(Taxpayer) v. *(Commissioner)*

405 F.2d 673 (2d Cir. 1968)

AN INDIVIDUAL MAY NOT USE A SINGLE WHOLLY OWNED CORPORATION TO TRANSFER INCOME AND OTHER TAX ATTRIBUTES BETWEEN SEPARATE AND UNRELATED BUSINESSES

■ **INSTANT FACTS** An entertainer sought to offset losses he incurred in a poultry business against profits he earned as an entertainer by assigning both to a wholly owned corporation, and contracting for a minimal salary.

■ **BLACK LETTER RULE** A single wholly-owned corporation may be comprised of two separate organizations, trades or businesses within the meaning of the Code for purposes of reallocating income between organizations, trades or businesses controlled by the individual.

■ **PROCEDURAL BASIS**

Appeal to the Second Circuit, challenging the decision of the Tax Court sustaining the Commissioner's allocation to the taxpayer of a portion of the compensation received by the taxpayer's wholly-owned corporation.

■ **FACTS**

Victor Borge (P), an entertainer, transferred a poultry business with substantial losses to his wholly owned corporation, Danica Enterprises, Inc. (Danica), in exchange for all its stock and a note. Borge (P) also entered into a contract with Danica to perform entertainment and promotional services for the corporation for five years at a salary of $50,000 per year. Prior to the transfers, Borge (P) operated the poultry business under the guise of ViBo Farms. Danica offset the poultry losses against the entertainment profits, which far exceeded the annual compensation it had contracted to pay Borge (P). Danica, however, did nothing to further Borge's (P) entertainment career. Indeed, Borge (P) was required to personally guarantee all entertainment services contracts.

■ **ISSUE**

May the Commissioner reallocate income between an individual and the individual's wholly owned corporation under the theory that the corporation is in fact two separate businesses, trades or organizations?

■ **DECISION AND RATIONALE**

(Hays, Cir. J.) Yes. A single wholly owned corporation may be comprised of two separate organizations, trades or businesses within the meaning of the Code for purposes of reallocating income between organizations, trades or businesses controlled by the individual. Section 482 of the Code provides: "In the case of two or more organizations, trades, or businesses owned or controlled directly or indirectly by the same interests, the Secretary may distribute, apportion, or allocate gross income, deductions, credits, or allowances between or among such organizations, trades or businesses, if he determines that such distribution, apportionment, or allocation is necessary in order to prevent the evasion of taxes or clearly to reflect the income of any of such organizations, trades, or businesses." Borge (P) argues that § 482 is inapplicable here because he is not a trade or business separate from his wholly owned corporation. But the cases Borge (P) relies upon have merely held that devoting one's time and energies to the affairs of a corporation is not itself a trade or business of the person so engaged. But that is not the case here because Borge (P) was in the business of entertainment, channeling his income to the corporation, not devoting his efforts to the corporation. We conclude that the Commissioner (D) could properly have found that for purposes of Section 482 Borge (P) owned or controlled two businesses, an entertainment business and a poultry business, both under the umbrella of one corporation.

Analysis:

Section 482 permits the IRS to allocate income and other tax attributes between businesses controlled by the same interests. What the court essentially holds here is that a single wholly owned corporation may actually be two or more separate businesses or trades within the meaning of § 482. The presence of tax avoidance motives played a large role in the courts' decisions that reallocation was permissible under § 482. The factors the court found important were that Danica played no role in Borge's (P) entertainment career and the salary received by Borge (P) from Danica was grossly inadequate considering the income generated by Borge's (P) entertainment services. But the question left open by the court was whether an individual as an employee can be a separate organization for purposes of § 482. The court avoids the issue by finding that there were indeed two organizations, a poultry business and an entertainment business.

CHAPTER FOURTEEN

Business Deductions

Welch v. Helvering

Instant Facts: The owner of a grain purchasing business sought to deduct from his income payments he made and that were directed to the creditors of a grain company for which he had served as secretary and which had all its debts legally discharged in bankruptcy.

Black Letter Rule: An "ordinary" expense is not one that is habitual, but rather one that is common in the taxpayer's particular industry or business.

Midland Empire Packing Co. v. Commissioner

Instant Facts: A meat packing company is adjudged to have made a deductible repair after lining the basement walls of its plant with concrete, in order to keep out oil from a nearby factory.

Black Letter Rule: Repairs to property made during the taxable year are deductible as an ordinary and necessary business expense.

INDOPCO, Inc. v. Commissioner

Instant Facts: The Commissioner sought to disallow a deduction taken by a company with respect to professional expenses incurred as a target corporation in a friendly takeover.

Black Letter Rule: The fact that an expenditure does not create or enhance a separate and distinct additional asset does not alone preclude the expenditure from being treated as a non-deductible capital expense.

Morton Frank v. Commissioner

Instant Facts: A taxpayer sought to deduct travel expenses incurred while conducting preliminary investigations into the purchase of a newspaper press.

Black Letter Rule: Travel expenses and legal fees spent in searching for a business to purchase cannot be deducted under the provisions of section 162(a).

Exacto Spring Corporation v. Commissioner

Instant Facts: The I.R.S. challenged a close corporation's CEO's salary as so excessive as not to be deductible as "reasonable" salary.

Black Letter Rule: Executives' salary is "reasonable" (and deductible) if it's proportional to investors' profits.

Harolds Club v. Commissioner

Instant Facts: The proprietors of a gaming establishment sought to pay a fixed percentage salaries, ranging from $350,000 to $560,000, paid to the establishment's manager, father of the proprietors, from 1952 to 1956.

Black Letter Rule: Where an employee dominates his employers, the lack of ability to bargain freely for salaries may exist even as between adults, thereby making the employee's salary non-deductible.

Rosenspan v. U.S.

Instant Facts: A traveling jewelry salesman, who had no permanent home, sought to deduct his expenses incurred while on the road.

Black Letter Rule: Living expenses paid by a single taxpayer who has no home and is continuously employed on the road may not be deducted in computing net income.

Andrews v. Commissioner

Instant Facts: A taxpayer who held separate businesses in New England and Florida sought to deduct as travel expenses the costs of maintaining a home in Florida.

Black Letter Rule: A taxpayer can have only one home for purposes of deducting travel expenses under section 162(a)(2).

Starr's Estate v. Commissioner

Instant Facts: The Commissioner disallowed a taxpayer a deduction for payments made on a sprinkler system he obtained through an agreement termed as a "lease," but which was, in reality, a sale.

Black Letter Rule: Where the foreordained practical effect of the rent is to produce title eventually, the rental agreement can be treated as a sale.

Hill v. Commissioner

Instant Facts: A certified school teacher sought to deduct her expenses incurred while attending summer school, which was one of two choices she had to renew her teaching license.

Black Letter Rule: Education expenses incurred to fulfill the requirements of a taxpayer's employment or profession are deductible as necessary and ordinary business expenses.

Coughlin v. Commissioner

Instant Facts: An attorney, whose partners relied on for matters relating to federal taxation, sought to deduct tuition and travel expenses incurred while attending a N.Y.U. tax seminar, but the government disallowed the deduction.

Black Letter Rule: A taxpayer may deduct education expenses incurred in maintaining or improving his professional skills.

Sharp v. United States

Instant Facts: The government sought to tax the partners in a partnership on a gain realized from the sale of an airplane, as used for personal and business purposes and upon which the partnership took allowable depreciation deductions in proportion to the extent it was used for business purposes.

Black Letter Rule: The gain or loss realized upon the sale of property that is used for both business and personal matters must be allocated in accordance with the property's percentages of business and personal use.

Simon v. Commissioner

Instant Facts: Professional violin players who purchased antique violin bows for use in their performances sought to take allowable depreciation deductions on the bows even though the bows actually appreciated in value in the hands of the taxpayers.

Black Letter Rule: Under the Accelerated Cost Recovery System the test for determining whether tangible property is of a character subject to the allowance for depreciation is whether the property will suffer exhaustion, wear and tear, or obsolescence in its use by a business.

Welch v. Helvering

(*Taxpayer*) v. (*Commissioner of Internal Revenue*)
290 U.S. 111, 54 S.Ct. 8 (1933)

BUSINESS EXPENSES ARE DEDUCTIBLE AS ORDINARY AND NECESSARY EXPENSES IF THEY ARE COMMON AND ACCEPTED, AND APPROPRIATE AND HELPFUL

■ **INSTANT FACTS** The owner of a grain purchasing business sought to deduct from his income payments he made and that were directed to the creditors of a grain company for which he had served as secretary and which had all its debts legally discharged in bankruptcy.

■ **BLACK LETTER RULE** An "ordinary" expense is not one that is habitual, but rather one that is common in the taxpayer's particular industry or business.

■ **PROCEDURAL BASIS**

Appeal to the United State Supreme Court from the decision of the Board of Tax Appeals, sustaining the Commissioner's ruling that payments made to establish credit are not deductible.

■ **FACTS**

Mr. Welch (P) served as secretary of the E.L. Welch Company, a corporation engaged in the grain business. The E.L. Welch Company was adjudged an involuntary bankrupt, and had all its debts discharged. Thereafter, Mr. Welch (P) contracted with the Kellogg Company to purchase grain on commission. In order to reestablish his relations with customers, Mr. Welch decided to pay the debts of the E.L. Welch Company. From 1923 to 1928 Mr. Welch (P) paid debts totaling nearly $50,000, all of which were deducted in the year they were made. The Commissioner ruled that these payments were not deductible as ordinary and necessary expenses because they were in the nature of capital expenditures for reputation and goodwill. The Board of Tax Appeals sustained the ruling.

■ **ISSUE**

Are payments by a taxpayer, who is in business as a commission agent, ordinary and necessary if made to the creditors of a bankrupt corporation in an endeavor to strengthen his own credit standing?

■ **DECISION AND RATIONALE**

(Cardozo, J.) No. We can assume that the payments made to the creditors of the E.L. Welch Company were necessary in the sense that they were appropriate and helpful. But we are also required to determine if the payments were "ordinary." An "ordinary" expense is not one that his habitual, but rather one that is common in the particular industry or business. The norms of the particular business or community make this inquiry objective. It is true that at time people pay the debts of others, but they do not do so ordinarily. We could even say that the payments made here were "extraordinary." The issue of ordinary is one of degree, not kind. There is no bright-line rule. Life itself must supply the answer. The Commissioner's ruling carries with it a presumption of correctness, and Mr. Welch has the burden of proving otherwise. He has failed to do so. Nothing in the record permits us to say that these expenses were ordinary and necessary according to the prevailing norms of business. In fact, reputation is akin to a capital asset, much like goodwill. The money spent in acquiring it is not an ordinary expense in the operation of a business. Affirmed.

Analysis:

Section 162 of the Internal Revenue Code allows a deduction for all the *ordinary and necessary* expenses paid or incurred during the taxable year in carrying on any trade or business. It is the statutory meaning of ordinary and necessary that the Court here attempts to address. The Court defines necessary as "appropriate and helpful," citing Justice Marshal's definition of the word as used in the Necessary and Proper Clause of the Constitution. This broad definition makes the "necessary" requirement easy to fulfill, since businesses rarely make expenditures that are not appropriate and helpful. The real issue, however, was the extent of the "ordinary" requirement. The Court eschews a restrictive definition that would require the payments to be habitual. Instead, Justice Cardozo adopts a factual inquiry that focuses on accepted business practices and norms. The thrust of the decision is that those payments that are common and accepted within a particular industry will be held "ordinary" within the meaning of the Code.

Midland Empire Packing Co. v. Commissioner

(Meat Packers) v. *(The IRS)*
14 T.C. 635 (1950)

EXPENDITURES MADE FOR THE PURPOSE OF KEEPING PROPERTY IN A NORMAL OPERATING
CONDITION ARE DEDUCTIBLE

■ **INSTANT FACTS** A meat packing company is
adjudged to have made a deductible repair after
lining the basement walls of its plant with concrete, in order to keep out oil from a nearby
factory.

■ **BLACK LETTER RULE** Repairs to property
made during the taxable year are deductible as
an ordinary and necessary business expense.

■ **PROCEDURAL BASIS**

Judgment by the Tax Court concerning expenditures made to repair a meat packing plant.

■ **FACTS**

For some 25 years prior to the taxable year, Midland Empire Packing Co. (Midland) (P) had used the
basement rooms of its plant as a place for the curing of hams and bacon and for the storage of meat
and hides. Although at times water would seep into this room, the basement had been entirely
satisfactory for this purpose. However, in the taxable year, it was found that oil, created by a
neighboring refinery, was also seeping through the concrete walls of the basement and could not be
drained out. For this reason, a thick scum of oil was left on the basement floor which gave off a strong
odor, permeated the air of the entire plant, and created a fire hazard with its fumes [to say nothing
about how it affected the taste of the hams]. Furthermore, the oil had also made its way into the water
wells which served to furnish water for Midland's (P) plant. As a result, the Federal meat inspectors
advised Midland (P) that it must discontinue the use of the water and oil-proof the basement, or else
shut down its plant. In response, Midland (P) undertook steps to oil proof its basement, by adding a
concrete lining to the walls from the floor to a height of about four feet, and also added concrete to the
floor of the basement. Midland (P) argues that the expenditure of $4868.81 for the concrete lining
should be deductible as an ordinary and necessary expense under 162(a) of the Internal Revenue
Code, on the theory that it was an expenditure for repair. Alternatively, Midland (P) argues that the
expenditure may be treated as the measure of loss sustained during the taxable year and not
compensated for by insurance or otherwise within the meaning of 165(a). The Commissioner (D) argues
that the expenditure is for a capital improvement that should be recovered through depreciation
charges, and not through deductions as an ordinary and necessary business expense or loss.

■ **ISSUE**

Are expenditures made for the purpose of keeping property in an ordinarily efficient operating condition,
deductible as ordinary and necessary business expense?

■ **DECISION AND RATIONALE**

(Arundell, J.) Yes. Repairs to property made during the taxable year are deductible as an ordinary and
necessary business expense. A repair is an expenditure made for the purpose of restoring property to a
sound state, or for keeping the property in an ordinarily efficient operating condition. It does not add to
the value of the property, nor appreciably prolong its life. On the other hand, expenditures for
replacements, alterations, improvements, or additions connotes substitution, which prolong the life of

property, increase its value, or make it adaptable to a different use. The basement was not enlarged by this work, nor did the oil-proofing serve to make the basement more desirable for its present purposes. Furthermore, the expenditure did not add to the value or prolong the expected life of the property beyond what it was before the event occurred. Although seepage of water was also stopped after the work, the presence of water had never been found objectionable. While it is conceded that the that the expenditure was "necessary," the Commissioner (D) contends that it was not an "ordinary" expense in petitioner's particular business. However, the fact that Midland (P) has not previously made a similar expenditure to prevent damage and disaster to its property does not remove that expense from the classification of "ordinary." Ordinary does not mean that expenses must be habitual or normal in the sense that the same taxpayer will have to make them often. It is enough that the situation is unique in the life of the taxpayer affected, but not in the life of the group or community which he is a part. Protecting a business building from the seepage of oil caused by a nearby factory, would seem to be a normal thing to do. We have previously allowed deduction for extensive expenditures made to prevent disaster, even when the repairs were of a type which had never been needed before and were unlikely to recur, on the ground that they were ordinary and necessary expenses. In American Bemberg Corporation [where a taxpayer hired engineers to inject grout into cavities beneath its manufacturing plant to prevent a cave-in], we found that the purpose of the expenses was not to improve or prolong the life of the original plant, but instead to enable the taxpayer to continue the plant in operation on the same scale and as efficiently as it had operated before. Therefore, in our opinion, the expenditure for lining Midland's (P) basement walls and floor was essentially a repair, deductible as an ordinary and necessary business expense. This holding makes it unnecessary to consider Midland's (P) alternative contention.

Analysis:

In order to deduct for losses, the loss must be "realized." In other words, there must be an identifiable event that justifies a current accounting. Therefore, a decline in value caused by, for example, wear and tear or a change in the economic environment will not give rise to a loss deduction. Furthermore, as this opinion states, in order to deduct for repairs, the expenses must be made for the purpose of keeping the property in an ordinarily efficient operating condition, rather than for improving, increasing the value of, or prolonging the life of the property. There may at times be a fine line between repair and capital improvement. The outcome of this case may have been different if the water had been a significant burden that needed to be dealt with, in order for the basement to be used for its originally intended purpose. Here, it could have been determined the concrete lining was a foreseeable part of the process of completing Midland's (P) initial investment, and therefore needed to be capitalized.

■ CASE VOCABULARY

REPAIRS: An expenditure made for the purpose of keeping or restoring property to its ordinarily efficient operating condition.

CAPITAL IMPROVEMENT: An expenditure made for the purpose of prolonging the life of property, increasing its value, or making it adaptable to a different use.

INDOPCO, Inc. v. Commissioner

(Taxpayer) v. *(Commissioner of Internal Revenue)*

503 U.S. 79, 112 S.Ct. 1039 (1992)

WHERE AN EXPENDITURE PRODUCES BENEFITS BEYOND ONE YEAR IT WILL LIKELY BE HELD A CAPITAL EXPENSE AND NOT DEDUCTIBLE

■ **INSTANT FACTS** The Commissioner sought to disallow a deduction taken by a company with respect to professional expenses incurred as a target corporation in a friendly takeover.

■ **BLACK LETTER RULE** The fact that an expenditure does not create or enhance a separate and distinct additional asset does not alone preclude the expenditure from being treated as a non-deductible capital expense.

■ **PROCEDURAL BASIS**

Appeal to the United State Supreme Court, challenging the decision of the Court of Appeals which affirmed the Tax Court's findings that professional expenses incurred in a friendly takeover were in the nature of capital expenditures.

■ **FACTS**

INDOPCO, Inc. (P), formerly National Starch and Chemical Company, was the target of a friendly take over by Unilever United States, Inc. After being informed of its fiduciary duties towards the shareholders, INDOPCO's (P) Board of Directors engaged Morgan Stanley & Co. to render a fairness opinion concerning the value of INDOPCO's (P) stock. Morgan Stanley charged a fee, including expenses, of over $2,000,000. The takeover was consummated in August of 1978. On its tax return, INDOPCO (P) claimed a deduction for the money paid to Morgan Stanley. The Commissioner (D) disallowed the deduction and issued a notice of deficiency. The Tax Court upheld the deficiency, holding that the expenditures were in the nature of capital expenses due to the long term benefits they produced. The Court of Appeals affirmed.

■ **ISSUE**

Are all expenditures deductible under Section 162 if they do not create or enhance a separate and distinct additional asset?

■ **DECISION AND RATIONALE**

(Blackmun, J.) No. The fact that an expenditure does not create or enhance a separate and distinct additional asset does not alone preclude the expenditure from being treated as a non-deductible capital expense. Because they are a matter of "legislative grace," deductions are to be narrowly construed and allowed only if there is a clear provision therefor. Section 162 of the Internal Revenue Code provides a deduction for "all the ordinary and necessary expenses paid or incurred during the taxable year in carrying on any trade or business." The question of whether an expenditure is an ordinary and necessary *expense* deductible under § 162, or whether it is in the nature of a non-deductible capital expense, often turns on the particular facts of the case. INDOPCO (P) argues that for an expenditure to be treated as a capital expense it is a prerequisite that an asset be created or enhanced. But IDOPCO confuses what is necessary with what is sufficient. Our cases have held that, for purposes of capitalization, it is sufficient that a taxpayer's expenditure serve to create or enhance a separate and distinct asset. But that does not mean that capitalization requires an asset to be created or enhanced.

Rather, a taxpayer's realization of benefits beyond the year in which the expenditure is incurred, although not controlling, is undeniably important in determining whether the expense will be held deductible under § 162, or whether capitalization is required. In applying these principles to this case, we conclude that INDOPCO (P) has not demonstrated that the professional expenses incurred in connection with the takeover were deductible as ordinary and necessary expenses. INDOPCO (P) realized benefits well beyond the tax year in question, including access to Unilever's resources and its transformation to a wholly-owned subsidiary, which lessened the company's administrative costs. Affirmed.

Analysis:

Generally speaking, § 263 prohibits deductions for costs incurred in making permanent improvements and restorations to property, as well as expenditures that add to the value or substantially prolong the life of property. These expenditures must be capitalized, which means they are added to a taxpayer's basis in the property with respect to which the expenses are made. The difference between capitalization and an expense deduction is mainly one of timing. A deduction gives the taxpayer a benefit for the year the expense was incurred. Capitalization, on the other hand, requires the taxpayer to wait until he disposes of the asset in order to realize the tax benefit as an increase in basis. The Court here rejects an asset-based approach to determining whether an expenditure is deductible or must be capitalized. Rather, the Court adopts a financial benefit approach. The approach seems to establish a presumption that expenditures should be capitalized if they produce benefits beyond one year.

Morton Frank v. Commissioner

(Taxpayer)
20 T.C. 511 (1953)

A TAXPAYER SEEKING TO START OR ACQUIRE A BUSINESS IS NOT "CARRYING ON" BUSINESS FOR DEDUCTION PURPOSES

■ **INSTANT FACTS** A taxpayer sought to deduct travel expenses incurred while conducting preliminary investigations into the purchase of a newspaper press.

■ **BLACK LETTER RULE** Travel expenses and legal fees spent in searching for a business to purchase cannot be deducted under the provisions of section 162(a).

■ **PROCEDURAL BASIS**

Not provided.

■ **FACTS**

In 1945, Morton Frank (P) began a trip to examine newspaper and radio properties, with the purpose to investigate and acquire a radio or newspaper. Prior to the trip, Frank (P) had worked for several newspapers. Both Frank (P) and his wife settled in Phoenix, Arizona, but continued their efforts to purchase a newspaper plant. Frank (P) conducted negotiations and made offers, eventually purchasing a newspaper in Canton, Ohio. Frank (P) incurred travel expenses and legal fees totaling $5,027.94 in connection with his investigation.

■ **ISSUE**

Are travel expenses and legal fees incurred in searching for a business to purchase deductible under section 162?

■ **DECISION AND RATIONALE**

(Van Fossan, J.) No. Travel expenses and legal fees spent in searching for a business to purchase cannot be deducted under the provisions of section 162(a). That section provides a deduction for "all ordinary and necessary expenses paid or incurred during the taxable year in *carrying on any trade or business.*" The Franks (P) were not engaged in any trade or business at the time the expenses were incurred. The expenses of investigating and looking for a new business and trips preparatory to entering a business are not deductible as an ordinary and necessary business expense incurred in carrying on a trade or business. We conclude that the petitioners may not deduct the expenses they have claimed.

Analysis:

Section 195 of the Internal Revenue Code provides that start-up expenditures may be deducted ratably over a period of at least five years. The expenses must meet all the "ordinary and necessary" requirements of § 162, and the taxpayer must have actually started the business; a failed acquisition or start-up does not qualify for the deferred deduction. The congressional generosity embodied in § 195 notwithstanding, this case is still important for its elucidation on the meaning of "carrying on a business," as used in § 162. Basically, the court requires that a taxpayer be engaged in an existing business or trade to be eligible for deduction under § 162. Expenses that are incurred in the start-up of a business are not eligible for a deduction under § 162. Similarly, expenses that are incurred in looking for a "first job" are generally not deductible, but those expenses incurred in obtaining another job in the same line of work are generally deductible.

Exacto Spring Corporation v. Commissioner

(Close Corporation) v. *(I.R.S.)*
196 F.3d 833 (7th Cir. 1999)

SEVENTH CIRCUIT PROCLAIMS TWO TESTS FOR "REASONABLE" SALARIES

■ **INSTANT FACTS** The I.R.S. challenged a close corporation's CEO's salary as so excessive as not to be deductible as "reasonable" salary.

■ **BLACK LETTER RULE** Executives' salary is "reasonable" (and deductible) if it's proportional to investors' profits.

■ **PROCEDURAL BASIS**

In I.R.S. challenge to deduction, appeal from Tax Court's denial of deduction.

■ **FACTS**

I.R.C. § 162(a)(1) allows businesses to deduct "ordinary and necessary" business expenses, including "reasonable allowance for salaries or other compensation for personal services actually rendered." Closely-held corporation Exacto Spring Corporation ("Exacto") (D) paid its co-founder/CEO/principal owner Heitz a salary of $1.3M one year, and $1M the next, when Exacto (D) earned only $1M in profits. The Internal Revenue Service (P) disallowed Exacto's (D) deduction of Heitz's salary as excessive, finding a reasonable salary was only $381K—$400K. Exacto (D) appealed in Tax Court. That court held for I.R.S. (P), finding Heitz's reasonable salary should be $700K—$900K. In so finding, the tax court applied a seven-factor test, considering the (i) rendered services' type and extent, (ii) scarcity of qualified employees, (iii) employee's qualifications and prior earnings, (iv) employee's contribution to the business, (v) employer's net earnings, (vi) comparable employees' prevailing compensation, and (vii) employer's business' peculiar characteristics. Exacto (D) appeals.

■ **ISSUE**

Is a closely held corporation's CEO's salary of $1M unreasonable?

■ **DECISION AND RATIONALE**

(Posner, J.) No. Executives' salary is "reasonable" (and deductible) if it is proportional to investors' profits. We reject the tax court's seven-factor test of "reasonable" compensation as unclear. This test is commonly applied in other circuits. However, we owe them no deference. First, this multi-factor test gives no indication of how the factors should be weighed, relative to each other. Also, many of its factors are vague. Second, the factors bear no clear relation to either each other, nor to *§ 162(a)(1)*'s purpose (to prevent non-deductible dividends/gifts to be disguised as deductible salaries). E.g., the multi-factor test would not necessarily prevent a huge salary paid to a qualified CEO who did no work, even though this is an obvious sham. Third, the test invites the Tax Court to decide what employees should be paid, based on its own subjective, untrained opinion. Fourth, since the test does not necessarily point to one result, it invites arbitrary decisions. Fifth, because the test yields unpredictable results, it impedes businesses' crucial salary-setting. Here, even under the seven-factor test, most factors support Exacto (D). Heitz (i) is indispensable / essential as its chief salesman and researcher, (ii) is a rare specialist, (iii) is qualified, and (iv) contributed to the corporation. The other factors are inconclusive. Thus, the Tax Court's decision is unfounded, and its calculated "reasonable" salary is arbitrary. I.R.S. (P) claims that Heitz's salary is unreasonable because it reduces Exacto's (D)

---

shareholders' return to below-market rates, but disallowing the deduction only reduces their return further. Thus, we reject the multi-factor test. Instead, we indorse an "indirect market test," where an executive's salary is presumed reasonable if he generates correspondingly high returns for investors. This presumption could be rebutted by showing the executive didn't contribute to the high returns, or that the salary was a disguised gift/dividend. Here, Heitz's returns justified his salary; the expected return was calculated at 13%, while Heitz's returns were 20%. There is no suggestion Heitz was not responsible, or received disguised dividends. Reversed; judgment for Exacto (D).

Analysis:

Note that *Exacto* is still the minority rule. It is the first decision rejecting the multi-factor test, instead replacing it with the "independent investor" standard. Other circuits have either kept the old multi-factor test or *combined* it with the "independent investor" standard. When reading *Exacto*, note its imbedded discussion of the seven factors, since this test is the law in most jurisdictions. Consider also why the *Tax Court* should concern itself with whether executives' salaries are reasonable. Generally, the Tax Court considers policy based on the needs of the government, versus fairness to the taxpayer. It doesn't usually consider whether the taxpayer corporation's *constituents*—such as shareholders—are affected by the taxpayer's decision. From a *tax* policy standpoint, the only reason to limit salary deductions to "ordinary and necessary" amounts is so that corporations do not evade dividends'/gifts' non-deductibility by disguising them as "salary." But Posner's pure "indirect market test"—considering whether investors are willing to pay the executive a high salary—is also irrelevant to the issue of whether that salary includes a premium representing a gift or dividend. Perhaps the issue, from the tax tribunal's perspective, should be limited to whether the salary was intended to contain a gift or dividend, and was inflated to obtain deductibility for it.

■ CASE VOCABULARY

CLOSELY HELD CORPORATION: Corporation whose shares are not traded publicly, and thus tend to be held by the same few people. The shareholders are usually the managers as well. Thus, there's potential for abuse, since the manager-shareholders can have the corporation pay them huge salaries, with no one to stop them.

DIVIDEND: Corporation's payment of corporate profits to shareholders. Dividends are deductible expenses for the corporation, but taxable income for the shareholder.

Harolds Club v. Commissioner

(Taxpayer) v. *(Commissioner of Internal Revenue)*

340 F.2d 861 (9th Cir. 1965)

THE AMOUNTS OF UNREASONABLE SALARIES PAID ARE NON–DEDUCTIBLE WITHOUT REGARD TO THE MOTIVE OR REASON FOR WHICH THE SALARY IS PAID

■ **INSTANT FACTS** The proprietors of a gaming establishment sought to pay a fixed percentage salaries, ranging from $350,000 to $560,000, paid to the establishment's manager, father of the proprietors, from 1952 to 1956.

■ **BLACK LETTER RULE** Where an employee dominates his employers, the lack of ability to bargain freely for salaries may exist even as between adults, thereby making the employee's salary non-deductible.

■ **PROCEDURAL BASIS**

Appeal to the Ninth Circuit, challenging the decision of the Tax Court which held that a deduction was not allowed for those portions of a salary that were held to be unreasonable.

■ **FACTS**

Harold and Raymond Smith were the proprietors of Harolds Club (P), a gaming establishment in Nevada. The business was in reality the continuation of one illegally operated in California by the Smiths' father, Although not a stockholder in Harolds Club (P), the Smith brothers' father was in charge of running the business. After the father took over the business the Club prospered significantly. In 1941, the Smith brothers and their father entered into an employment contract, which would pay the elder Smith an annual salary of $10,000 plus twenty percent of the yearly profits. Due to the success of Harolds Club (P), the amounts paid pursuant to the contract between 1952 and 1956 ranged from $350,000 to $560,000. During the same period, Harold and Raymond Smith were paid salaries ranging from $60,000 to $75,000. Competitors testified that the salary contract was reasonable, and that Smith was worth everything that was paid to him.

■ **ISSUE**

Were salaries of $350,000 to $560,000 paid to the father of the owners of a gaming establishment pursuant to a "free bargain"?

■ **DECISION AND RATIONALE**

(Hamley, Cir. J.) No. Where an employee dominates his employers, the lack of ability to bargain freely for salaries may exist even as between adults. Section 162 allows a deduction for reasonable salaries paid. The reasonableness of salaries paid should be judged at the time the contract was entered into. Under the Treasury Regulations, if a salary is for an amount greater than would ordinarily be paid, it will nonetheless be held reasonable if pursuant to an arm's length free bargain. The Tax Court held that this particular arrangement was not pursuant to a free bargain due to the family relationship and other circumstances indicating that the elder Smith dominated his employers. The fact that Smith was invaluable to Harolds (P) only strengthens this conclusion. Although Smith's services were extremely valuable, that fact does not lead to the conclusion that the entire salary paid was reasonable. Contrary to Smith's argument, the fact that the payments were not disguised dividends is of no consequence. The statute disallows all unreasonable salaries, without regard to the motive for paying them. Salaries must be reasonable to be deductible. To the extent they are not reasonable, they are non-deductible.

Analysis:

The question of the reasonableness of salaries usually comes up in the context of closely held corporations or family owned businesses. The reason is that the owners of these types of businesses often attempt to disguise dividend payments as salaries. Dividend payments are non-deductible by the corporation, while salaries are. Moreover, dividends received by a shareholder are taxed at a different rate than compensation income received. But the court here rejects reading this policy limitation into the statute. In its view, all unreasonable salaries are non-deductible, whether they are a disguised dividend payment, a gift, or simply an exorbitant salary. But problems in this area should always be tackled with an eye towards disguised dividends or like payments. Reasonableness in this context is a question of fact, so the Ninth Circuit was very willing to defer to the Tax Court's determination. Important to the court's analysis was the domination of the elder Smith over his sons and the value of Smith's services. The former was a major reason for finding that the employment contract was not pursuant to a free bargain, while the latter served only to determine the extent to which the salary was reasonable.

Rosenspan v. U.S.

(Taxpayer) v. *(Government)*
438 F.2d 905 (2d Cir. 1971)

BECAUSE DEDUCTIONS ARE ALLOWED FOR BUSINESS RELATED TRAVEL IN ORDER TO OFFSET THE COSTS OF DUPLICATED LIVING EXPENSES, A TAXPAYER MUST HAVE A PERMANENT HOME IN ORDER TO BE ELIGIBLE FOR TRAVEL EXPENSE DEDUCTIONS

■ **INSTANT FACTS** A traveling sales-man, who had no permanent home, sought to deduct his expenses incurred while on the road.

■ **BLACK LETTER RULE** Living expenses paid by a single taxpayer who has no home and is continuously employed on the road may not be deducted in computing net income.

■ **PROCEDURAL BASIS**

Appeal to the Second Circuit from the dismissal on the merits of an action in District Court for refund of income taxes.

■ **FACTS**

Robert Rosenspan (P) was a jewelry salesman who traveled by automobile for some 300 days a year, staying at motels and eating at restaurants. Rosenspan (P) would periodically return to New York-his original home—to meet with his employers, check orders, and perform other services essential to his work. After he left New York to enter the jewelry business, Rosenspan (P) used his brother's Brooklyn home as a permanent address, registering, voting, and filing his income taxes from there. While in New York on business, however, Rosenspan (P) would stay at a hotel, not his brother's home. Rosenspan (P) sought to deduct the costs associated with his meals and lodging, but the Commissioner disallowed the deductions on account of the fact that Rosenspan (P) had no "home" to be away from. Rosenspan (P) countered by arguing that his home for tax purposes was his business headquarters, New York City. The Commissioner responded that normally a "home" means "business headquarters," but that in situations like this, home should be given its natural meaning of permanent residence.

■ **ISSUE**

May living expenses paid by a single taxpayer who has no home and is continuously employed on the road be deducted in computing net income?

■ **DECISION AND RATIONALE**

(Friendly, Cir. J.) No. Living expenses paid by a single taxpayer who has no home and is continuously employed on the road may not be deducted in computing net income. Section 162(a) of the Internal Revenue Code provides a taxpayer a deduction for "all the ordinary and necessary expenses paid or incurred during the taxable year in carrying on any trade or business, including . . . traveling expenses (including amounts expended for meals and lodging other than amounts which are lavish or extravagant under the circumstances) while away from home in the pursuit of a trade or business." But there is nothing to indicate that the statute was meant to address the situation where a business traveler has no home. The Supreme Court has held that for a travel expense to be deductible three conditions must be met: (1) The expense must be a reasonable and necessary traveling expense; (2) the expense must be incurred "while away from home"; and (3) the expense must be incurred in the pursuit of a business. These requirements have been held as establishing a general rule that a taxpayer is entitled to travel deductions only when travel is required by the "exigencies of the business." Nevertheless, the Court has never addressed the question we are faced with here, whether "home" means a taxpayer's residence or his employer's business headquarters. Both the Treasury and the lower courts are in disagreement on this point. Although we believe that the word "home" should be given its ordinary meaning of residence, the facts of this case do not require us to decide this point. Instead, we find it impossible to read the words "away from home" out of the statute, as Rosenspan (P), in effect would have us do and allow a deduction to a taxpayer who had no "home" in the ordinary sense. Rosenspan (P) simply had no expenses which were duplicated. It is enough for us to decide that "home" means "home" and Rosenspan (P) had none. He, therefore, has not fulfilled the second requirement announced by the Supreme Court, that expenses must be incurred while "away from home." Affirmed.

Analysis:

Section 162 expressly provides a deduction for business travel expenses incurred while away from home. The question here was whether Rosenspan (P), an itinerant salesman with no permanent residence, was entitled to travel expense deductions under § 162. Consistent with the Treasury's long-held position, Rosenspan (P) argued that his home was his employer's headquarters, and that being away from those headquarters for the bulk of the year entitled him to the deductions sought. The Treasury made an about face, arguing that normally an employee's home is his employer's headquarters, but that in this case the word home should be coterminous with a principal residence. The court first discusses the prerequisites for obtaining the deduction, as elucidated by the Supreme Court. In *C.I.R. v. Flowers*, the Court announced a three-part test for deductibility. The test requires that the travel expenses be: (1) reasonable and necessary; (2) incurred while away from home; and (3) required by the exigencies of the business. The last of these requirements addresses a situation where, as in *Flowers*, the taxpayer works in one city but chooses to live in another, in which case a deduction is not allowed. The fact that Rosenspan (P) had no home, be it a residence or a principal place of business, means that he could not fulfill the second requirement announced in *Flowers*.

Andrews v. Commissioner

(Taxpayer) v. *(Commissioner of Internal Revenue)*

931 F.2d 132 (1st Cir. 1991)

FOR PURPOSES OF DEDUCTING TRAVEL EXPENSES, A TAXPAYER MAY HAVE ONLY ONE "TAX HOME"

■ **INSTANT FACTS** A taxpayer who held separate businesses in New England and Florida sought to deduct as travel expenses the costs of maintaining a home in Florida.

■ **BLACK LETTER RULE** A taxpayer can have only one home for purposes of deducting travel expenses under section 162(a)(2).

■ **PROCEDURAL BASIS**

Appeal to the First Circuit, challenging the holding of the Tax Court sustaining the disallowance of a deduction for travel expenses.

■ **FACTS**

Edward Andrews (P) was the president and CEO of a swimming pool construction business in New England, a seasonal business. Andrews (P) established a horse racing and breeding business, which he eventually moved to Florida. Consequently, Andrews (P) purchased a condominium in Florida close to the raceway where he maintained the horse business. Andrews (P) used the condominium as his residence during the racing season. The Tax Court concluded that in 1984 Andrews worked primarily in his horse business for six months, and in his pool business for the rest of the year. Andrews claimed a one hundred percent business usage on his Florida house, taking depreciation deductions thereon. Andrews also characterized tax, mortgage interest, utilities, insurance, and other miscellaneous expenses as "lodging expenses," which he deducted in connection with this Florida horse racing business. After stating its general rule that a taxpayer's home for purposes of § 162(a)(2) is his principle place of business, the Tax Court held that Andrews had two tax homes, basing its decision on the fact that Andrews' (P) businesses in New England and Florida were both recurrent, rather than temporary.

■ **ISSUE**

May a taxpayer have two homes with in the meaning of the word "home" as used in section 162(a)(2)?

■ **DECISION AND RATIONALE**

(Campbell, Cir. J.) No. A taxpayer can have only one home for purposes of deducting travel expenses under section 162(a)(2). The Tax Court's decision to the contrary is in error. For a taxpayer to be eligible for deductions under § 162(a)(2), the travel expenses must be: (1) reasonable and necessary; (2) incurred while away from home; and (3) incurred in pursuit of business. The Tax Court held that because Andrews had two tax homes he was never "away from home," and thus could not fulfill the second requirement. The meaning of the word "home" as used in § 162 has engendered much difficulty. The Treasury maintains a position that "home" means the taxpayer's principle place of business. Whether "home" as used in § 162 means residence or primary place of business, the effectuation of the travel expense provision must be guided by the policy underlying the provision that costs necessary to producing income should ordinarily be deductible. Where the "exigencies of the business" require that a taxpayer maintain two places of abode, the cost of duplicating expenses should be deductible. The Tax Court's conclusion that Andrews had two "tax homes" is clearly

---

inconsistent with this policy. Thus, Andrews could have only one home for purposes of § 162(a)(2). We do not, however, instruct the Tax Court how to determine which house was Andrews' "tax home." The length of time spent at each should normally be the determinative factor. Vacated and remanded.

Analysis:

The court here had to determine whether Andrews (P) met the requirement under § 162(a)(2) that travel expenses be incurred "while away from home." The Tax Court had held that Andrews had not met this requirement because he had two "tax homes," and was consequently never "away from home." The First Circuit rejects the notion that a taxpayer can have two homes. Much like the court in *Rosenspan v. U.S.*, the First Circuit bases its holding on the guiding principle behind the deduction allowed for business travel expenses, namely that a taxpayer should be able to deduct duplicate living expenses incurred in the production of income. The court's concern was that if a taxpayer could have multiple tax homes, § 162 would be rendered meaningless in many cases, for the whole point behind travel deductions is to offset these kinds of expenses.

Starr's Estate v. Commissioner

(Taxpayer's Estate) v. *(Commissioner of Internal Revenue)*
274 F.2d 294 (9th Cir. 1959)

A TAXPAYER MAY NOT SEEK BUSINESS DEDUCTIONS FOR NECESSARY RENTAL PAYMENTS IF THE RENTAL OR LEASE AGREEMENT IS, IN SUBSTANCE, A SALE

■ **INSTANT FACTS** The Commissioner disallowed a taxpayer a deduction for payments made on a sprinkler system he obtained through an agreement termed as a "lease," but which was, in reality, a sale.

■ **BLACK LETTER RULE** Where the foreordained practical effect of the rent is to produce title eventually, the rental agreement can be treated as a sale.

■ **PROCEDURAL BASIS**

Appeal to the Ninth Circuit, challenging the decision of the Tax Court sustaining the Commissioner's disallowance of deductions taken on monthly payments pursuant to an installment contract.

■ **FACTS**

Delano Starr (P), owner of the Gross Manufacturing Company, entered into an agreement with Automatic Sprinkler of the Pacific, Inc. (Automatic) for the installation of a sprinkler system in Gross Manufacturing's plant. The agreement was entitled a "Lease Form of Contract," providing for annual rentals of $1,240 for five years, with the option to renew for an additional five years at a rental of $32.00 per year. The agreement gave Automatic the right to remove the sprinkler system, which was custom made, if Starr (P) did not renew. No provisions addressed the status of the system in the eleventh year. The Tax Court held that the five payments of $1,240 were a capital expense and not deductible rental, but it did allow for a annual depreciation deduction of $269.60.

■ **ISSUE**

Are payments made under a lease contract that has the effect of a sale deductible as necessary rental payments?

■ **DECISION AND RATIONALE**

(Chambers, Cir. J.) No. Where the foreordained practical effect of the rent is to produce title eventually, the rental agreement can be treated as a sale. It is true that the agreement in question did not by its terms pass title to Mr. Starr (P), but the internal revenue service is not always bound by form and can often recast a contract according to the practical realities. The sprinkler system in question was tailor made for Gross Manufacturing. There was never any real threat that Automatic would remove the system, for its salvage value thereafter would be negligible. It is obvious that the rental payments after five years of $32.00 were only a maintenance fee. The Commissioner (D) was entitled to recast the "lease" as a sale, disallowing rental payment deductions taken there on. However, we do find it necessary for the Tax Court to consider interest paid on the contract as a deductible item. The normal selling price of the system was $4,960, while the total rental payments amounted to $6,200. The difference could be regarded as interest for the five years on an amortized basis. In any event, after an allowance has been made for depreciation and interest, the attack this lease seems to be a zero sum game. Reversed and remanded.

Analysis:

Section 162(a)(3) provides: "There shall be allowed as a deduction all the ordinary and necessary expenses paid or incurred during the taxable year in carrying on any trade or business, including— rentals or other payments required to be made as a condition to the continued use or possession, for purposes of the trade or business, of property to which the taxpayer has not taken or is not taking title or in which he has no equity." Parties often choose to rent or lease equipment solely for the purpose of taking the deductions provided under § 162(a)(3). The court here thought that the payments made were an installment purchase even though title did not pass. In the court's view, the fact that Starr would likely possess the sprinkler forever was enough to treat the agreement as a sale, thus disallowing a deduction on the yearly installments of $1,240. But even as a sale, the contract provides Starr (P) with some tax benefits, specifically depreciation and interest deductions. At the end of its opinion, the court suggests that the government comes out the same whether the contract is treated as a lease or installment purchase. But that is not the case. The totals come out the same, but once the present value of money is figured into the equation, taking lease deductions over five years significantly outweighs the sum of interest deductions over five years and depreciation deductions allowed over twenty years. Nevertheless, this difference matters little under today's rule, for the Code now permits a taxpayer to take accelerated depreciation.

Hill v. Commissioner

(Taxpayer) v. *(Commissioner of Internal Revenue)*
181 F.2d 906 (4th Cir. 1950)

EDUCATION EXPENSES INCURRED TO FULFILL THE REQUIREMENTS OF A TAXPAYER'S EMPLOY-
MENT OR PROFESSION ARE DEDUCTIBLE AS NECESSARY AND ORDINARY BUSINESS EXPENSES

■ **INSTANT FACTS** A certified school teacher sought to deduct her expenses incurred while attending summer school, which was one of two choices she had to renew her teaching license.

■ **BLACK LETTER RULE** Education expenses incurred to fulfill the requirements of a taxpayer's employment or profession are deductible as necessary and ordinary business expenses.

■ **PROCEDURAL BASIS**

Appeal to the Fourth Circuit, from a decision of the Tax Court affirming a determination of deficiency due to the disallowance of deductions for education expenses.

■ **FACTS**

Nora P. Hill (P) was a Virginia school teacher for twenty seven years. The State required for the renewal of her certificate, the highest issued by the State, that Hill (P) present evidence that she had been a successful teacher, had read five books from an approved reading list, and either had taken college credits within her academic field during the life of her certificate or passed an examination on the five books. In 1945, after being informed of the impending expiration of her certificate, and in an effort to meet the requirements for renewal, Hill (P) attended summer school at Columbia University, and deducted the cost.

■ **ISSUE**

May a teacher deduct education expenses incurred for the renewal of her certificate?

■ **DECISION AND RATIONALE**

(Dobie, J.) Yes. Education expenses incurred to fulfill the requirements of a taxpayer's employment or profession are deductible as necessary and ordinary business expenses. Ms. Hill (P) was faced with two alternatives for the renewal of her certificate. She could acquire college credits or take an exam. She chose the former and attended summer school. Section 162 of the Internal Revenue Code provides that "there shall be allowed as a deduction all the ordinary and necessary expenses paid or incurred during the taxable year in carrying on any trade or business." The statute clearly sets out three requirements: (1) That expenses be paid or incurred within the taxable year; (2) that the expenses be incurred in carrying on a trade or business; and (3) that the expenses be ordinary and necessary. Ms. Hill (P) has met all three requirements. It cannot be said that the expenses were not "ordinary" simply because most teachers chose to take the exam instead of attend college. The course chosen by Ms. Hill (P) was one that a reasonable person would take under specific circumstances, and that is all that is required. The Tax Court erred by requiring Ms. Hill (P) to show that she was employed to continue in her position as teacher when she incurred the expenses. It sufficed that she had continuously been so employed for decades, had not resigned her position, and that no practical advantage would accrue to her upon renewal other than the privilege to continue as a teacher. Ms. Hill (P) went to school to maintain her present position; to preserve, not to expand or increase; to carry on, not to commence. We conclude

---

that the expenses incurred by Ms. Hill (P) were incurred in carrying on a business or trade, were ordinary and necessary, and were not personal in nature. Reversed.

Analysis:

Before this case was decided, educational expenses were thought to be nondeductible due to dictum from Justice Cardozo's opinion in *Welch v. Helvering*, which stated that learning was akin to a capital asset, and the expenses incurred therefor were not "ordinary" within the meaning of the statute. Educational expenses are deductible like any other expense so long as the requirements of § 162 are met. Notice that the court expressly notes that Ms. Hill (P) went to summer school to maintain her position, or as the court put it "to preserve, not to expand or increase; to carry on, not to commence." The court seemingly holds as nondeductible both education expenses incurred in entering a profession, and those incurred in expanding the scope of one's profession. The former proposition generally remains true; the latter, however, is challenged by the following case.

Coughlin v. Commissioner

(*Taxpayer*) v. (*Commissioner of Internal Revenue*)

203 F.2d 307 (2d Cir. 1953)

A TAXPAYER MAY DEDUCT EDUCATION EXPENSES INCURRED IN MAINTAINING OR IMPROVING HIS PROFESSIONAL SKILLS

■ **INSTANT FACTS** An attorney, whose partners relied on for matters relating to federal taxation, sought to deduct tuition and travel expenses incurred while attending a N.Y.U. tax seminar, but the government disallowed the deduction.

■ **BLACK LETTER RULE** A taxpayer may deduct education expenses incurred in maintaining or improving his professional skills.

■ **PROCEDURAL BASIS**

Appeal to the Second Circuit, from the decision of the Tax Court upholding a the Commissioner's disallowance of a deduction for education expenses on the ground that the expenses were personal in nature.

■ **FACTS**

Mr. Coughlin (P) was an attorney in a general practice law firm. As the firm's federal tax "expert," Mr. Coughlin attended a tax seminar sponsored by New York University, incurring tuition, travel, lodging, and meal expenses of $305, which he claimed as an allowable business deduction under what is now Section 162(a).

■ **ISSUE**

May a taxpayer deduct education expenses incurred in taking special courses or training within his profession, but which are not required to maintain employment?

■ **DECISION AND RATIONALE**

(Chase, Cir. J.) Yes. A taxpayer may deduct education expenses incurred in maintaining or improving his professional skills. Mr. Coughlin (P) relies on the general provision of Section 162, which allows a taxpayer a deduction for "all the ordinary and necessary expenses incurred during the taxable year in carrying on any trade or business." If it is usual for lawyers in practice to incur such expenses they are "ordinary." The expenses are also "necessary" if they are appropriate and helpful. Although there is dictum in *Welch v. Helvering* [Supreme Court holds that a taxpayer could not deduct payments made to creditors of a bankrupt corporation in order to establish his own reputation] which implies that education expenses are nondeductible personal expenses, the passage was intended to illustrate the point then under decision, not to establish a generally applicable rule. Here, Mr. Coughlin, although not required to attend the seminar in order to maintain his license, was morally bound to his partners to keep abreast of the ever changing tax laws. The seminar was a way well adapted to fulfill his professional duty to keep sharp the tools he actually used in his trade. The knowledge gained may have increased his general fund of learning, but that is incidental to the true purpose his attendance. Reversed and Remanded.

Analysis:

Although language in *Hill v. Commissioner* implied that education expenses incurred in expanding the scope of a taxpayer's professional skills are not deductible as ordinary business expenses, the Second Circuit, nevertheless, extends the rationale of *Hill* to allow for the deduction of education expenses that are not required for the trade or profession, but that maintain or improve the taxpayer's skills. Today, this type of deduction is expressly allowed by § 1.162–5 of the Treasury Regulations, which provides that education expenses are deductible if "the education maintains or improves the skills required by the individual in his employment or other trade or business." This section should not be read too broadly, however. An accountant seeking to expand his knowledge of federal tax laws could not deduct expenses incurred in obtaining a law degree, but in all likelihood a tax attorney could deduct expenses incurred in obtaining an LL.M. The general point is this: the education must be within the taxpayer's field; it cannot train him for another profession, even if such training is helpful to his trade.

Sharp v. United States

(Taxpayer) v. *(Government)*

199 F.Supp. 743 (D. Del. 1961)

PROPERTY THAT IS SUBJECT TO BOTH BUSINESS AND PERSONAL USE IS ELIGIBLE FOR BUSINESS RELATED DEDUCTIONS IN PROPORTION TO THE EXTENT THE PROPERTY IS USED FOR BUSINESS

■ **INSTANT FACTS** The government sought to tax the partners in a partnership on a gain realized from the sale of an airplane, as used for personal and business purposes and upon which the partnership took allowable depreciation deductions in proportion to the extent it was used for business purposes.

■ **BLACK LETTER RULE** The gain or loss realized upon the sale of property that is used for both business and personal matters must be allocated in accordance with the property's percentages of business and personal use.

■ **PROCEDURAL BASIS**

District Court ruling on cross motions for summary judgment in an action to recover alleged overpayments of federal income taxes.

■ **FACTS**

Hugh Sharp and Baynard Sharp ("Sharps") (P), equal partners in a partnership, purchased an airplane for $45,875. After making additional capital expenditures with respect to the airplane, the Sharps' (P) basis in the aircraft increased to $54,273.50. During their ownership, the Sharp's used the plane 73.654% for personal use and 26.346% for business purposes. Thus, the partnership was allowed depreciation on the basis of $14,298.90, or 26.346% of the total cost of the plane. Accordingly, the partnership took depreciation deductions totaling $13,777.92 over six years. In 1954, the Sharps (P) sold the plane for $35,380. The government sought to tax the partnership for a gain as a result of the sale. The government argued that the partnership's adjusted basis in the airplane was reduced to $520.98, after subtracting the total depreciation deductions from the partnership's basis in the plane, and that upon sale of the plane the partnership realized an amount of $9,321.21, or 26.346% of $35,380. In the government's view, the difference between $9321.21, the amount allegedly realized upon sale by the partnership, and $520.98, the adjusted basis in the plane, netted the partnership a gain of $8,800.23.

■ **ISSUE**

Must the proceeds from the sale of property that is used for both business and personal matters be allocated in accordance the percentages of business and personal use?

■ **DECISION AND RATIONALE**

(Layton, D.J.) Yes. The gain or loss realized upon the sale of property that is used for both business and personal matters must be allocated in accordance with the property's percentages of business and personal use. It is well settled that a thing normally regarded as a single entity may be divisible for tax purposes. For example, upon the sale of a building, which is depreciable, together with land, which is non-depreciable, the selling price must be allocated between the land and building and the gain or loss separately determined upon each. The Sharps (P) argue that a plane is not as easily divisible. However, that is why courts employ legal fictions. The fact that the Code itself does not provide for this allocation does not mean Congress intended to exempt from taxation profits from the sale of property used for both business and pleasure. If the Sharps (P) had their way there would be a lack of uniformity in tax treatment between those who use property solely for business and those who use property for business and pleasure, with the latter receiving an exemption not afforded the former. The government's position is "plainly" fair [excuse the pun]. The Sharps (P) were allowed depreciation deductions on the airplane to the extent it was used for business purposes. The government seeks nothing more than to tax the Sharps (P) for a gain realized on the sale of the airplane to the extent is was used for business purposes. The Sharps received a tax benefit which they must now pay for.

Analysis:

Section 167 of the Internal Revenue Code allows taxpayers a deduction for exhaustion and wear and tear on business property. Section 1016 requires that the taxpayer's basis in depreciable property be reduced by the amount of depreciation deductions allowed—not necessarily taken—during the life of the property. Therefore, when property used in a business is sold, the adjusted basis used to determine gain will be far less than the taxpayer's cost basis. The reason for adjusting basis for depreciation deductions is simple. Depreciation is meant to compensate the taxpayer for the loss of value over the life of the property. If the allowable depreciation deductions exceed the actual loss of value, the difference will be taxed upon the sale of the property. The question here was whether an amount realized from the sale property held for both business and personal use had to be allocated according to the percentage of business and personal use. The court held that such allocation was necessary.

Simon v. Commissioner

(Taxpayer) v. *(Commissioner of Internal Revenue)*

68 F.3d 41 (2d Cir. 1995)

A TAXPAYER MAY TAKE DEPRECIATION DEDUCTIONS ON PROPERTY THAT APPRECIATES IN VALUE

■ **INSTANT FACTS** Professional violin players who purchased antique violin bows for use in their performances sought to take allowable depreciation deductions on the bows even though the bows actually appreciated in value in the hands of the taxpayers.

■ **BLACK LETTER RULE** Under the Accelerated Cost Recovery System the test for determining whether tangible property is of a character subject to the allowance for depreciation is whether the property will suffer exhaustion, wear and tear, or obsolescence in its use by a business.

■ **PROCEDURAL BASIS**

Appeal to the Second Circuit, from the decision of the Tax Court allowing depreciation deductions to be taken on appreciable property.

■ **FACTS**

The Simons (P) were professional violin players who purchased two antique violin bows at a cost of $30,000 and $21,500. Simons used the bows regularly in their performances. The Tax Court found that the bows suffered from wear and tear when used regularly. The bows in effect become "played out." This wear and tear notwithstanding, the bows were appraised five years after their purchase at $45,000 and $35,000, respectively. Nevertheless, the Simons claimed depreciation deductions under the Accelerated Cost Recovery System (ACRS) in the amount of $6,300 and $4,515. The Tax Court allowed the depreciation deductions. The Commissioner appealed.

■ **ISSUE**

May a taxpayer claim depreciation deductions for wear and tear under the ACRS even though the taxpayer cannot demonstrate that the property has a "determinable useful life?"

■ **DECISION AND RATIONALE**

(Winter, Cir. J.) Yes. Under the Accelerated Cost Recovery System (ACRS) the test for determining whether tangible property is of a character subject to the allowance for depreciation is whether the property will suffer exhaustion, wear and tear, or obsolescence in its use by a business. Section 168 of the Internal Revenue Code provides a depreciation deduction for "recovery property" placed into service after 1980. Recovery property is defined as "tangible property of a character subject to the allowance for depreciation" when "used in a business or trade." Both parties agree that the phrase "of a character subject to depreciation" must be read in the light of the Section 167 allowances for "exhaustion, wear and tear, and . . . obsolescence." Consequently, the Simons (P) argue that all that is required is that the property be subject to exhaustion, wear and tear, or obsolescence. The Commissioner, on the other hand, argues that the phrase "of a character subject to depreciation" requires more, namely that the property have a "determinable useful life," as required by section 167. But the Commissioner's argument must fail for two reasons. First, under the ACRS the depreciation recovery period is wholly unrelated to the useful life of the asset; ergo the term "accelerated." Second, the ACRS was enacted specifically to simplify the rules concerning depreciation by eliminating the need to adjudicate matters such as useful life and salvage value. Basically, Congress has overhauled the regulatory system in this area; and it is, therefore, improper for us to retain an isolated element from the previous regime. We realize that the result of this holding gives favorable tax treatment to those you use appreciable property for business purposes. But Congress wanted to stimulate business property investment, and it is not our duty to draw subjective lines between the wasteful and the productive. Affirmed.

■ **DISSENT**

(Oakes, Sen. Cir. J.) I cannot believe that with the adoption of the ACRS, Congress intended to abandon the concept underlying depreciation, namely that the property must have a useful life capable of being estimated. The courts holding today, as the Commissioner points out, renders meaningless the phrase "of a character subject to the allowance for depreciation." The purpose behind the ACRS was to shorten recovery periods and ease the administration of the depreciation deductions, not to reward those who use appreciable property for business purposes. I hereby dissent.

Analysis:

This case was decided under the pre–1986 ACRS. The court's task here was to fill a gaping hole left open by Congress when it adopted the ACRS. Under the system used prior to the ACRS, it was inherently necessary for the property to have a determinable useful life, because deductions were taken with reference to the salvage value, i.e., the value of the property after the taxpayer had made full use of it over its useful life. If the property had a salvage value higher than the taxpayer's basis—if it was appreciable property—then no deductions could be taken. But the ACRS did away with the need to determine the salvage value of depreciable property. Therefore, the question left open was whether under the ACRS business property must have a determinable useful life—in other words, whether it must actually depreciate in value. The court here answered no. The majority equated Congress's decision to eliminate the need to calculate salvage value with an intent to eliminate the need for depreciable property to have a "useful life capable of being estimated." The majority's reasoning is proper in light of the fact that there is little sense in calculating the useful life of the property when the deductions are taken without reference to that very useful life. The problem with this, as the dissent points out, is that is gives an unintended advantage to those who use appreciable property in their business.

CHAPTER FIFTEEN

Deductions for Profit–Making, Nonbusiness Activities

Higgins v. Commissioner

Instant Facts: Taxpayer claimed deductions for expenses associated with monitoring personal investments.

Black Letter Rule: Expenses incurred in managing personal investments are not deductible as business expenses.

Bowers v. Lumpkin

Instant Facts: Taxpayer claimed deductions for expenses incurred in defending litigation brought by South Carolina Attorney General to invalidate purchase of stock from trustees who were to open an orphanage.

Black Letter Rule: Nonbusiness expenses incurred for production or collection of income must meet restrictions applicable to business expenses in order to be deductible.

Surasky v. United States

Instant Facts: Taxpayer claimed deductions for expenses incurred in proxy fight as nonbusiness expenses.

Black Letter Rule: Showing of proximate relationship between nonbusiness expenses and producing or managing income producing property not necessary to claim nonbusiness deduction so long as expenses are ordinary and necessary.

Meyer J. Fleischman v. Commissioner

Instant Facts: Taxpayer deducted legal expenses incurred in defending lawsuit brought by his wife to void an antenuptial agreement.

Black Letter Rule: Legal expenses incurred defending or bringing a claim that arises out of one's personal life are not deductible.

William C. Horrmann v. Commissioner

Instant Facts: Taxpayer claimed deductions for depreciation, maintenance and loss of home he inherited from his mother, lived in for two years and then abandoned.

Black Letter Rule: Deductions for depreciation and maintenance are allowed when property is held for production of income, but a loss is not allowed unless the property constitutes a transaction entered into for profit.

Lowry v. United States

Instant Facts: Taxpayer put summerhouse up for sale immediately after stopping personal use and claimed deductions for maintenance expenses for the newly converted income-producing property.

Black Letter Rule: Whether a personal residence has been converted into income-producing property is not determined by whether or not it was rented before sold, but rather by looking at all of the relevant facts and circumstances, including whether the taxpayer had an expectation of profit.

Higgins v. Commissioner

(Taxpayer) v. *(IRS)*

312 U.S. 212, 61 S.Ct. 475 (1941).

EXPENSE OF MANAGING PERSONAL INVESTMENTS THROUGH YOUR EMPLOYEES IS NOT DEDUCTIBLE

■ **INSTANT FACTS** Taxpayer claimed deductions for expenses associated with monitoring personal investments.

■ **BLACK LETTER RULE** Expenses incurred in managing personal investments are not deductible as business expenses.

■ **PROCEDURAL BASIS**

Taxpayer appealed decision of the IRS denying deductions for expenses incurred in monitoring his personal investments.

■ **FACTS**

Mr. Higgins (P) owned and operated a real estate business in New York while living in Paris, France. His personal financial affairs were conducted, pursuant to his directions, by his office in New York. The New York office kept records, received securities, interest and dividends, prepared reports, deposited checks and generally managed Mr. Higgins' (P) personal investments according to his directions. During tax years 1932 and 1933, Mr. Higgins (P) claimed the expenses and salaries associated with monitoring his investments as well as those associated with running his real estate business as business deductions pursuant to § 23(a) of the Revenue Act of 1932, as he had for the past thirty years. [§ 23(a) allowed deductions for "all the ordinary and necessary expenses paid or incurred ... in carrying on any trade or business". It is now § 162(a).] The IRS (D) denied the deductions for these tax years for those expenses attributable to monitoring personal investments, despite having never objected to similar deductions in the past. Mr. Higgins (P) appealed to the Board of Tax Appeals, which affirmed the decision of the IRS (D). Mr. Higgins (P) then appealed to the Circuit Court of Appeals, which also affirmed. Finally, he appealed to the United States Supreme Court.

■ **ISSUE**

Is managing personal investments "carrying on a business" for which expenses would be deductible?

■ **DECISION AND RATIONALE**

(Reed, J.) No. Mr. Higgins (P) argues that the activities of monitoring his personal investments are much larger and more continuous than those of a small investor and, as such, constitute carrying on a business for which the deductions should be allowed. The IRS (D) disagrees, arguing that mere personal investment activities can never constitute carrying on a business. There are no regulations or previous rulings that define "carrying on a business". [If there were, this would be a much easier case.] While there are some rulings that indicate the IRS (D) has accepted the proposition that managing personal investments may constitute carrying on a business if the activities are continuous and on a large scale, these are not controlling here and are not persuasive. The practice evidenced by these rulings is neither substantially uniform nor long-standing. Moreover, there is no reason to believe that simply because the IRS (D) has challenged similar deductions in other cases on the grounds that the activities were sporadic, it would not challenge deductions in a case such as this on other grounds. In fact, in three other cases the IRS (D) has taken the same position as it has taken here: that personal investment activities never constitute carrying on a business. Mr. Higgins (P) argues that the definition of business in *Flint v. Stone* [business is everything about which a person can be employed] should apply here. However, the issue in *Flint* was whether a corporation engaged in buying and selling real estate was conducting business such that it was subject to the corporations tax. The issue here is unrelated to that inquiry and therefore the definition of business in *Flint* is not applicable here. Whether a taxpayer's activities constitute carrying on a business requires an examination of the facts in each case. Such an examination is the duty of the IRS (D), subject only to limited review by the Board of Tax Appeals and the courts. Here, the IRS (D) determined that Mr. Higgins' (P) activities in monitoring his personal investments did not constitute carrying on a business. The Board of Tax Appeals and the courts have affirmed that determination. The decision is supported by the record and will not be reversed by this Court. As a matter of law, managing personal investments, regardless of how continuous or on what scale it is done, does not constitute carrying on a business. Finally, Mr. Higgins (P) argues that the deductions should be allowed because the expenses were incurred simultaneously with running a legitimate real estate business. In other words, Mr. Higgins (P) contends that since his was a unified business, the deductions should not be severed and allocated to the real estate business on one hand and his personal investments on the other. Despite his objections, there is no reason why expenses that can be apportioned to a certain activity, one that is deductible and one that is not, should be allocated to the appropriate activity and severed for purposes of determining deductions. Affirmed.

Analysis:

In response to the result reached here, Congress added § 212 to the Code. Section 212 allows deductions for expenses associated with income-producing activities, such as managing personal investments, even if not incurred in carrying on a business. Notice, though, that Congress did not step in and clear up the confusion surrounding exactly what constitutes a business or trade for purposes of deductions allowed by § 162(a). If Congress had chosen to define trade or business instead of adding § 212, there would be no discretion on the part of the IRS. Allowing the IRS to make determinations on a case-by-case basis gives it the flexibility necessary to avoid unjust results that often occur when per se rules apply. Finally, this case, in addition to providing the background to why § 212 was added, demonstrates the degree of deference courts give to administrative agencies like the IRS. If administrative decisions have a rational basis, courts will not be quick to overturn them.

■ CASE VOCABULARY

PROMULGATED: Issued or made.

SECURITIES: Stocks or bonds that show ownership in a public company.

Bowers v. Lumpkin

(IRS) v. *(Taxpayer)*
140 F.2d 927 (4th Cir. 1944), cert. denied 322 U.S. 755, 64 S.Ct. 1266 (1944)

NONBUSINESS EXPENSE DEDUCTIONS SUBJECT TO SAME RESTRICTIONS AS BUSINESS EXPENSE DEDUCTIONS

■ **INSTANT FACTS** Taxpayer claimed deductions for expenses incurred in defending litigation brought by South Carolina Attorney General to invalidate purchase of stock from trustees who were to open an orphanage.

■ **BLACK LETTER RULE** Nonbusiness expenses incurred for production or collection of income must meet restrictions applicable to business expenses in order to be deductible.

■ **PROCEDURAL BASIS**

IRS appeals the judgment of the District Court Judge in favor of taxpayer for $22,680.10 in overpaid income taxes.

■ **FACTS**

Mrs. Lumpkin (D) inherited a life estate in a trust consisting of half of the stock in a corporation that owned valuable rights to the sale and distribution of coca cola syrup from her late husband. The other half of the corporation's stock was bequeathed to a group of trustees who were to open and manage an orphanage. Mrs. Lumpkin (D) purchased the stock from the trustees for $255,885. Thereafter, the Attorney General of South Carolina brought an action against Mr. Lumpkin (D), seeking to invalidate the sale and to force Mrs. Lumpkin (D) to account for profits. Mrs. Lumpkin (D) successfully defended the lawsuit, but incurred litigation expenses of $255 in 1936 and $26,798.22 in 1937. She deducted these expenses from her gross income on her income tax returns for those years. The IRS (P) disallowed these deductions. The IRS (P) also assessed additional taxes and interest, which Mrs. Lumpkin (D) paid under protest. She then brought this action seeking reimbursement of the alleged overpaid income taxes. Judgment was entered in her favor after a trial to the court and the IRS (P) appeals.

■ **ISSUE**

Are litigation expenses incurred in defending purchase of income producing property deductible as nonbusiness expenses?

■ **DECISION AND RATIONALE**

(Soper, J.) No. Mrs. Lumpkin (D) argues that the 1942 amendment of § 23(a), which allows for deduction of ordinary and necessary expenses paid or incurred for the management, conservation or maintenance of property held for the production of income, permits the deductions taken for litigation expenses here. The purpose of the 1942 amendment was to allow deductions for certain nonbusiness expenses related to earning or collecting income, such as managing personal investments. It was not the intent of Congress, however, to remove any other restrictions or limitations on allowable deductions under § 23(a). Prior to the amendment, legal expenses incurred for defending or protecting title to property were deemed not deductible because they were not "ordinary and necessary." This principle has been consistently applied throughout the years by IRS Regulations, the courts and has been retained by Congress, who adopted the same language in the amendment as had been previously used. As a result, it is clear that Congress intended by using the same phrase "ordinary and necessary" in the amendment for nonbusiness expenses that the same restrictions and limitations apply to deductions for nonbusiness expenses as have always applied to deductions for business expenses. Mrs. Lumpkin (D) argues that the phrase was meant to be more expansive in the amended section because it authorizes deductions for management, conservation and maintenance of property held for the production of income. She argues that this language authorizes the deductions here because the litigation expenses were incurred in "conserving" the stock—protecting it from adverse attack. It is Mrs. Lumpkin's (D) position that if her interpretation is not adopted, conservation of property is impossible thereby rendering its use in the amendment meaningless. To the contrary, however, property can be conserved even if the word conservation is limited to expenses incurred in only ordinary and necessary activities. Applying Mrs. Lumpkin's (D) interpretation loses sight of the clear intent of Congress that prior limitations on deductions still apply—intent that is clear by Congress' use of the same language. Additionally, Regulation 19.23(a)–15 supports this conclusion. [§ 19.23(a)–15 provides that a deduction under the nonbusiness expense amendment is subject to all the restrictions and limitations of business expense deductions, and states that expenses incurred in perfecting or defending title to property are not deductible.] Judgment reversed.

Analysis:

Congress enacted what is now § 212 to allow deductions for expenses incurred in conducting personal income-producing activities that had been determined by the IRS not to constitute carrying on a business. In doing so, however, Congress did no more than say those certain nonbusiness expenses were now deductible. As this case points out, it did not change the rules, restrictions, or limitations on when the deduction applies. It is not necessarily important to remember that litigation expenses incurred in defending purchases of income-producing property, in this case stock, were not allowed as nonbusiness deductions. Rather, it is important to notice that the same rules, restrictions, and limitations that apply to business expense deductions under what is now § 162(a) apply to nonbusiness expense deductions under § 212. Since the issue of litigation expenses had already been dealt with under business expense deductions, the Court here had little trouble saying the deductions Mrs. Lumpkin (D) wanted were not allowed. Whether litigation expenses are incurred in business or nonbusiness activities, they are said to be not ordinary and necessary.

■ CASE VOCABULARY

BEQUEATHED: Property gifted to a person by a decedent in his will.

CAPITAL GAIN OR LOSS: Income received from the sale of investments that is over the price the investment was purchased for is a capital gain; if under the purchase price is it a capital loss.

LIFE INTEREST: An interest in property that ends when the person who owns the life interest dies.

Surasky v. United States

(Taxpayer) v. *(IRS)*

325 F.2d 191 (5th Cir. 1963)

EXPENSES INCURRED IN BATTLING FOR CONTROL OF CORPORATION DEDUCTIBLE

■ **INSTANT FACTS** Taxpayer claimed deductions for expenses incurred in proxy fight as nonbusiness expenses.

■ **BLACK LETTER RULE** Showing of proximate relationship between nonbusiness expenses and producing or managing income producing property is not necessary to claim nonbusiness deduction so long as expenses are ordinary and necessary.

■ **PROCEDURAL BASIS**

Taxpayer challenged judgment of the District Court following a bench trial that monies contributed to stockholders' committee as part of a proxy battle were not deductible as ordinary and necessary nonbusiness expenses.

■ **FACTS**

Based on the recommendation of Mr. Wolfson and his aggressive plans for managing the company, Mr. Surasky (P) purchased 4,000 shares of Montgomery Ward & Co. stock in 1954 and 1955 for $296,870.20. When Mr. Wolfson was unable to discuss his plans with the current management of Montgomery Ward, he, Mr. Surasky (P) and other stockholders formed a committee, whose objective was to advocate Mr. Wolfson's aggressive plans for the company and to mount a proxy fight for control of the Board of Directors. To that end, Mr. Surasky (P) contributed $17,000 to the committee, believing the contribution would increase the income potential of his stock. Although the committee failed to gain control of the board, it was successful in placing three directors on the board, forcing the resignation of the President of the company and the Chairman of the Board of Directors. The sales and earnings of the company increased and dividends also increased. Mr. Surasky (P) deducted the $17,000 he contributed as nonbusiness expenses. The IRS (D) denied the deductions. Following a trial to the court, the District Court agreed with the IRS (D), concluding that the expenses incurred in the proxy fight were not deductible. It is from that judgment that Mr. Surasky (P) appeals.

■ **ISSUE**

Is a showing of a proximate relationship between the expense claimed and the income produced from property required for a nonbusiness expense to be deductible?

■ **DECISION AND RATIONALE**

(Tuttle, J.) No. In reaching the conclusion that Mr. Surasky's (P) contribution to the committee was not deductible, the District Court relied on its finding that there was no proximate relationship between the contribution and the production of the income. It was the trial court's opinion that when the contribution was made it was purely speculative whether income from the stock would increase. The trial court also found that the contribution was not an ordinary and necessary expense. Mr. Surasky's (P) argument that the trial court applied too rigid of a standard here in requiring a proximate relationship between the expense incurred and the income produced is persuasive. It is undisputed that Congress added § 212 to correct the inequity that resulted in allowing certain expenses because they were related to a business but denying other expenses because they were only related to nonbusiness income-producing property. [§ 212 allows a deduction for all ordinary and necessary expenses incurred for the production or collection of income or for the management, conservation or maintenance of income-producing property.] It is also undisputed that the ordinary and necessary requirement of § 162 applies with equal force to § 212. [§ 162 allows a deduction for all ordinary and necessary expenses incurred in carrying on a trade or business.] It is clear from the trial court's emphasis on the absence of a proximate relationship between the expense and the income here that it placed too much weight on the language in regulation 1.212–1(d). [Reg. 1.212–1(d) states that expenses must be reasonable in amount and bear a reasonable and proximate relation to the production or collection of income.] In construing the statute, in light of this regulation, as requiring a proximate relationship between the expense claimed and the income-producing property, the trial court has applied a much stricter standard than is required by the statute. The trial court's standard is akin to the proximate cause requirement in common law tort cases. [Bet you didn't expect to see proximate cause in a tax course!] In adding § 212, Congress intended to allow deductions for expenses incurred in the exercise of reasonable business judgment in an attempt to produce income. Such expenses bear little relationship to the income that may be produced, and certainly would fail the trial court's proximate cause standard. Additionally, there is nothing in the statute or relevant case law that requires a showing of a proximate relationship. All that is required is that the expenses be ordinary and necessary. It was held in *Harris & Co. v. Lucas* that the ordinary and necessary requirement is not a strict, technical requirement, but rather is to be construed broadly such that "any necessary expenses, not actually a capital investment, incurred in good faith in a particular business," is to be considered a deductible expense. According to the United States Supreme Court in *Welch v. Helvering,* expenses are said to be necessary if they were appropriate and helpful. Additionally, whether expenses are ordinary is a question to be decided in light of the way of life rather than the rule of law. In this case, Mr. Surasky (P) made his contribution to the committee with the belief that doing so would increase the income from his stock. For reasons similar to those expressed in the Tax Court decision of *Alleghany Corporation,* Mr. Suraksy's (P) contribution was an ordinary and necessary expense of protecting his income-producing property and was deductible under § 212. [*Alleghany Corporation* held that expenses incurred in a proxy solicitation and other related activities in a railroad reorganization were deductible business expenses even though had the proxy been successful it would have diluted the taxpayer's stock and decreased his income.] Judgment reversed.

Analysis:

For a nonbusiness expense to be deductible, it must be ordinary and necessary, as shown by *Bowers v. Lumpkin,* but it is not essential that there be a proximate relationship between the expense and the possibility of producing income. This means that it is unnecessary for a taxpayer to show that a proximate result of the expense is an increase in income. To be ordinary, the expense must only be appropriate and helpful in the good business judgment of the taxpayer. To be necessary, again the courts are only looking at whether the expense was needed in light of the factual circumstances, but not necessarily whether the expense was a necessity as that term is defined in the law. The requirements applicable to business deductions under § 162 also apply to deductions under § 212.

■ **CASE VOCABULARY**

DIVIDEND: A share of a corporation's profits paid to shareholders based on the number and type of shares owned.

IN PARI MATERIA: In relation to the same subject matter; statutes on the same subject matter are construed together even if enacted at different times since they relate to the same matter.

PROXY: A written authorization to act on behalf of someone else; a written authorization to vote for another shareholder.

Meyer J. Fleischman v. Commissioner

(*Taxpayer*) v. (*Internal Revenue Commissioner*)

45 T.C. 439 (1966)

BUT/FOR ORIGIN OF CLAIM TEST ADOPTED TO DETERMINE WHEN LEGAL FEES ARE DEDUCTIBLE AS NONBUSINESS EXPENSES

■ **INSTANT FACTS** Taxpayer deducted legal expenses incurred in defending lawsuit brought by his wife to void an antenuptial agreement.

■ **BLACK LETTER RULE** Legal expenses incurred defending or bringing a claim that arises out of one's personal life are not deductible.

■ PROCEDURAL BASIS

From decision of the IRS denying deduction of legal expenses, taxpayer appeals to the Tax Court.

■ FACTS

The day before they were married in Cincinnati, Ohio, Mr. Fleischman (P) and Ms. Francis entered into a antenuptial agreement that provided for Mr. Fleischman (P) to pay Ms. Francis $5,000 in exchange for her releasing all interest in his property if they were to divorce. Six years later, Ms. Francis filed for divorce. Contemporaneously with the divorce proceeding, Ms. Francis filed a lawsuit seeking to set aside the antenuptial agreement. The second lawsuit was necessary because the issue of the validity of the agreement was outside the jurisdiction of the divorce court under Ohio law. Mr. Fleischman (P) successfully defended the action to invalidate the antenuptial agreement. In doing so, he incurred $3,000 in legal expenses, which he deducted as nonbusiness expenses. The IRS disallowed the deduction, and Mr. Fleischman (P) appealed.

■ ISSUE

Are legal expenses incurred in defending an action to invalidate an antenuptial agreement deductible as nonbusiness expenses?

■ DECISION AND RATIONALE

(Simpson, J.) No. Mr. Fleischman (P) argues that the deduction he took is allowed by *Carpenter v. United States* [deduction for legal expenses incurred in course of divorce proceeding allowed because they were for a tax lawyer and were incurred in connection with the determination of a tax]. *Carpenter* is irrelevant to the issue here, however. There is not even a suggestion that Mr. Fleischman (P) incurred the legal expenses here in connection with determining tax matters. Additionally, the opinion in *Carpenter* was based on § 212(3) [ordinary and necessary expenses incurred in connection with the determination, collection, or refund of any tax are deductible], and not the other subsections]. Since § 212(3) is not involved here, and is based on a much different policy than at issue here, *Carpenter*'s discussion of § 212(3) is of no consequence to this Court. Moreover, *Carpenter* concluded that legal expenses would not be deductible under § 212(2) [ordinary and necessary expenses incurred for the management, conservation, or maintenance of property held for the production of income are deductible]. Finally, although *Carpenter* stands for the proposition that in certain cases the legal expenses associated with a divorce proceeding can be deducted, it offers no guidance in determining whether the legal expenses deduced by Mr. Fleischman (P) fall into one of those cases. Mr. Fleischman (P) next argues that *Erdman v. Commissioner* [legal expenses incurred in defending title to property held in trust not deductible] may be helpful in resolving this issue. However, since the issues involved in *Erdman* are so different than those involved here, it is of little guidance. Mr. Fleischman (P) may deduct his legal expenses only if they fall within § 212. Since the legal expenses incurred here do not concern tax matters, they do not fall within § 212(3). Since Mr. Fleischman (P) did not incur these legal expenses for the production or collection of income, they do not fall within § 212(1) [ordinary and necessary expenses incurred in connection with production or collection of income are deductible]. Therefore, if these legal expenses are deductible, they must fall within § 212(2). In determining whether Mr. Fleischman's (P) legal expenses are deductible under § 212(2), it is important to understand the purpose and history of that section. Prior to its enactment, legal expenses were only deductible if they were directly connected to running a business. If the expenses were personal they were simply not deductible. Even though certain personal activities generate taxable income, expenses attributable to those activities were not deductible because they were not expended in connection with a business. To equalize this disparity, Congress enacted what is now § 212. At the same time, it also enacted sections that required a spouse to include alimony in her gross income. Since deductions under § 212 are analogous to business deductions under § 162 [all ordinary and necessary expenses paid or incurred during the taxable year in carrying on any trade or business are deductible], the same rules and restrictions that apply to § 162 deductions have been applied with equal force to § 212 deductions. Applying the limitations regarding deduction of legal expenses proved difficult, however. Courts held that a wife could deduct her legal expenses in seeking to obtain alimony, but a husband defending such a suit could not, even if required to pay the wife's expenses. The Supreme Court eventually stepped in, expressing at first the general intent of Congress in not permitting taxpayers to deduct personal expenses. Thus, just because a lawsuit may have some effect on a taxpayer's liability did not render legal expenses incurred therein deductible. Finally, in 1963, the Supreme Court decided *United States v. Gilmore* [legal expenses incurred in defending claim for community property made by wife in divorce proceeding not deductible since underlying claim did not arise out of profit-seeking activities], which established a straightforward test for determining when legal expenses in divorce proceedings could be deducted as nonbusiness expenses. In *Gilmore,* the Supreme Court adopted the "origin of claim" test used to determine whether legal expenses were deductible as business expenses. Under the test, if a suit against a taxpayer is directly connected or proximately related to the business, the legal expenses are deductible. Thus, for legal expenses to be deductible as nonbusiness expenses, the suit against the taxpayer must be directly connected to or proximately related to the production or collection of income, or the management, conservation or maintenance of income-producing property. Otherwise, the legal expenses are personal and not deductible pursuant to § 262 [no deduction shall be allowed for personal, living, or family expenses]. The Supreme Court's decision in *Gilmore* rested upon two grounds. First, conservation of property was said to concern actions performed with respect to property and not retention of ownership. Second, legislative history indicates a policy that limitations applicable to business deductions be applied to nonbusiness deductions as well. In *United States v. Patrick* [legal expenses incurred in fighting to uphold property settlement entered into prior to divorce not deductible because lawsuit arises out of rights obtained during marriage], the Supreme Court made it clear that the *Gilmore* test did not just apply to actions regarding community property. It is of little consequence that *Gilmore* was decided under the 1939 code and *Patrick* under the 1954 code. The provision that is now § 212 is linguistically the same as in both prior versions of the code. Following *Gilmore,* however, the Tax Court was faced with several more cases where wives were allowed to deduct legal expenses incurred in seeking alimony payments, like *Jane U. Elliott* and *Ruth K. Wild.* In *Elliott,* no mention was made of *Gilmore* and *Patrick.* However, in *Wild, Gilmore* and *Patrick* were distinguished on the grounds that they had not addressed deductions under § 212(1). Additionally, regulations permitted deduction of legal expenses for obtaining alimony had not been changed or rescinded by the IRS and the IRS had not indicated its acquiescence to *Elliott* had been withdrawn. Thus, a wife may still deduct her legal expenses incurred in obtaining alimony payments under § 212(1), but only those related to obtaining alimony that will be includable in the wife's gross income. Here, however, Mr. Fleischman (P) seeks to deduct his legal expenses in defending his wife's suit to invalidate the antenuptial agreement under § 212(2). In order to do so, he must demonstrate that his case is different from *Gilmore* and *Patrick.* Mr. Fleischman (P) argues that his case is different because his expenses were incurred in defending a separate action from the divorce proceeding. This is not persuasive. Even though a separate suit was brought, viewed in its entirety, Ms. Francis' claims are directed at obtaining support above and beyond that provided for in the agreement. The fact that Ohio law does not allow the issue of the validity of the agreement to be raised in divorce proceedings should not be a meaningful distinction for purposes of tax deductions. Clearly, Ms. Francis' claims arise out of her marriage to Mr. Fleischman (P). The fact that those claims have consequences affecting Mr. Fleischman's (P) income-producing property does not change their origin. Consider Ms. Francis' claims in light of the but/for origin of claim test set forth in

Gilmore. If Ms. Francis' claim could not exist but for the marriage, the claim is personal in origin. Here, had Ms. Francis and Mr. Fleischman (P) not been married, Ms. Francis would have no claims against him for support. Thus, her claims are personal in origin. In both this case and *Gilmore,* the wife sought an award of property based upon a right obtained by virtue of the marriage. In both cases, legal expenses incurred in defending the claim are not deductible. Similarly, in both this case and *Patrick,* the agreements entered into prior to the marriage were intended to effect rights that would accrue during the marriage. In both cases, claims arising from the contracts originate from the marriage and are personal in nature. Therefore, it becomes clear that Mr. Fleischman's (P) legal expenses incurred in defending the action brought by Ms. Francis to invalidate the antenuptial agreement may not be deducted. The Tax Court's opinion in *David G. Joyce* [legal expenses incurred in defending postnuptial agreement from attack by wife not deductible because rights limited by contract existed solely by virtue of the marriage] supports this conclusion. Affirmed.

Analysis:

The Tax Court does a good job of laying out the law regarding the deductibility of legal expenses, and in particular focuses on deductibility of expenses incurred in divorce proceedings. For legal expenses to be deductible, the claim being defended must be directly connected or proximately related to (1) the carrying on of a business or trade; (2) the production or collection of income; (3) the management, conservation or maintenance of income-producing property; or (4) obtaining advice regarding tax matters. If connected to (1), expenses are deductible under § 162. If connected to (2), (3) or (4), expenses are deductible under § 212. It is not enough to show that a claim will affect income-producing property or a business. Rather, it must be shown that but for the income-producing property or business, the claim would not exist. When alimony payments are sought, legal expenses incurred are deductible under § 212(1) because the claim seeks to collect income. Notice that this deduction does not include claims for property, presumably because property is not income. Note also that § 212(2) applies to the "management, conservation or maintenance," but not collection of income-producing property.

■ CASE VOCABULARY

ALIMONY: Payments made to a spouse to maintain the spouse's financial status after divorce.

ANTENUPTIAL AGREEMENT: A contract entered into between a couple in contemplation of marriage providing for division of property and assets after marriage.

CAPITALIZED: Computing periodical payments by determining their value as a whole.

William C. Horrmann v. Commissioner

(Taxpayer) v. *(Internal Revenue Commissioner)*

17 T.C. 903 (1951)

ABANDONED RESIDENCE RESULTS IN DEDUCTIONS FOR DEPRECIATION AND MAINTENANCE BUT NOT LOSS

■ **INSTANT FACTS** Taxpayer claimed deductions for depreciation, maintenance and loss of home he inherited from his mother, lived in for two years and then abandoned.

■ **BLACK LETTER RULE** Deductions for depreciation and maintenance are allowed when property is held for production of income, but a loss is not allowed unless the property constitutes a transaction entered into for profit.

■ **PROCEDURAL BASIS**

Taxpayer appeals the decision of the IRS denying deductions for depreciation, maintenance and loss resulting from the sale of property.

■ **FACTS**

Mr. Horrmann (P) inherited a home from his mother in 1940. At that time, the home was worth $60,000. Mr. Horrmann (P) sold his previous residence, redecorated the home he had inherited and lived in it for two years. However, in 1942, Mr. Horrmann (P) abandoned the home because it was too large and expensive. [Gee thanks, mom.] At the time of abandonment, the home was worth $45,000. Following abandonment, Mr. Horrmann (P) made numerous efforts to rent or sell the home. Finally, in 1945, the home was sold for a net profit of $20,800. As a result of this transaction, Mr. Horrmann (P) claimed deductions for depreciation in value of the home and maintenance expenses for 1943, 1944 and 1945. He also claimed a deduction equal to the capital loss sustained at the time of the sale in 1945. The IRS denied the deductions, and Mr. Horrmann (P) appealed to the Tax Court.

■ **ISSUE**

Does the abandonment and subsequent sale of a personal residence at a loss entitle the homeowner to a deduction for the loss?

■ **DECISION AND RATIONALE**

(Black, J.) No. Mr. Horrmann (P) is entitled to deductions for depreciation in value and maintenance expenses because those deductions are for property that was held for the production of income. In the case of depreciation, §§ 167(a)(2) and 168(a) allow a deduction when the property that has depreciated was held for the production of income. Mere abandonment of a personal residence does not render that property one held for production of income. But where, as here, continuous efforts are made to rent or sell the property, the property is said to be held for the production of income and the deduction for depreciation is allowed. In the case of maintenance expenses, § 212(2) allows a deduction for the management, conservation or maintenance of income-producing property. Again, the requirement is that the property be held for production of income and the same analysis applies. The analysis changes, however, when determining whether a deduction for a capital loss is allowed. In order for a capital loss to be deductible, the loss must have occurred in a transaction entered into for profit. [See § 165(c)(2).] Under this standard, the abandonment of property may lead to a different result than the sale of a personal residence after numerous attempts to sell or rent. Generally, when property has been used as a personal residence, it must be converted to a transaction entered into for profit. To show such a conversion, the owner must do more than abandon the property and try to rent or sell it. Mr. Horrmann (P) argues that whether or not a person rents his house prior to selling it rather than abandoning it should not be the sole criteria for determining if conversion to a transaction for profit has taken place. However, contrary to abandonment, renting the house removes the possibility that the homeowner can change his mind about converting the use to a profit-making one from a personal residence. Thus, while renting is not the sole criteria, it is more persuasive than abandonment. This is in accord with the regulations that require that the personal residence be converted or appropriated to another profit-making use. While actual rental is not required, more than mere abandonment is. In the prior cases of *Estate of Maria Assmann* and *Mary E. Crawford,* the Tax Court has held that abandonment followed by demolition is sufficient to show conversion or appropriation to a profit-making use. Here, however, the situation is different from those cases. Here, Mr. Horrmann (P) simply abandoned the home and then tried to rent or sell it, finally selling it at a loss. Additionally, this occurred after a two year period when Mr. Horrmann (P) took actions consistent only with an intent to use the home as a personal residence rather than as a profit-making transaction. Therefore, he is not entitled to claim a deduction for the capital loss sustained upon selling the home. Decision affirmed.

Analysis:

When looking at taking a deduction for a capital loss under § 165(c)(2), the issue is not just whether the property is intended to produce income, but rather whether it was obtained for the express purpose of obtaining a profit. The difference is slight, but important. Not all income-producing property was obtained with the express intent of making a profit. Take the house at issue here. By simply renting a personal residence, property can become income-producing. However, that same property may not be meant to render a profit. For instance, one could rent a home for an amount equal to a mortgage payment, thereby producing income but not gaining a profit. Thus, showing a transaction is entered into for profit requires more than a showing that the property is income-producing. As a result, deductions under § 165 are not as easy to claim as those under § 212 for nonbusiness expenses.

■ CASE VOCABULARY

ABANDON: Withdrawing entirely from something; to leave something completely.

APPROPRIATION: Taking possession of something to the exclusion of others.

CONVERSION: Changing something's character or use.

DEPRECIATION: The decrease in value of property due to use, time, weather, or the like.

Lowry v. United States

(Taxpayer) v. *(IRS)*
384 F.Supp. 257 (D. N.H. 1974)

ONE CAN TURN ONE'S PERSONAL RESIDENCE INTO INCOME–PRODUCING PROPERTY WITHOUT RENTING IT

■ **INSTANT FACTS** Taxpayer put a summer house up for sale immediately after stopping personal use and claimed deductions for maintenance expenses for the newly converted income-producing property.

■ **BLACK LETTER RULE** Whether a personal residence has been converted into income-producing property is not determined by whether or not it was rented before sold, but rather by looking at all of the relevant facts and circumstances, including whether the taxpayer had an expectation of profit.

■ **PROCEDURAL BASIS**

Taxpayer brought action in the Federal District Court seeking reimbursement of an alleged overpayment of taxes assessed by the IRS that resulted when deductions for maintenance expenses were disallowed.

■ **FACTS**

Mr. and Mrs. Lowry (P) acquired a summer home in Martha's Vineyard from Mr. Lowry's (P) father in 1942. The home was located in a cooperative community formed by the Seven Gates Corporation. The corporation owns all of the homes in the community, and each homeowner, including Mr. and Mrs. Lowry (P), owns a certain number of shares in the corporation. The corporation then leases the homes to the homeowners. The term of the lease is for life, with an express provision that if the corporation terminates, the lease is turned into fee title to the home. Thus, the shareholders are treated as the de facto owners of their respective summerhouse. Mr. and Mrs. Lowry (P) used their summer home in Martha's Vineyard every summer up until 1967, when they decided to sell the home. They immediately placed it on the market for $150,000, and continued to maintain it until it finally sold for the list price in 1973. As a result of the sale, Mr. and Mrs. Lowry (P) recognized a capital gain of over $100,000. Mr. and Mrs. Lowry (P) claimed their expenses in maintaining the summer home from 1967 until it was sold in 1973 as nonbusiness expenses. The IRS (D) denied the deductions, and Mr. and Mrs. Lowry (P) brought this action seeking reimbursement of the taxes they paid under protest.

■ **ISSUE**

Can a personal residence be converted into income-producing property without first renting it?

■ **DECISION AND RATIONALE**

(Bownes, J.) Yes. To determine whether a personal residence has been converted into income-producing property for purposes of nonbusiness expense deductions, the Tax Court has adopted a simple test. To convert a personal residence under this test, the taxpayer must first make a bona fide offer to rent the property. This test was adopted to avoid taxpayers listing a house for sale and then, after claiming deductions, reoccupying it, to provide a clear and convenient test and because of language in the regulations that referred to deduction for property held as rental property. [See § 1.212–1(h), allowing deductions for ordinary and necessary expenses paid or incurred in connection with the management, conservation or maintenance of property held by the taxpayer as rental property.] In *Hulet P. Smith* [an offer for sale plus an abandonment converted property into income-producing], however, the Tax Court abandoned this test. Shortly thereafter, it began using the *Newcombe* test. Under the *Newcombe* test, a variety of factors must be weighed, including the length of time the owner occupied the house, availability of the house for personal use during abandonment, recreational character of the property, attempts to rent and whether attempts to sell were made with the intent to realize appreciation. Thus, the key question under this test is whether, in light of all the circumstances, the taxpayer expected a profit. This test represents the better approach. It removes the inflexibility of the prior test and conforms with other sections and regulations that provide that deductions are available even if the property is not producing or likely to produce income. Applying the *Newcombe* test here, it is clear that the property was converted into a transaction entered into for profit. Although the property was immediately listed for sale after abandonment, it was not sold until the market price reflected the asking price. Moreover, Mr. Lowry (P) has substantial knowledge of real estate transactions and had the foresight to know the market prices in the area would rise substantially. Under these circumstances, it is clear Mr. and Mrs. Lowry (P) intended to take advantage of this unusual escalation in property values when they put their summer home on the market. Decision reversed.

Analysis:

Under the *Newcombe* test applied here, if it appears under all the circumstances the owner intended to gain a profit, even if not renting the property, the property can still be deemed income producing and the benefits of that characterization recognized. Remember, the benefits of characterizing property as income producing include deductions for maintenance and conservation of the property. It is interesting that the court chose to ignore the rule applied by the Tax Court. The benefit of having such a rule is that it provides uniformity of law and consistency of its application. If a court such as this one can ignore a rule when it so chooses, as courts often do when justice so requires, what is the point of having any such rule? This is a similar argument to form over substance: rule over flexibility. Keep in mind the court here had some justification for ignoring the rule and taking a different approach. The Tax Court itself had, in some cases, abandoned its own rule, as *Newcombe* demonstrates. Additionally, regulations included language that indicated that receiving income is not necessary to characterizing property as income producing. This case provides insight into the long-standing debate over *per se* rules versus flexible, fact-based standards.

■ **CASE VOCABULARY**

APPRECIATE: An increase in value from the amount paid.

BONA FIDE: In good faith.

DE FACTO: In fact, not by right.

FEE TITLE: Outright ownership with all benefits accorded to a true owner.

SINE QUA NON: Literally, without which it is not; an absolute requirement.

CHAPTER SIXTEEN

Deductions Not Limited to Business or Profit–Seeking Activities

J. Simpson Dean v. Commissioner

Instant Facts: Taxable income assessed to taxpayers for economic benefit derived from interest-free use of money borrowed from a corporation they controlled.

Black Letter Rule: An interest-free loan results in no taxable income to the borrower.

Cramer v. Commissioner

Instant Facts: Taxpayer deducted property taxes paid on three houses, one she owned, one she sold and the third she was given by her mother.

Black Letter Rule: Property taxes may only be deducted if they are assessed to the taxpayer claiming the deductions.

J. Simpson Dean v. Commissioner

(Taxpayer) v. *(Internal Revenue Commissioner)*

35 T.C. 1083 (1961)

NO INCOME IMPUTED TO BORROWER OF INTEREST–FREE LOAN

■ **INSTANT FACTS** Taxable income assessed to taxpayers for economic benefit derived from interest-free use of money borrowed from a corporation they controlled.

■ **BLACK LETTER RULE** An interest-free loan results in no taxable income to the borrower.

■ **PROCEDURAL BASIS**

From deficiencies assessed to their income taxes by the IRS due to imputed income from interest-free loans from corporation, taxpayers appeal to the Tax Court.

■ **FACTS**

Mr. and Mrs. Dean (P) owned a substantial amount of no par common stock in Nemours Corporation. Mr. and Mrs. Dean (P) both owed several loans totaling over $2,000,000 to Nemours Corporation. The loans were secured by non-interest bearing notes. Based in part on a statement made by the Tax Court in a prior case also involving Mr. and Mrs. Dean (P) that lending over two million dollars without interest might [that's an understatement!] be looked at as a means of escaping income insofar as reasonable interest is not required, the IRS (D) assessed additional income taxes against Mr. and Mrs. Dean (P) based on the amount of interest they were not paying. It is from this assessment that Mr. and Mrs. Dean (P) appeal.

■ **ISSUE**

Does an interest-free loan result in taxable income being imputed to the borrower?

■ **DECISION AND RATIONALE**

(Raum, J.) No. There are no cases, administrative rulings or regulations that have recognized the position taken by the IRS (D) here, that interest-free loans result in taxable income being imputed to the borrower. Nevertheless, the IRS (D) argues that the series of cases holding that rent-free use of corporate property may result in imputed income apply with equal force to interest-free loans. In both situations, it is said, property is being used for free. While that is true, the difference between an interest-free loan situation such as the case here and rent-free use of property is that if interest were being paid by a borrower, that interest would be deductible under § 163 [all interest paid on indebtedness is deductible]. Thus, the net result of an interest-free loan versus an interest-bearing loan is zero. The deduction therefore differentiates an interest-free loan case from a rent-free use case. Since interest-free loans result in no deductions for the borrower, it is equally true that they result in no taxable income to the borrower. Assessment of additional taxes reversed. [Before you obtain that interest-free loan, read further in the Chapter—this is no longer the law.]

■ **CONCURRENCE**

(Opper, J.) While the result reached by the majority is correct, the reasons for that result are much broader than necessary and set a dangerous precedent. It is not necessary to say that interest-free loans result in no taxable income being imputed to the borrower to find that Mr. and Mrs. Dean (P) do not owe the additional taxes assessed by the IRS (D). Here it is true that the deductions Mr. and Mrs. Dean (P) could take if they were paying interest on these loans offsets any income imputed to them based on nonpayment of interest. However, to say that in all cases interest-free loans result in no taxable income being imputed is unwarranted. Would that generalization hold true if deductions were allowed for business or nonbusiness expenses on rental property being used rent-free such that rent-free use no longer results in taxable income? Certainly not since to so hold would ignore an entire line of cases setting forth the opposite rule. Moreover, since the burden is upon the IRS (D) to show a deficiency in the amount of taxes paid, all conclusions and inferences must be in favor of Mr. and Mrs. Dean (P) thereby making the broad generalization of the majority even less necessary to resolution of this case.

■ DISSENT

(Bruce, J.) The result the majority reaches is inconsistent with prior case law holding that use of property rent-free results in income to the user. Interest represents compensation for the use, forbearance or detention of money, and as such may be likened to rent paid for use of the money. Additionally, the broad generalization that interest-free loans never result in income to the borrower is unnecessary and certainly unsupported in this case. § 163 allows interest paid on indebtedness to be deducted, but § 265(2) limits that deduction to interest on indebtedness not incurred or continued to purchase or carry obligations. Thus, not all interest is deductible. Here, because the facts were stipulated to, it was upon Mr. and Mrs. Dean (P) to prove that they would be entitled to deduct interest if paid on the loans in question. This they failed to do. Having failed to prove they would be entitled to a deduction, it is far from clear that inclusion of foregone interest in Mr. and Mrs. Dean's (P) gross income would not have resulted in the deficiency assessed.

Analysis:

This case illustrates the competing theories at play regarding interest-free loans. As the majority points out, one theory is that not imputing income to the borrower equal to the amount of interest he does not have to pay is justified because any such imputed income would be deductible under § 163. In other words, imputing income that will be deducted results in a zero gain in taxes. The problem with this theory, however, is that it assumes all interest payments would be deductible. Such is not the case, as the dissent points out. Thus, while it may be that the interest payments imputed to the Deans (P) would be deductible, which the dissent does not believe was proven, it is incorrect to say all interest payments would be deductible so there is never taxable income. If the majority's position is the rule, then anytime a loan would result in interest not being deductible and taxes having to be paid, using an interest-free loan will negate those taxes. Additionally, if no income is imputed to the borrower, then no income can be imputed to the lender. Thus, while the lender has essentially given a gift of the amount of interest he would be entitled to, no gift taxes are assessed since no income changed hands. Eventually, the amount of taxes being avoided by interest-free loans came to a head and Congress and the courts stepped in. The Supreme Court, recognizing the potential gift present in interest-free loans, decided *Dickman v. Commissioner*, (holding that an interest-free loan to the family is a transfer of property by gift), and Congress enacted § 7872 (providing that interest-free and below-market loans result in imputed income to both the lender and borrower).

■ CASE VOCABULARY

NO PAR COMMON STOCK: Ordinary stock usually issued by a corporation that has no special rights or privileges beyond those attendant to a normal shareholder and has no par value.

PAR VALUE: The face value of one share of stock, usually fixed at the time of issuance and usually $1.00.

PRIME RATE: The lowest interest rate available at a particular time usually available only to the largest credit-worthy consumers.

Cramer v. Commissioner

(Taxpayer) v. *(IRS)*
55 T.C. 1125 (1971)

NOT ALL PROPERTY TAXES ARE DEDUCTIBLE

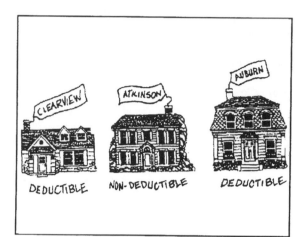

■ **INSTANT FACTS** Taxpayer deducted property taxes paid on three houses, one she owned, one she sold and the third she was given by her mother.

■ **BLACK LETTER RULE** Property taxes may only be deducted if they are assessed to the taxpayer claiming the deductions.

■ **PROCEDURAL BASIS**

Taxpayer appeals the decision of the IRS to assess a deficiency in her income taxes due to deductions for property taxes which the IRS determined were not allowed.

■ **FACTS**

Ms. Cramer (P) sold her residence on Auburn Street under a land sale contract whereby the purchaser agreed to make monthly payments to her and to pay the property taxes. Title to the property remained in Ms. Cramer (P). Shortly thereafter, Ms. Cramer (P) purchased a new home on Clearview Street. In 1964 and 1965, the purchaser failed to make the monthly payments or to pay the property taxes, so Ms. Cramer (P) paid the property taxes, foreclosed against the purchaser and retook possession of the property in 1966. Later that year, she sold the Auburn Street house but realized no gain on the sale. Around the same time, in 1965 and 1966, Ms. Cramer (P) paid the property taxes on her mother's home on Atkinson Street. In 1967, Ms. Cramer's (P) mother quitclaimed the Atkinson house to her. Ms. Cramer (P) [needing some relief after paying all those property tax bills] deducted the property taxes she paid on all three houses. The IRS (D) denied the deductions for the Atkinson and Auburn houses, however, and Ms. Cramer (P) appealed to the Tax Court.

■ **ISSUE**

May all property taxes paid be deducted?

■ **DECISION AND RATIONALE**

(Featherston, J.) No. Ms. Cramer (P) is not entitled to claim the property taxes paid on the Atkinson property as a deduction. § 164 allows a deduction for real property taxes, but they are only deductible by the person upon whom they are assessed. Ms. Cramer's (P) mother owned the Atkinson property, up until 1967. More importantly, at the time Ms. Cramer (P) paid the property taxes on the Atkinson property, her mother owned it. Since property taxes are assessed against the owner or occupant of the property, here Ms. Cramer's (P) mother, only the owner or occupant who pays the taxes can claim the deduction. If someone else pays the property taxes, like Ms. Cramer (P) did here, they have done so as a gift to the person assessed the taxes. [Now that's a unique gift!] Regarding the Auburn property, however, taxes are assessed against the owner or the occupier. At the time Ms. Cramer (P) paid the property taxes on the Auburn Street property, she was the record owner. Since she paid the property taxes despite the purchaser's contractual obligation to do so, she may claim the deduction for the years she owned the home. It is noted that Ms. Cramer (P) sold the home in 1966. § 164(d)(1) provides that if property is sold, the property taxes are apportioned between the buyer and the seller. Thus, although Ms. Cramer (P) paid all of the property taxes for 1966, she may only claim a deduction for the portion of property taxes assessed while she was the owner of the property. Decision reversed in part and affirmed in part.

Analysis:

This case provides a good illustration of how to determine when property taxes are deductible under § 164 and when they are not. In general, if the property taxes are imposed on the taxpayer claiming the deduction, the deduction will be allowed. In some states, the owner and the occupier, if not the same, are responsible for payment of property taxes. In that situation, then, whoever pays the property taxes may claim the deduction. For the most part, determining deductions for property taxes is relatively simple, assuming you know upon whom the property tax was imposed. The tricky part is applying the same rule to other taxes, such as sales, use, gasoline, and other similar taxes.

■ CASE VOCABULARY

ESCROW: Property held in trust to be turned over to the buyer only upon satisfaction of certain requirements.

FORECLOSURE: A legal remedy by which someone's rights in the property are extinguished.

QUITCLAIM DEED: A legal document by which an owner of land transfers his interest, whatever it is, to the recipient without making any guarantee as to what type of interest he is transferring.

CHAPTER SEVENTEEN

Restrictions on Deductions

Engdahl v. Commissioner

Instant Facts: The IRS denied the petitioners' deductions for losses incurred in a horse-breeding operation, finding that the operation was more of a hobby than a business for profit, and the petitioners appealed.

Black Letter Rule: When a taxpayer engages in an activity with the bona fide purpose of turning a profit, losses incurred from that activity are fully deductible.

Commissioner v. Tellier

Instant Facts: Taxpayer deducted expenses incurred in unsuccessfully defending criminal fraud charges brought against him.

Black Letter Rule: Public policy does not bar otherwise valid deductions for ordinary and necessary legal expenses incurred in defending criminal charges arising out of carrying on a business.

Engdahl v. Commissioner

(Taxpayer) v. *(IRS)*

72 T.C. 659 (1979)

A HORSE–BREEDING VENTURE WAS OPERATED "FOR PROFIT" EVEN THOUGH IT ONLY PRO-DUCED LOSSES

stus.com

Nothing but losses, and now the IRS is trying to label us just a "hobby"!

■ **INSTANT FACTS** The IRS denied the petitioners' deductions for losses incurred in a horse-breeding operation, finding that the operation was more of a hobby than a business for profit, and the petitioners appealed.

■ **BLACK LETTER RULE** When a taxpayer engages in an activity with the bona fide purpose of turning a profit, losses incurred from that activity are fully deductible.

PROCEDURAL BASIS

Tax court review of a determination of deficiencies.

FACTS

Engdahl (P) was an orthodontist. His children enjoyed riding and showing horses, which the Engdahls (P) kept at a local stable. As his retirement neared, Engdahl (P) thought about what kind of new business he might like to get involved in, and after consulting with several experts he decided to start a horse-breeding operation. The Engdahls (P) purchased a ranch and erected a seven-stall stable, fenced pastures, and a corral. Mr. and Mrs. Engdahl (P) spent thirty-five to fifty-five hours per week caring for the horses and maintaining the ranch. They hired a professional trainer to train the horses and enter them in horse shows. Despite these efforts, the venture showed operating losses from 1964 through 1975. The Engdahls (P) claimed that the losses arose from the fact that American saddle-breds were losing popularity, while the costs of running their operation had dramatically increased. They had also lost several horses due to illness, an accident, and stillbirth. Ultimately, the Engdahls (P) decided to wind up the horse operation and put the ranch on the market. During the years of operation, the Engdahls (P) had deducted losses of about $17,000 to $18,000 per year from their income. The IRS issued a notice of deficiency, disallowing these losses because the horse operation was not an "activity engaged in for profit." The taxpayers appealed.

ISSUE

Was the Engdahls' (P) horse-breeding operation an "activity . . . not engaged in for profit" under the Tax Code?

DECISION AND RATIONALE

(Hall, J.) No. When a taxpayer engages in an activity with the bona fide purpose of turning a profit, losses incurred from that activity are fully deductible. The Tax Code provides that if an individual engages in an activity, and that activity is *not* engaged in for profit, no deduction attributable to that activity will be allowed. Breeding and raising horses may or may not constitute a business venture; whether such an operation qualifies in this regard depends on whether the venture was engaged in with the predominant purpose of making a profit. Relevant considerations include (1) the manner in which the taxpayer carried on the activity, (2) the expertise of the taxpayer and his or her advisers, (3) the time and effort expended by the taxpayer, (4) the expectation that assets used in the activity will increase in value, (5) the taxpayer's success in other similar or dissimilar activities, (6) the taxpayer's history of income or loss with respect to the activity, (7) the amount of occasional profits earned, (8) the financial status of the taxpayer, and (9) whether elements or personal pleasure or recreation are involved. The question is one of fact, to be decided based on all the facts and circumstances.

With regard to the manner in which the taxpayer carried on the activity, it is relevant whether the taxpayers maintained complete and accurate books and records, whether the activity was conducted in a manner similar to other comparable businesses that are profitable, and whether changes were made in an attempt to improve profitability. Here, the horse operation receipts were deposited in a separate savings account, and a CPA reviewed the operation's books and records on a quarterly basis. The accountant monitored Engdahl's (P) financial management of the business and found it suitable. The Engdahls (P) advertised their operation by exhibiting their horses at shows and in other manners, indicating the venture was more than a hobby. They made many changes to their operating methods over the years in an attempt to increase profitability. They bought the ranch so they could keep their horses on site rather than boarding them, and made reasoned breeding and purchasing decisions with regard to the horses. The petitioners' manner of operation indicates an intent to make a profit.

In addition, the petitioners sought the advice of experts in running their operation. Veterinarians, trainers, and others involved in the horse business advised the Engdahls (P) on their horse-breeding operation. Their informal but continuous consultations with these experts indicate an intent to engage in a horse-breeding business for profit. The facts also indicate that the Engdahls (P) had a bona fide expectation that their assets, including the ranch and horses, would appreciate in value. Tolerating losses during the early years of an operation does not indicate that profits are not ultimately expected. Nor does the fact that Dr. Engdahl (P) still earned income from his orthodontic practice indicate that the horse operation was a hobby. Although the fact that the taxpayer has no other income indicates that a venture is engaged in for profit, the fact that he has other income against which losses from a separate venture are charged does not mean the venture is not for profit. The essential question remains whether there was genuine hope of actual profit. Here, the Engdahls (P) were looking at the horse-breeding operation as a means of earning retirement income. They worked hard at it, mucking out stalls and building fences themselves. They did not engage in the activity for pure pleasure; indeed, they did not even ride their horses or use the ranch for social activities. Viewing the record as a whole, we conclude that the Engdahls (P) engaged in their horse activities with the bona fide intent to derive a profit, and that therefore the losses incurred in such activities were fully deductible.

Analysis:

The IRS reviews decisions of the Tax Court to determine whether an appeal should be taken. In this case, IRS counsel acquiesced to the Tax Court's decision. *See In re Engdahl*, AOD–1979–177, 1979 WL 53223 (IRS AOD Sept. 28, 1979). The opinion notes that the Tax Court applied the factors listed in Treas. Reg. § 1.183–2(b) to the facts of the case, concluding that the petitioners engaged in their horse-related activity with the bona fide intent to derive a profit therefrom and that the losses incurred in the activity were therefore fully deductible. Because this issue is factual and the court's determination was not clearly erroneous, no appeal was recommended. The Commissioner's acquiescence in a decision of the Tax Court relates only to the issue or issues decided adversely to the Government. An acquiescence should be relied on by revenue officers and others only with regard to the application of the law to the facts in that particular case. "Caution should be exercised in extending the application of the decision to a similar case unless the facts and circumstances are substantially the same . . ." *See id.*, 1979–2 C.B. 1, 1979 WL 194017 (IRS ACQ Dec. 31, 1979). Note, too, that acquiescence in a decision means acceptance by the Service of the conclusion reached, but not necessarily of any of the reasons given by the court for its conclusion. *Id.*

Commissioner v. Tellier

(IRS) v. *(Taxpayer)*
383 U.S. 687, 86 S.Ct. 1118 (1966)

PUBLIC POLICY DOES NOT BLOCK DEDUCTION OF EXPENSES INCURRED IN DEFENDING CRIMINAL FRAUD CHARGES

■ **INSTANT FACTS** Taxpayer deducted expenses incurred in unsuccessfully defending criminal fraud charges brought against him.

■ **BLACK LETTER RULE** Public policy does not bar otherwise valid deductions for ordinary and necessary legal expenses incurred in defending criminal charges arising out of carrying on a business.

■ **PROCEDURAL BASIS**

The IRS appeals the decision of the Second Circuit Court of Appeals reversing the decision of the Tax Court affirming the IRS' disallowance of Taxpayer's claimed deduction.

■ **FACTS**

Mr. Tellier (D) was in the business of underwriting public stock offerings and purchasing stock for resale. In 1956, Mr. Tellier (D) was charged with and convicted of securities fraud, mail fraud and conspiracy to commit securities and mail fraud. Mr. Tellier (D) was sentenced to four and a half years in prison and an $18,000 fine. In unsuccessfully defending the charges, Mr. Tellier (D) incurred legal expenses totaling $22,964.20, which he deducted under § 162(a). [§ 162(a) allows deductions for ordinary and necessary expenses incurred in carrying on a business or trade.] The IRS (P) disallowed the deduction on public policy grounds, and the Tax Court affirmed. The Second Circuit Court of Appeals reversed, and the IRS (P) appealed to the United States Supreme Court.

■ **ISSUE**

May expenses incurred defending a criminal prosecution be deducted under § 162(a)?

■ **DECISION AND RATIONALE**

(Stewart, J.) Yes. Clearly the expenses deducted by Mr. Tellier (D) were expenses incurred in connection with his securities business, as the IRS (P) concedes. Under *Gilmore,* expenses that originate from business activities are deductible; those that originate from personal activities are not. The charges Mr. Tellier (D) incurred in defending originated from his business activities as a securities broker. Therefore, those expenses qualify as expenses incurred in carrying on a business. Those expenses were also ordinary and necessary expenses within the meaning of § 162(a). Under *Welch v. Helvering,* to be necessary, expenses must only be appropriate and helpful in the development of business activities. To be ordinary, expenses must be of the type that are deductible and not capital expenditures. Here, Mr. Tellier's (D) legal expenses were not capital expenditures. Thus, Mr. Tellier's (D) legal expenses are clearly deductible under § 162(a). The IRS (P), which concedes the expenses were ordinary and necessary business expenses, disallowed the deduction on public policy grounds. While that view finds support in prior administrative and judicial decisions, it finds no support whatsoever in any regulation, statute or opinion of the Supreme Court. As such, and under the plain provisions of § 162(a), no such public policy exception is warranted. First, income taxes are a means of taxing income, not punishing wrongful conduct. This is evident from the fact that taxes are assessed against all income, whether obtained legally or illegally. The same is true of deductions. Deductions, as stated in

Commissioner v. Sullivan [deduction for rent and wages paid by operators of illegal gambling enterprise allowed] *Lilly v. Commissioner* [deductions claimed by opticians for amounts paid as kickbacks to doctors who prescribed eyeglasses sold by them allowed despite obvious ethical considerations] and *Commissioner v. Heininger* [deductions claimed by dentist for legal expenses incurred in unsuccessfully defending against administrative mail fraud hearing allowed], are not limited by whether losses were legitimate. Obviously, otherwise valid deductions may be disallowed by specific legislation. However, where Congress has chosen not to enact legislation or has remained silent on the subject, "it is only in extremely limited circumstances" that a court should create exceptions where none exist. Only where allowing the deduction would "frustrate sharply defined national or state policies proscribing particular types of conduct" should such public policy exceptions be created. To warrant creation of a public policy exception, courts should be sure the policy frustrated is one evidenced by a governmental declaration. Additionally, the test for nondeductability should always be the severity and immediacy of frustration that will result from allowing the deduction, as set forth in *Tank Truck Rentals v. Commissioner* and *Hoover Express Co. v. United States* [deductions for fines assessed for violating statutes disallowed]. Applying these standards to Mr. Tellier's (D) case, it becomes evident that the legal expenses deducted fall outside those limited circumstances where a public policy exception to deductibility would apply. Public policy is not offended when a man faced with criminal charges exercises his constitutional right to hire a lawyer to defend him. Moreover, Congress has authorized certain punishments for those found guilty of criminal charges and we see no reason to assess further financial punishment than Congress saw fit to assess. Such an additional financial punishment would also be inconsistent with determining punishment based on the severity of the offense since the financial burden would depend not on the crime but on the cost of defending the charges. Judgment affirmed.

Analysis:

It is the province of the legislature to create and define public policy by enacting laws. This premise is evidenced by the Supreme Court's statement that if an exception is warranted, Congress should create it. The executive branch also has a role in making public policy through enforcement of those laws. The judiciary, however, as evidenced by this opinion, should not play a role in creating public policy. Therefore, exceptions to statutes or rules based solely on public policy should not be enforced unless clearly articulated by another branch of government. This is an important concept since courts often employ public policy as a means of reaching an end the law does not allow them to reach. This has led to widespread debate of the appropriate role of public policy in judicial decisions, both on a constitutional and on a practical level. From a constitutional standpoint, judicial creation of public policy is troubling and discouraged, as the Supreme Court states in this opinion. However, as a practical matter, if law results in an inequitable result and justice demands a different result, public policy is often the only means of getting there in an albeit questionably legitimate manner. Keep in mind, however, that the Supreme Court did not hold that public policy exceptions may never be created by the courts. In a limited sense, the Court left the door open for courts to recognize public policy exceptions that the IRS may not have recognized. As a result, public policy remains a viable restriction on otherwise valid deductions.

■ CASE VOCABULARY

MAIL FRAUD: Using the postal system to deceive another by a trick or scheme intended to deprive another of a legal right.

SECURITIES FRAUD: Violating the fraud provisions of the 1933 Securities Act; deceiving another through the use of stocks or bonds.

CHAPTER EIGHTEEN

Deductions for Individuals Only

Raymon Gerard v. Commissioner

Instant Facts: Taxpayer deducted cost of installing central air conditioning unit in his home at recommendation of his ill daughter's doctor as a medical expense.

Black Letter Rule: Expenditures that constitute a permanent addition to a home are deductible as medical expenses only insofar as they do not increase the value of the home.

Commissioner v. Banks

Instant Facts: Two taxpayers excluded the amounts paid to their attorneys as contingent fees from their annual income tax returns.

Black Letter Rule: A taxpayer who owns or controls an income-producing asset may not anticipatorily assign the income to avoid tax liability for the income.

Raymon Gerard v. Commissioner

(Taxpayer) v. *(Internal Revenue Commissioner)*

37 T.C. 826 (1962)

INSTALLATION OF CENTRAL AIR CONDITIONING DEDUCTIBLE AS MEDICAL EXPENSE

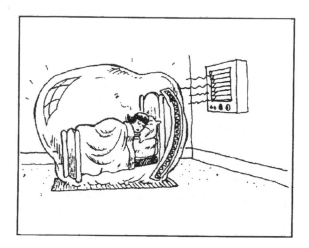

■ **INSTANT FACTS** Taxpayer deducted cost of installing central air conditioning unit in his home at recommendation of his ill daughter's doctor as a medical expense.

■ **BLACK LETTER RULE** Expenditures that constitute a permanent addition to a home are deductible as medical expenses only insofar as they do not increase the value of the home.

■ **PROCEDURAL BASIS**

Appeal to the Tax Court of IRS' decision to deny deduction of installing central air conditioning unit as a medical expense.

■ **FACTS**

At the recommendation of his daughter's doctor, Mr. Gerard (P) installed a room air conditioning unit to help alleviate his daughter's cystic fibrosis, a disease which requires a special diet and special antibiotics given by mouth and aerosol through a tent-device in which those inflicted with the disease sleep. The room air conditioner restricted the daughter's movements to only one room in Mr. Gerard's (P) home. This was determined to be bad for the daughter psychologically and so her doctor recommended that Mr. Gerard (P) install a central air-conditioning unit, thus enabling her to move about the entire house. Mr. Gerard (P) did so and deducted the $1,300 cost as medical expenses under § 213 [authorizes medical expense deductions]. The IRS [showing its lack of compassion] denied the deduction, and Mr. Gerard (P) appealed.

■ **ISSUE**

Are expenses incurred in installing a central air conditioning unit pursuant to a doctor's recommendation deductible as medical expenses?

■ **DECISION AND RATIONALE**

(Mulroney, J.) Yes. § 213 allows expenses paid for medical care to be deducted. Medical care is defined by § 213(e)(1) as amounts paid for the diagnosis, care, mitigation, treatment or prevention of disease. Here, it is clear that some form of temperature and humidity control was a medical necessity for Mr. Gerard's (P) daughter. As such, the $1,300 expenditure for the central air-conditioning unit recommended by the daughter's doctor is deductible under § 213. This does not end the inquiry, however, because § 263 disallows a deduction for permanent improvements made to increase the value of property. Generally, a medical expenditure that is essentially a permanent addition to the taxpayer's home is not deductible as a medical expense. However, the mere fact that a medical expenditure is also a capital expenditure does not automatically disqualify the expenditure as a medical expense deduction. Whether a capital expenditure is deductible as a medical expense depends on whether it increased the value of the home. For instance, in *Berry v. Wiseman,* expenses incurred in installing an elevator for a housewife suffering from acute coronary insufficiency were deemed deductible as medical expenses because the elevator did not increase the value of the home. The IRS has acquiesced in this decision. [See Revenue Ruling 59–411.] The reasons for this value-based test were set forth in *Frank S. Delp,* in which we stated that if a capital expenditure increases the value of the home, the taxpayer has already been compensated for the expense such that a deduction would render a double benefit. It follows from this rule that if the taxpayer can show the increase in the value of the home was less than the amount of the capital expenditure, the difference should be allowed as a deduction. Here, Mr. Gerard (P) spent $1,300 installing the central air conditioning unit. The expenditure increased the value of his home by $800. Thus, $500 of the expense is deductible as a medical expense under § 213 [better $500 than nothing]. Decision reversed.

Analysis:

As this case demonstrates, not all medical-expense deductions may be allowed if the effect of allowing the deduction results in a double benefit to the taxpayer. When, as here, a taxpayer's medical expenditure results in a permanent addition to his home, a question arises as to whether the expenditure is a deductible medical expense. The test is whether the expenditure increased the value of the home above the amount of the expenditure. If so, no deduction is allowed. However, the mere fact that the expenditure increased the value of the home does not automatically render the deduction moot; the expenditure is deductible only insofar as it exceeded the increase in value.

■ CASE VOCABULARY

EXPENDITURE: Payment of money for an expense or contribution.

MITIGATION: Lessening or decreasing.

Commissioner v. Banks

(*IRS Commissioner*) v. (*Taxpayer*)

543 U.S. 426, 125 S.Ct. 826 (2005)

DAMAGES, INCLUDING CONTINGENT FEE AMOUNTS, ARE TAXABLE INCOME TO LITIGANTS

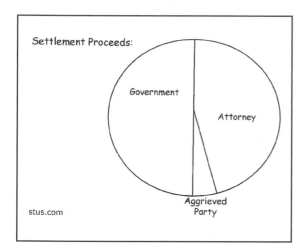

Settlement Proceeds:

Government

Attorney

Aggrieved Party

stus.com

■ **INSTANT FACTS** Two taxpayers excluded the amounts paid to their attorneys as contingent fees from their annual income tax returns.

■ **BLACK LETTER RULE** A taxpayer who owns or controls an income-producing asset may not anticipatorily assign the income to avoid tax liability for the income.

■ **PROCEDURAL BASIS**

Certiorari to review consolidated decisions of the Sixth Circuit and Ninth Circuit.

■ **FACTS**

Two cases were consolidated for review. In the first, John W. Banks, II (D) successfully settled an employment discrimination suit for $464,000, with $150,000 payable to his attorney as part of their contingent-fee agreement. Banks (D) did not include any of the settlement proceeds as income on that year's tax return. Seven years later, the Commissioner (P) issued him a notice of deficiency. The Tax Court concluded that Banks (D) should treat the entire $464,000 as income. The Sixth Circuit reversed in part, holding that only his net proceeds constituted income. In so reasoning, the court acknowledged that the contingent-fee agreement is not akin to an assignment of income, but rather resembles an assignment of an income-producing asset, regardless of any special property interests in the litigation bestowed upon the attorney by state law.

In the other case, Banaitis (D) successfully litigated interference with contract and breach of fiduciary duty claims, earning nearly $5 million for himself and nearly $4 million as a contingent fee for his attorney. Banaitis (D) reported as income on his tax return only the portion he personally received, prompting a notice of deficiency from the Commissioner (P). The Tax Court agreed with the Commissioner (P) that the contingent fee was taxable to Banaitis (D) as well. However, the Ninth Circuit reversed, reasoning that whether the fee is taxable to the successful litigant depends on state law. Where state law grants the attorney a lien or other property interest in the judgment, he receives a partial transfer of the client's property. Accordingly, the client is not liable for the tax on the contingent fee.

■ **ISSUE**

Is the portion of a money judgment or settlement paid to a plaintiff's attorney under a contingent-fee agreement income to the plaintiff under the Internal Revenue Code?

■ **DECISION AND RATIONALE**

(Kennedy, J.) Yes. As a general rule, when a litigant's recovery constitutes income, the litigant's income includes the portion of the recovery paid to the attorney as a contingent fee. Under the Tax Code, "gross income" is "all income from whatever source derived." A taxpayer's income includes any economic gain earned and cannot be reduced by an anticipatory assignment of income. While the anticipatory assignment of income doctrine ensures that one who earns income does not avoid tax liability by creatively assigning the income to another, the doctrine does not permit consideration of the actual motive for the assignment. Rather, the question to be considered when an assignment is involved is whether the taxpayer retains control not of the income, but of the income-producing asset. He "who owns or controls the source of the income, also controls the disposition of that which he could have received himself and diverts the payment from himself to others as the means of procuring the satisfaction of his wants."

In litigation, the income-producing asset is the cause of action retained by the plaintiff. Although the value of the cause of action is speculative when the income is assigned via the contingent-fee agreement, the anticipatory assignment doctrine is not affected by the uncertainty of the income to be derived. Neither is the doctrine affected by the attorney-client partnership formed to generate the income. While the client's cause of action is joined by the attorney's effort and expertise to create the income, the cause of action remains controlled by the client. He must decide whether to settle or proceed to trial and make other important choices. The attorney employs his effort and expertise not independently, but on behalf of the client. He is a paid agent serving his principal's best interests. State laws affecting the strength of the attorney's interest in the outcome of the client's case do not affect his status as the client's agent. Because the taxpayer retains control and dominion over his income-producing cause of action, the entire amount of damages received is treated as income. Reversed.

Analysis:

As the Court emphasized in its opinion, "there was no indication in Banks' contract with his attorney, or in the settlement agreement with the defendant, that the contingent fee paid to Banks' attorney was in lieu of statutory fees." While the Court declined to address exactly how its holding is affected by fee-shifting statutes, it strongly suggested that if Banks' attorney had the foresight to consider the tax treatment of the contingent fee, Banks may have been spared the tax liability.

■ CASE VOCABULARY

AGENT: One who is authorized to act for or in place of another; a representative.

ASSIGNMENT: The transfer of rights or property.

CONTINGENT FEE: A fee charged for a lawyer's services only if the lawsuit is successful or is favorably settled out of court.

ORDINARY INCOME: For individual income tax purposes, income that is derived from sources such as wages, commissions, and interest (as opposed to income from capital gains).

PRINCIPAL: One who authorizes another to act on his or her behalf as an agent.

CHAPTER NINETEEN

Fundamental Timing Principles

Charles F. Kahler v. Commissioner

Instant Facts: The Tax Court held that a cash method taxpayer who actually received a check on December 31, 1946, must include the value of the check in income for that year despite the fact that it was impossible to cash the check before the end of the taxable year.

Black Letter Rule: The value of a check actually received is includable in the year of receipt despite the fact the check can not be converted to cash in the year of receipt.

Williams v. Commissioner

Instant Facts: The Tax Court held that a taxpayer who actually received an unsecured promissory note did not realize income the year he received the promissory note as the taxpayer established that the promissory note was not payment for his services nor did the promissory note have any fair market value in the year of receipt.

Black Letter Rule: An unsecured promissory note (which has no fair market value) is not the equivalent of cash and is not includable in the income of a cash method taxpayer in the year of receipt.

Cowden v. Commissioner

Instant Facts: Cowden (D), entered into leasing contract with an oil company for the mineral rights to some of his land with the payments set forth in a "supplemental agreement" which provided for payment to him and his family over the course of a few years, and then assigned the "supplemental agreement" to a bank for cash before the payments came due.

Black Letter Rule: A readily marketable agreement (obligation/promise) to make future payments is the equivalent of cash and thus, currently taxable.

Hornung v. Commissioner

Instant Facts: Green Bay Packers football player (Paul (D)) was awarded a Corvette from Sport Magazine on December 31, 1961, but which he did not actually receive until 1962, and which he did not include as income at any time; held not to be constructively received in 1961, included and taxable in 1962.

Black Letter Rule: Constructive receipt occurs when income is credited, set apart, or otherwise made available to a taxpayer unless the taxpayer's control of its receipt is subject to substantial limitations or restrictions.

Commissioner v. Boylston Market Ass'n

Instant Facts: The 5th Circuit found that Boylston (D), a cash method taxpayer, could take a deduction equal to the prorated cost of its insurance premiums over the life of the policies, and was not required to only take a deduction for the amount actually paid in the taxable year.

Black Letter Rule: Taxpayers (even cash method taxpayers) must prorate expenses related to the creation of an asset which has a useful life substantially beyond the taxable year and may not take the full deduction for the expense in the year of actual payment.

Cathcart v. Commissioner

Instant Facts: The Tax Court determined that the taxpayer (Cathcart) (D) was not allowed to deduct as "interest paid" the points withheld on a mortgage loan in the year of the loan.

Black Letter Rule: Prepaid interest withheld from a mortgage loan is not currently deductible as prepaid interest, but must be deducted ratably over the life of the loan.

Vander Poel, Francis & Co., Inc. v. Commissioner

Instant Facts: A cash method taxpayer (Vander) (D) was denied a current deduction for salary it "paid" to its officers as the payment was credited to their accounts, but not actually paid, in the taxable year.

Black Letter Rule: Deductions are only permitted under specific statutes and only when actually paid.

Spring City Foundry Co. v. Commissioner

Instant Facts: Although Spring (D) was unable to collect an amount due from a purchaser of its goods, the amount due was held to be includable in its gross income under the accrual method of accounting.

Black Letter Rule: For the accrual method taxpayer, income is included in gross income when the right to receive such income is fixed and can be determined with reasonable accuracy.

North American Oil Consolidated v. Burnet

Instant Facts: Net profits earned by North American Oil Consolidated (NorthAm) (D) in 1916 while under a (partial) receivership were held not to be income to NorthAm (D) until 1917 when the receivership was vacated and the net profits paid over to the company.

Black Letter Rule: A taxpayer with a claim of right over an amount earned must include that amount in income in the year the claim of right accrues, which is not necessarily the year the amount is earned.

New Capital Hotel, Inc. v. Commissioner

Instant Facts: A taxpayer resisted the IRS' decision to declare a receipt of rent for the last year of a multi-year lease as income in the year in which it was received as opposed to the last year of the lease, which is the year when it was earned.

Black Letter Rule: Cash received as an advance payment of rent must be included in income in the year received, even if it is not used until later on when the money is earned.

Artnell Co. v. Commissioner

Instant Facts: The owners of the Chicago White Sox had to pay taxes on all revenues received in a particular year, even if some of those revenues (stemming from the sale of season tickets) would not technically be earned until a subsequent year (when the games paid for were actually paid).

Black Letter Rule: An accrual taxpayer may defer taxes due on prepayments for services until those services are actually rendered so long as the services are to be rendered at a fixed time and in the year following the year of receipt.

Schuessler v. Commissioner

Instant Facts: The IRS objected to a taxpayer's attempt to take as a future deduction the costs of future expenses, the income for which was maintained in a reserve account.

Black Letter Rule: When the use of a reserve account accurately reflects a taxpayer's income on an annual accounting basis, the tax code permits its use.

Charles F. Kahler v. Commissioner

(Bank Holiday Taxpayer) v. *(IRS)*

18 T.C. 31 (1952)

THE VALUE OF A CHECK IS INCLUDED IN INCOME IN YEAR OF ACTUAL RECEIPT

■ **INSTANT FACTS** The Tax Court held that a cash method taxpayer who actually received a check on December 31, 1946, must include the value of the check in income for that year despite the fact that it was impossible to cash the check before the end of the taxable year.

■ **BLACK LETTER RULE** The value of a check actually received is includable in the year of receipt despite the fact the check can not be converted to cash in the year of receipt.

■ **PROCEDURAL BASIS**

Not Stated.

■ **FACTS**

Taxpayer Kahler (D) received a commission check after 5:00 p.m. on December 31, 1946, and claimed that because he could not cash the check it was not income within that year. Kahler (D) argues that the mere receipt of the check does not constitute income. Kahler (D) relies upon *Fisher* [check received on last day of 1942 found not to be income until 1943 because check was subject to substantial restriction]. Kahler (D) also relies upon the *Lavery* and *Ostenberg* cases [although checks delivered on December 30, and December 31, respectively, found to be included in year of delivery, dicta suggests different result if unable to cash checks in same year as delivery]. The IRS (P) relies upon its regulations [Reg. §§ 1.61–2(d) and 1.446–1(a) and (c)] which provide that all items of gross income shall be included in the taxable year in which received by the taxpayer, and that where services are paid for other than by money, the amount to be included as income is the fair market value of the thing taken in payment.

■ **ISSUE**

Is actual receipt of a check sufficient to cause the value of the check to be included in income even though it is impossible to cash the check before the next taxable year?

■ **DECISION AND RATIONALE**

(Rice, J.) Yes. The cases relied upon by Kahler (D) to support his position [mere receipt of a check does not constitute income within the same year of receipt if the check is not received in sufficient time to convert the check into cash] are distinguishable from this case. In *Fisher*, the delivery of the check was subject to a substantial restriction. The parties had an oral agreement at the time of delivery that the check was not to be cashed for a few days because the drawer (writer) of the check was short of funds. In *Lavery*, and *Ostenberg*, the checks delivered to the taxpayer were found to be income in the year of delivery. Kahler (D) relies on the dicta from both cases which notes that the result might have been different if the taxpayer could have shown that he could not have cashed the checks in the year drawn. We fail to see how the fact that it might be impossible to cash the check in the same year as actual delivery of the check changes the result [inclusion in income]. By way of analogy, a check that is written and delivered in year one then cashed in year two is a deduction to the writer of the check in year one. Under the negotiable instruments law, payment by check is a conditional payment subject to the condition that it will be honored upon presentation; and once such presentation is made and the check is honored, the date of payment *relates back* to the time of delivery. [The idea here is that assuming that the check is honored the delivery of the check is the moment in time that is relevant for inclusion and/or deduction of income.] It is immaterial that delivery of a check is made too late in the taxable year for the check to be cashed in that year. Kahler (D) realized income upon receipt of the commission check on December 31, 1946. Decision for the IRS (P).

■ CONCURRENCE

(Murdock, J.) While I concur with the result that receipt of a check is regarded as payment and income unless it is subject to some restriction, the present case is a weak case to find such a result. Although the evidence showed that the check could not be cashed at the drawee's (checkwriter's) bank, there was no evidence presented that showed that the check could not have been cashed somewhere other than that bank, that the check could not have been deposited at the drawee bank, or that the check could not have been used to discharge an obligation, all within the year of receipt.

Analysis:

There could be many reasons Kahler (D) would care that his commission check is included in his 1947 income rather than 1946. The value of the check may have been such that it increased his income to the point of placing him in a higher tax bracket, thus increasing the amount of money he would owe to the IRS (P). In addition to paying fewer taxes in 1946, he could invest his commission check over the course of 1947 and possibly earn sufficient interest to pay any taxes due on that money for the tax year 1947 (this is an example of the time value of money). Another possibility is that Kahler (D) might have had a smaller income in 1947 and that even with the addition of the commission check to his income (if any) he was in a lower tax bracket than in 1946, thus owing less tax. The reason the IRS (P) wants the commission check included in 1946 is that it wants all the money it can get as soon as it can get it. It would rather have the commission check included in the tax year that results in the highest amount of taxes paid, which, although there is no statement of facts included in the case, one might presume is 1946. The item *actually received* here is just a piece of paper. It is a piece of paper, however, that is considered in personal and business reality as a transfer of money or the same as cash. As long as the check is honored in the normal course of business, the inclusion relates back to the date of delivery. The underlying "issue" for all of the cases about timing of inclusion is "*when* did the taxpayer realize income?"

Williams v. Commissioner

(Timberland Taxpayer) v. *(IRS)*

28 T.C. 1000 (1957)

UNSECURED PROMISSORY NOTE IS NOT CASH EQUIVALENT—NOT INCOME TO CASH METHOD TAXPAYER

■ **INSTANT FACTS** The Tax Court held that a taxpayer who actually received an unsecured promissory note did not realize income the year he received the promissory note as the taxpayer established that the promissory note was not payment for his services nor did the promissory note have any fair market value in the year of receipt.

■ **BLACK LETTER RULE** An unsecured promissory note (which has no fair market value) is not the equivalent of cash and is not includable in the income of a cash method taxpayer in the year of receipt.

■ **PROCEDURAL BASIS**

Not Stated.

■ **FACTS**

In 1951, the taxpayer Jay A. Williams (D) (Williams) was in the business of locating marketable parcels of timberland for prospective purchasers of timber. He provided such information to Lester McConkey and J.M. Housley (Housley). On May 5, 1951, J.M. Housley gave to Williams (D) an unsecured, non-interest-bearing promissory note for $7,166.60, which was not payable for 240 days. It was understood at the time the promissory note was given to Williams (D) that Housley had no funds, and that no payment could be made until Housley acquired and sold at least part of the timber property which Williams (D) had located. In need of money, Williams (D) tried to sell the promissory note to banks or finance companies 10 or 15 times but was unable to do so. In 1954, he finally collected $6,666.66 from Housley in discharge of the debt represented by the note. Williams (D) reported the $6,666.66 as income in 1954. Williams (D) asserts that the receipt of the promissory note was not payment for services (and thus, not includable in income in 1951), but merely as evidence of indebtedness, and even if it was considered payment it had no fair market value and thus, was not the equivalent of cash. The Commissioner (P) asserts that the receipt by Williams (D) of the promissory note in 1951, constitutes taxable income in that year.

■ **ISSUE**

Does a cash method taxpayer realize income when he actually receives an unsecured promissory note?

■ **DECISION AND RATIONALE**

(Not Stated.) No. Under § 22(a) of the 1939 Code, promissory notes or other evidence of indebtedness received as payment for services constitute income to the extent of their fair market value. Williams' (D) uncontradicted testimony, however, is that the promissory note was not received as payment, but merely as an evidence of indebtedness. The Commissioner (P) points out that Williams (D) testimony is self-serving and without supporting evidence his testimony is not worthy of belief. However, it is not our province to disregard the unimpeached and uncontradicted testimony of a taxpayer. As there is no conflicting evidence from the record, Williams (D) has established to our satisfaction that the promissory note was not received in payment for his services. A note received only as security, or as an evidence of indebtedness, and not as payment, may not be regarded as income at the time of receipt. The promissory note here represented nothing more than a debt owed to Williams (D). This note payable was no different from an account payable. A simple change in the form of indebtedness from an account payable to a note payable is insufficient to cause the realization of income by the creditor. Even if Williams (D) had not shown that the promissory note was not intended as payment, it would still not be income in 1951 as the Commissioner (P) asserts. The promissory note bore no interest and was unsecured. In addition, Housley had no funds to pay the note at the time it was written, the note itself was not payable until 1952, and Williams (D) was unable to sell the note to financial institutions. Williams (D) has shown that the note had no fair market value in 1951 and consequently it cannot be held to be the equivalent of cash during the year of receipt. The receipt by Williams (D) of the promissory note in 1951 does not constitute taxable income realized during that year.

Analysis:

A promissory note that can't be exchanged for cash, or something else of value (such as property), has little or no value. A promise to pay an amount in the future isn't even enforceable under contract law until the note becomes due and even then it might not be financially savvy to sue on a note that the holder knows the writer of the note can't pay. In this case it is even an unsecured promissory note, which means there is nothing backing it up. The point here is that a promissory note is not a check. When one writes a check there is the underlying presumption that the check is tied to a bank account with money in it and the bank will honor the check. The promissory note here was an "IOU" that basically set forth that Housley would pay some money sometime later if and when he had it. Receipt of a piece of paper that isn't worth the paper its written on doesn't constitute realization of income. The promissory note here is not the equivalent of cash, because the note does not have a fair market value, or to be more exact, the fair market value is zero.

■ CASE VOCABULARY

PROMISSORY NOTE: A signed, written promise to pay a specific amount of money on a specific date to a named individual.

PROVINCE: The field or subject area over which a person has the authority and obligation to properly manage.

Cowden v. Commissioner

(Texas Land Owner) v. *(IRS)*

289 F.2d 20 (5th Cir. 1961)

READILY MARKETABLE "SUPPLEMENTAL AGREEMENT" HELD TO BE CASH EQUIVALENT AND CURRENTLY TAXABLE

■ **INSTANT FACTS** Cowden (D), entered into a leasing contract with an oil company for the mineral rights to some of his land with the payments set forth in a "supplemental agreement" which provided for payment to him and his family over the course of a few years, and then assigned the "supplemental agreement" to a bank for cash before the payments came due.

■ **BLACK LETTER RULE** A readily marketable agreement (obligation/promise) to make future payments is the equivalent of cash and thus, currently taxable.

■ **PROCEDURAL BASIS**

On appeal to the 5th Circuit Court of Appeals from the Tax Court remanding for reconsideration of whether an obligation of future payments is cash equivalent.

■ **FACTS**

In 1951, Frank Cowden, Sr. (D) (Cowden) and his wife (on behalf of themselves and their children) entered into a lease agreement with Stanolind which gave Stanolind oil, gas and mineral rights to some of their Texas land. By a related supplemental agreement. Stanolind agreed to make "bonus" or "advance royalty" payments in an aggregate amount of $511,192.50. The supplemental agreement provided that $10,233.85 was payable upon execution, the sum of $250,484.31 was due "no earlier than" January 5 "nor later than" January 10, 1952, and $250,484.34 was stipulated to be paid "no earlier than" January 5 "nor later than" January 10, 1953. One half of each payment was to be paid to Cowden (D) and his wife, and one-sixth to each child. The deferred payment agreement stated that the obligation for payment was a "firm and absolute personal obligation of [Stanolind] which was not in any manner conditioned upon development or production [from the land] but that such payments shall be made in all events." On November 30, 1951, Cowden (D) assigned the payments due in 1952 to the First National Bank of Midland, of which Cowden (D) was a director. [How convenient.] On November 20, 1952, Cowden (D) assigned the payments due in 1953 to the bank. The bank paid the face value of the amount assigned for 1952 discounted by $257.43 in the case of Cowden (D) and his wife, and $85.81 in the case of each of the children. For the 1953 amount assigned, the discounts were $313.14 for Cowden (D) and his wife, and $104.38 for each of the children. The taxpayers (Cowden (D), wife and children) reported the amounts received by them from the assignments as long-term capital gains. The Commissioner (P) determined that Stanolind's contractual obligations to make payments in the future represented ordinary income, subject to depletion, to the extent of the fair market value of the obligations at the time they were created. The Commissioner (P) computed a 1951 equivalent of cash value of $487,647.46 for the bonus payments paid in 1951, and determined that Cowden (D) should be taxed that year on that amount as ordinary income. The Tax Court found in favor of the Commissioner (P) of federal income tax liability of Cowden (D) (his wife and children) for the years 1951 and 1952. The Tax Court decided that the entire amounts of the bonus payments, $511,192.50, were taxable in 1951, as ordinary income.

■ **ISSUE**

Is an agreement to make future payments the equivalent of cash and taxable as current income?

■ DECISION AND RATIONALE

(Jones, J.) Yes. A majority of the Tax Court was convinced that the bonus payments here were not only readily but immediately convertible to cash and were the equivalent of cash, and had a fair market value equal to their face value. The Tax Court did state, as a general proposition, "that executory contracts to make future payments in money do not have a fair market value." The Tax Court, however, found that the facts of this case distinguished it from the general proposition. The facts as found by the Tax Court (and which we find, over the objection of Cowden (D), are sustained by substantial evidence) are as follows: Stanolind was perfectly willing and able at the time of the execution of the agreement to pay the bonuses in a lump sum payment; to pay the bonus immediately at all times thereafter until the due dates; that Cowden (D) believed the bonus agreements had a market value at the time of their execution; that a bank in which he was an officer and depositor was willing to and in fact did purchase such rights at a nominal discount; the bank considered such rights to be bankable and to represent direct obligations of the payor (Stanolind); that the bank generally dealt with such contracts where it was satisfied with the financial responsibility of the payor and looked only to the payor for payment; and that the sole reason why the bonuses were not immediately paid in cash upon execution of the agreement was the refusal of the lessor (Cowden (D)) to receive such payments. The majority stresses the fact that Stanolind was willing and able to make the entire bonus payment upon execution of the agreement. The dissenting opinion of the Tax Court states that the conclusion reached by the majority "is in effect that the taxpayers are not free to make the bargain of their choice." Cowden (D) asserts that the Tax Court held that a constructive receipt, under the equivalent of cash doctrine, resulted from the willingness of Stanolind to pay the entire amount, and the unwillingness of himself (even if for the sole reason to postpone taxes) to receive the full amount. A taxpayer has a legal right to avoid or decrease his tax liability by means which the law permits. As a general rule a tax avoidance motive is not to be considered in determining the tax liability resulting from a transaction. Cowden (D) had a right to enter into the agreement to lease the mineral rights to his land under the condition that the bonus payments were to be paid in future installments. A tax liability would not necessarily arise because the lessee (Stanolind) was willing and able to pay the entire payment upon the execution of the lease. While it is true that parties can make legal arrangements with the hope of avoiding taxation, it is also true that if a consideration for which one of the parties bargains is the equivalent of cash it will be subjected to taxation to the extent of its fair market value. In *Kleberg v. Commissioner* [similar case decided in 1941 by Board of Tax Appeals] it was stated that "where no notes, bonds, or other evidences of indebtedness other than the contract were given, such contract had no fair market value." In this case, the literal test of *Kleberg* is met in that the agreement *was evidenced by an instrument other than the contract of lease.* The supplemental agreement here is not, however, the kind which falls into the classification of notes or bonds. Cowden (D) asserts that there can be no "equivalent of cash" obligation unless it is a negotiable instrument. Such a test, to be determined by the form of the obligation, is as unrealistic as it is formalistic. The income tax deals in economic realities, not legal abstractions, and the reach of the income tax law is not to be delimited by technical refinements or mere formalism. A promissory note, negotiable in form, is not necessarily the equivalent of cash. The maker of a promissory note could be insolvent, or for other reasons, the note may not be accepted in the market place. We are convinced that if a promise to pay of a solvent obligor is unconditional and assignable, not subject to set-offs, and is of a kind that is frequently transferred to lenders or investors at a discount not substantially greater than the generally prevailing premium for the use of money, such promise is the equivalent of cash and taxable in like manner as cash would have been taxable had it been received by the taxpayer rather than the obligation. The principle that negotiability is not the test of taxability in an equivalent of cash case (such as this case) is consistent with the rule that men may, if they can, so order their affairs as to minimize taxes, and points up the doctrine that substance and not form should control in the application of income tax laws. In making its decision of Cowden's (D) tax liability, the Tax Court gave too much weight to its finding that Stanolind was willing and able to make full payments upon execution of the lease and that Cowden (D) requested the deferment of payment. In addition, the Tax Court's determination of the cash equivalent, it used its own calculations based upon what Cowden (D) could have received if he had made a different contract, rather than the fair market value cash equivalent of the obligation for which Cowden (D) bargained in the contract he actually (and legally) made. We are unable to say whether or not the Tax Court, if it disregarded, as we think it should have done, the facts as it found them as to the willingness of the lessee to pay and the unwillingness of the taxpayer Cowden (D) to receive full bonus on execution of the leases, would have still determined that the deferred bonus obligations were taxable in the year of the agreements as the equivalent of cash. This is primarily a fact issue. The case is remanded to the Tax Court for reconsideration in light of this opinion.

Analysis:

On remand, the contractual obligations were held to be the equivalent of cash. This means the income was currently taxable. The Fifth Circuit basically said that the Tax Court didn't use the right test; it relied too heavily on Stanolind's ability to pay and Cowden's (D) desire to put off payment. Although the IRS (P) is more than willing to recharacterize a taxpayer's transactions, courts are not so willing to rewrite parties' contracts. The relevant issue here isn't that Stanolind was solvent and willing to pay, but rather that Cowden (D) was able to immediately assign the "supplement agreement." This is an example of the IRS (P) looking to substance over form, or recharacterizing an event. Promissory notes and contract obligations are scrutinized under the Cash Equivalency doctrine to determine whether they have readily ascertainable fair market value. An obligation or promise to pay is a cash equivalent if: (1) the obligor is solvent; (2) there is an assignable and unconditional promise to pay, not subject to set-offs; and (3) the obligation is of a type normally transferable to lenders at a discount not substantially greater than the prevailing premium for money. If so, the obligation or promise is the equivalent of cash, and taxable just as if cash had been received.

■ CASE VOCABULARY

CONSTRUCTIVE RECEIPT: A taxpayer is in constructive receipt of income when income has been made available to the taxpayer, and there are no substantial limitations or restrictions on the taxpayer's ability to control its receipt. (Reg. 1.451–2(a)).

DEPLETION: To decrease the amount of something; to price a future payment at its current value.

NEGOTIABLE INSTRUMENT: A writing, signed by the maker, of an unconditional promise to pay a specific amount of money on demand, or at a fixed time, to the bearer (person who the promise of payment is made).

NOMINAL: A minimal amount or fee for services or products.

Hornung v. Commissioner

(Green Bay Packer MVP) v. *(IRS)*

47 T.C. 428 (1967)

CONSTRUCTIVE RECEIPT OF INCOME OCCURS WHEN THERE ARE NO SUBSTANTIAL LIMITATIONS ON A TAXPAYER'S ABILITY TO CONTROL ITS RECEIPT

■ **INSTANT FACTS** Green Bay Packers football player (Paul (D)) was awarded a Corvette from Sport Magazine on December 31, 1961, but which he did not actually receive until 1962, and which he did not include as income at any time; held not to be constructively received in 1961, included and taxable in 1962.

■ **BLACK LETTER RULE** Constructive receipt occurs when income is credited, set apart, or otherwise made available to a taxpayer unless the taxpayer's control of its receipt is subject to substantial limitations or restrictions.

■ **PROCEDURAL BASIS**

Not Stated.

■ **FACTS**

The taxpayer, Paul (D), a well-known professional football player for the Green Bay Packers in 1962, was selected by the editors of Sport Magazine (Sport) as the most valuable player (MVP) immediately after that year's National Football League Championship game and was awarded a Corvette. At the end of the 1962 championship game between the Green Bay Packers and the New York Giants, Sport issued a press release announcing the award. At approximately 4:30 p.m. on December 31, 1961 (the day of the game), the editor in chief of Sport informed Paul (D) that he was selected as the MVP and winner of the Corvette. The editor in chief did not have the key or the title to the Corvette and Paul (D) did not request or demand immediate possession of the car at that time but he did accept the award. Paul (D) was invited and agreed to attend an award presentation in New York (business office of Sport) on January 3, 1962, at which time he actually received the Corvette. Paul (D) posed for photographs with the Corvette which Sport used along with an article about Paul (D), his achievements, the game, and the Corvette in a subsequent issue of the magazine. Paul (D) was not required to attend the lunch or to pose for photographs or perform any service for Sport as a condition or as consideration for his receipt of the car. Sport purchased the Corvette in September of 1961 and it was kept (as it always was) at a New York Chevrolet dealership until presentation to the chosen winner. Prior to 1961, if the championship game was played in New York, the dealer would have the Corvette at the football stadium during the game. However, the championship game of 1961 was played in Green Bay, Wisconsin, and the car remained in New York and was not presented to Paul (D) until 1962. Sport used the award to promote sales of the magazine and its cost was deducted by the publisher for Federal income tax purposes as a promotion and advertising expense. Paul (D) did not include the fair market value of the Corvette ($3,331.04) [golly!] on his 1961 income tax return. He did report the sale of the Corvette [ungrateful slob] on his 1962 Federal income tax return in Schedule D as a gain. Paul (D) reported that he acquired the Corvette in 1962, sold it in 1962 at the fair market value price, at zero cost and zero gain. The Commissioner (P) issued an income tax deficiency against Paul (D) in the amount of $3,163.76 for the tax year 1962. Paul (D) concedes an issue regarding a travel deduction, and the only remaining question concerns the inclusion of the value of the Corvette in the taxable year 1962.

■ ISSUE

Is a taxpayer deemed to have constructively received income if he does not have unfettered control of such income and the income has not been set apart for him and/or is subject to substantial limitations or restrictions?

■ DECISION AND RATIONALE

(Hoyt, J.) No. Paul (D) alleges in his petition that the Corvette was received by him as a gift in 1962. However, at trial and in his brief, he argues that the car was constructively received in 1961, prior to the taxable year for which the deficiency is being assessed (1962). Paul (D) relies on the editor in chief's statement at trial that as far as Sport was concerned the Corvette was "available" to Paul (D) on December 31, 1961, when the award was announced. Generally, under the cash method of accounting, all items which constitute gross income (whether in the form of cash, property, or services) are to be included for the taxable year in which actually or constructively received. Reg. § 1.451–2(a) provides "Income although not actually reduced to a taxpayer's possession is constructively received by him in the taxable year during which it is credited to his account, set apart for him, or otherwise made available so that he may draw upon it at any time, or so that he could have drawn upon it during the taxable year if notice of intention to withdraw had been given. However, income is not constructively received if the taxpayer's control of its receipt is subject to substantial limitations or restrictions." Under *Ross v. Commissioner* [IRS may subject income to taxation when the only thing preventing its reduction to possession is the volition of the taxpayer], the doctrine of constructive receipt may be asserted by a taxpayer as a defense to a deficiency assessment even though the item in controversy had not been reported for the taxable year of the alleged constructive receipt. [This is exactly what Paul (D) did. He did not report the value of the Corvette in 1961, but he now argues, as the court says he may, that the Corvette was indeed constructively received in 1961, even though he reported the "date acquired" as 1962 when he reported the sale of the Corvette on his 1962 tax return.] When items are deemed constructively received in a taxable year, they will be considered as income in that year, and the taxpayer must be allowed to assert that the items were taxable only in the year of constructive receipt. [This means that *if* the Corvette was constructively received in 1961, it *cannot* be included in 1962 as the IRS (P) wants it to be.] The basis of constructive receipt is essentially the unfettered control by the recipient (taxpayer) over the date of actual receipt. However, Paul (D) has failed to convince us that he possessed such control on December 31, 1961, over the receipt of the Corvette. The evidence establishes that the Corvette was not presented to Paul (D) until January 3, 1962, that it was in the possession of a car dealer in New York on December 31, 1961, that on that date the editor in chief of Sport did not have the keys or the title to the Corvette, and nothing was given to Paul (D) to evidence his ownership or right to possession of the car at that time. In addition, December 31, 1961, was a Sunday, the car dealership was closed and in New York, Paul (D) and the editor in chief were in Wisconsin, and even if the editor in chief made an effort (which he did not) to deliver the vehicle, it is likely that it could not have been delivered until the next day. The car had not been set aside for Paul's (D) use, and delivery was not dependent solely upon the volition of Paul (D). The doctrine of constructive receipt is not applicable, and we hold that Paul (D) received the Corvette for income tax purposes in 1962 as he originally alleged in his petition and as he reported in his 1962 income tax return.

Analysis:

The court here found that the Corvette was not a gift, but was a prize or award that is required to be included in income at its fair market value. The subsequent sale of the Corvette was a separate issue. The issue of whether the Corvette was constructively received in 1961 is probably related to the statute of limitations. If the tax year of 1961 is outside the running of the statute of limitations, then it is too late for the IRS (P) to audit or claim a deficiency for that year's tax return. The statute of limitations must not have run yet for the tax year of 1962 when the IRS (P) issued the deficiency against Paul (D). The idea behind constructive receipt is to keep taxpayers from holding off income until the next taxable year by simply not taking income which is available for them to take. If the check is on the table and the taxpayer simply walks away from it and doesn't pick it up until the next taxable year, the IRS (P) says the value of the check is constructively received when the check is made available to the taxpayer. If the only thing keeping a taxpaying from receiving income is the action (or inaction) of the taxpayer, the income is deemed constructively received.

■ CASE VOCABULARY

VOLITION: By one's own will; the act of choosing or exercising one's will.

Commissioner v. Boylston Market Ass'n

(IRS) v. *(Property Management Company)*

131 F.2d 966 (1st Cir. 1942)

CASH METHOD TAXPAYER MUST PRORATE EXPENSES TIED TO CAPITAL ASSETS

■ **INSTANT FACTS** The 5th Circuit found that Boylston (D), a cash method taxpayer, could take a deduction equal to the prorated cost of its insurance premiums over the life of the policies, and was not required to only take a deduction for the amount actually paid in the taxable year.

■ **BLACK LETTER RULE** Taxpayers (even cash method taxpayers) must prorate expenses related to the creation of an asset which has a useful life substantially beyond the taxable year and may not take the full deduction for the expense in the year of actual payment.

■ **PROCEDURAL BASIS**

On appeal to the U.S. Court of Appeals, 5th Circuit upholding Board of Tax Appeals finding for Boylston (D).

■ **FACTS**

Boylston (D), a cash method taxpayer, is in the business of managing real estate which it owns. Boylston (D) purchases from time to time fire and other insurance policies covering periods of three or more years. Since 1915, it has deducted each year as insurance expenses the amount of insurance premiums applicable to carrying insurance for that year regardless of the year in which the premium was actually paid. This method was required by the Treasury Department prior to 1938. In 1936, Boylston (D) deducted $4,421.76 as the prorated amount for insurance premiums; it had paid $6,690.75 prior to 1936 and paid $1,082.77 in 1936. In 1938, Boylston (D) deducted $3,284.25 as the prorated amount for insurance premiums; it had paid $6,148.42 prior to 1938 and paid $890.47 in 1938. The Commissioner (P) in his notice of deficiency only allowed for the amounts actually paid during the years at issue on the basis that deductions for insurance expenses of a taxpayer on the cash receipts and disbursements basis is limited to premiums paid during the taxable year. The Commissioner (P) determined a deficiency in Boylston's (D) income tax for 1936 (of $835.34) and for 1938 (of $431.84). The Board of Tax Appeals reversed the Commissioner's (P) determination. The Commissioner (P) appeals.

■ **ISSUE**

Must an expense for an asset with a life substantially beyond the taxable year be prorated over the life of the asset?

■ **DECISION AND RATIONALE**

(Mahoney, J.) Yes. The government, on the basis of this court's decision in *Welsh v. De Blois* [taxpayer was entitled to take a full deduction for the prepayment of insurance premiums he paid as an ordinary and necessary business expense in the year payment was made despite the fact that the insurance covered a three-year period], changed its earlier rule which had required a taxpayer to prorate prepaid insurance premiums. The Board of Tax Appeals has refused to follow *Welsh* in this and other cases. The arguments in *Welsh* in favor of treating prepaid insurance as an ordinary and necessary business expense are persuasive. Nevertheless, we are unable to find a real basis for distinguishing between prepayment of rentals, bonuses for the acquisition or cancellation of leases, and prepaid insurance.

These types of cases are not as clear cut as a permanent improvement to a building which is a capital expenditure. In such a case there is a creation of a capital asset which has a life extending beyond the taxable year and which depreciates over a period of years. The taxpayer regardless of his method of accounting can only take deductions for depreciation over the life of the asset. Whether we consider advance rentals, bonuses for acquisition of leases, etc., to be the cost of the exhaustible asset, as in the case of advance rentals, or the cost of acquiring the asset, as in the case of bonuses, the payments are prorated primarily because the life of the asset extends beyond the taxable year. To permit the taxpayer to take a full deduction in the year of payment would distort his income. Prepaid insurance presents the same problem and should be resolved in the same way. The payments are easily prorated over the three years, and the policy may be surrendered at any time. It is clearly an asset having a longer life than a single tax year. The line to be drawn between capital expenditures and ordinary and necessary business expenses is not always an easy one [understatement]; but we are satisfied that in treating prepaid insurance as a capital expense we are obtaining a degree of consistency in these matters. [Are you similarly satisfied?] *Welsh* is incorrect and is overruled. The decision of the Board of Tax Appeals finding against the Commissioner (P) is affirmed.

Analysis:

Boylston (D) prorated the cost of his insurance premiums over a number of years as had previously been required. In 1938, a decision by this court (subsequently agreed to by the government) provided that a taxpayer was not required to prorate, but was entitled to take the full deduction in the year actually paid. The Commissioner (P) (presumably following this law) would only allow a deduction for the amount actually paid in the years at issue. The Board of Tax Appeals (disregarding precedent) said the Commissioner (P) was wrong—that Boylston (D) should prorate the deduction over the number of years the insurance covered. This court agreed with the Board of Tax Appeals that the cost of the premiums must be prorated (and deducted) over time. The court says that the premiums are like other costs that are required to be prorated. There are various expenses that the Code requires taxpayers to prorate, such as prepaid interest. However, there is an exception for prepaid interest paid ("points") when buying a principal residence. In addition, case law provides for a "one-year rule" that allows, in some circumstances, a current deduction for an expense that happens to fall within two taxable years, but the expense must be related to a time frame that does not exceed one year.

■ CASE VOCABULARY

CAPITAL ASSET: [Technically, all assets are capital assets except those listed in I.R.C. § 1221. Helpful definition, huh?] Generally, items of property such as your house or stocks are capital assets, but there are many detailed exceptions such as business property held for resale; to be a capital asset the item does not have to be connected with a trade or business and the time which the taxpayer holds the items is immaterial.

CAPITAL EXPENDITURE: The spending of money related to a capital asset.

PRORATE: To distribute or divide the total of a thing (interest, taxes, [pie]) into parts over time or between people.

Cathcart v. Commissioner

(Loan Recipient) v. *(IRS)*
36 T.C.M. 1321 (1977)

POINTS *WITHHELD* FROM A MORTGAGE LOAN ARE NOT CONSIDERED *PAID* BY THE BORROWER TAXPAYER AND ARE NOT DEDUCTIBLE AS "INTEREST PAID" IN THE YEAR OF THE LOAN

■ **INSTANT FACTS** The Tax Court determined that the taxpayer (Cathcart) (D) was not allowed to deduct as "interest paid" the points withheld on a mortgage loan in the year of the loan.

■ **BLACK LETTER RULE** Prepaid interest *withheld* from a mortgage loan is not currently deductible as prepaid interest, but must be deducted ratably over the life of the loan.

■ **PROCEDURAL BASIS**

Not Stated.

■ **FACTS**

The taxpayer, Cathcart (D), obtained a net proceeds mortgage loan from Southern Federal (Southern) on January 15, 1973. Cathcart (D) received $55,039.92 from Southern, yet the face amount of the loan was $57,600, bearing 7% interest over 29 years. The difference between the amounts ($2,560.08) was withheld by Southern and used to pay various services, and to pay points totaling $1,086.60. Although points sometimes represent a hidden service charge, the parties agree that the points represent interest charges. Cathcart (D) contends that the entire $1,086.60 charged for points is fully deductible in 1973. The Commissioner (P) contends that Cathcart (D) did not fully pay the points amount in 1973, but that the amount is included in the monthly mortgage payments over the 29–year term of the loan. The Commissioner (P) contends that Cathcart (D) must prorate the points over the life of the loan. If prorated, the interest deduction for 1973 would be $34.34.

■ **ISSUE**

If points on a mortgage loan are not paid out of the borrower's pocket, but instead are withheld by the lender from the total amount of the loan, is that amount deductible by the borrower taxpayer as "interest paid" in the year of the loan?

■ **DECISION AND RATIONALE**

(Judge Not Identified.) No. I.R.C. § 163 provides that "there shall be allowed as a deduction all interest paid or accrued within the taxable year on indebtedness." Despite this section, cash method taxpayers may not take interest expense deductions for prepaid interest if such deduction materially distorts their income. The IRS, and subsequently Congress, recognized an administrative exception to the material distortion argument when dealing with taxpayers who prepay interest or points on a home mortgage. Now, if a cash method taxpayer prepays points on their home mortgage with their own funds (or funds not from the lender), he is entitled to deduct the entire amount in the year paid. In this case, however, the amount used for points was *withheld* by the lender. Because the points were withheld by the lender (Southern), rather than *paid* by Cathcart (D), we conclude Cathcart (D) is not entitled to deduct the entire $1,086.60 in 1973. Rather, Cathcart (D) may only deduct $34.34, that pro rata portion of the points attributable to 1973. We base our finding on *Rubnitz v. Commissioner* ["Loan fee" (agreed to be interest) withheld from amount of loan by savings and loan association before issuing loan to borrower was not "paid" by borrower in the year of the loan and thus, not fully deductible in that year]. In *Rubnitz*, the taxpayer, Branham Associates (Branham) received (in 1970) a loan from a savings and loan association in order to construct an apartment complex. The face amount of the loan was $1,650,000, but Branham only received $1,592,220. The $57,750 difference was *withheld* by the savings and loan as a "loan fee" which the parties agreed represented interest. Branham did not *pay* $57,750 of interest in 1970, but signed a promissory note that postponed payment until sometime in the future. The withheld amount was to be paid ratably by Branham over the life of the loan as part of the monthly installment payments. Since Branham did not pay the $57,750 in 1970 he could not deduct that amount as "interest paid" during 1970.

Analysis:

Generally speaking, a cash method taxpayer must prorate the value of prepaid interest over the life of a loan. However, if the prepaid interest is part of a loan for the taxpayer's principal residence, that amount of interest is deductible in the year paid if the taxpayer paid the interest out of his own pocket. Lenders often add points to a loan. Some or all of the points represent interest paid up front instead of over the life of the loan. The deduction issue arises when a taxpayer borrows the amount of the points and adds it to the amount of the loan instead of paying for the points out of his own pocket. This is what Cathcart (D) did. Cathcart (D) borrowed, in addition to the loan itself, the amount needed to pay for the points. When the points are part of the total loan, each mortgage payment is proportionately payment for the points and the underlying loan. This means that the points are paid over the life of the loan and correspondingly may only be deducted over the life of the loan.

■ CASE VOCABULARY

POINTS: Prepaid interest, as charged for home mortgages. Banks may demand points either to pay expenses, or to effectively charge a higher-than-stated interest rate (because the bank is charging interest on money it never paid out to the borrower).

Vander Poel, Francis & Co., Inc. v. Commissioner

(Nonpaying Corporation) v. (IRS)

8 T.C. 407 (1947)

THERE IS NO DOCTRINE OF CONSTRUCTIVE PAYMENT; PAYMENTS ARE ONLY DEDUCTIBLE WHEN ACTUALLY MADE

■ **INSTANT FACTS** A cash method taxpayer (Vander) (D) was denied a current deduction for salary it "paid" to its officers as the payment was credited to their accounts, but not actually paid, in the taxable year.

■ **BLACK LETTER RULE** Deductions are only permitted under specific statutes and only when actually paid.

■ **PROCEDURAL BASIS**

Not Stated.

■ **FACTS**

A cash method taxpayer corporation (Vander) (D) which regularly and duly voted for salaries to its officers, credited the officers' accounts for salary in 1942, but did not actually pay the full amount in cash or property in 1942.

■ **ISSUE**

Is there a doctrine of "constructive payment" that corresponds to the accepted doctrine of constructive receipt?

■ **DECISION AND RATIONALE**

(Judge Not Identified) No. The officers of the taxpayer corporation, Vander Poel and Francis, correctly reported the receipt of their salaries on their 1942 tax returns under the doctrine of "constructive receipt." However, Vander (D) is not allowed to deduct the payment of the salaries as they were not actually paid in 1942. Although it seems logical that if the recipient of the credited salary must include it as income, the payer of the credited salary should be allowed to take a corresponding deduction, the Code itself and not logic dictates the rule here. Deductions are a matter of legislative grace and only permitted under the terms of the controlling statute. The Code does not provide for a doctrine of "constructive payment." Although a taxpayer may be taxed on income that he has not actually received, there is no corresponding deduction for payment which is not actually paid. The Commissioner (P) is sustained.

Analysis:

The idea of constructive receipt is to make sure taxpayers properly account for realization of income and to limit abuses. There is no corresponding assumption underlying permitted deductions; that is, the IRS is not concerned about taxpayers not accounting for available deductions. Constructive receipt is logical in that, for example, when someone receives a check that they can cash at any time, it makes sense that for all intents and purposes he has received income. In contrast, the idea of constructive payment does not have a corresponding underlying assumption about the nature of payment. A payment isn't payment until it is actually paid. This is simply the rule. Both businesses and individuals often use and accept checks in the same manner as cash. Under the cash method of accounting, when a taxpayer pays by check (assuming it clears in the normal course of business), it is a deduction, just as if he paid by cash. Payment by check is deemed to be made as of the date of mailing. Businesses and individuals now use credit cards, which are often more readily accepted than checks. To reflect this reality, the IRS issued Rev. Rul. 78–38, which permits an allowable deduction to be taken by a taxpayer in the year in which the charge is made to the credit card. However, the deductions depend on the type of credit card used by the taxpayer. If a taxpayer buys items at a department store using that department store's credit card, any allowable deduction is not permitted until the credit card bill is paid. If a bank-issued credit card is used to make a payment to a third party, the permitted deduction is taken in the year the charge is made, not the year the taxpayer pays off the credit card.

■ CASE VOCABULARY

DULY: In due course.

LEGISLATIVE GRACE: A law created or approved by the legislature to grant a right or privilege to persons, taxpayers, corporations, etc. that does not otherwise exist under the law.

Spring City Foundry Co. v. Commissioner

(Gypped Company) v. *(IRS)*

292 U.S. 182, 54 S.Ct. 644 (1934), rehearing denied 292 U.S. 613, 54 S.Ct. 857

AN ACCRUAL METHOD TAXPAYER MUST INCLUDE INCOME WHEN THE RIGHT TO RECEIVE INCOME BECOMES FIXED

■ **INSTANT FACTS** Although Spring (D) was unable to collect an amount due from a purchaser of its goods, the amount due was held to be includable in its gross income under the accrual method of accounting.

■ **BLACK LETTER RULE** For the accrual method taxpayer, income is included in gross income when the right to receive such income is fixed and can be determined with reasonable accuracy.

■ PROCEDURAL BASIS

On appeal to the United States Supreme Court upholding the Commissioner's (P) determination of inclusion of income.

■ FACTS

The taxpayer corporation (Spring) (D) uses the accrual method of accounting. Spring (D) sold goods in 1920 on open account. The purchaser went bankrupt and a receiver was appointed. By the end of the year it was clear that Spring (D) would not be paid in full for the goods. The Commissioner (P) disallowed Spring's (D) bad debt deduction and its decision was upheld by the Court. The Court also rejected Spring's (D) assertion that the partially worthless debt affected its gross income.

■ ISSUE

Is an amount due and owing to an accrual method taxpayer included in its gross income even if that amount is uncollectible?

■ DECISION AND RATIONALE

(Hughes, J.) Yes. We see no merit in Spring's (D) contention that to the extent the 1920 debt was worthless it was not includable in gross income. Under the accrual method of accounting it is the right to receive income and not the actual receipt of income that determines the inclusion of the amount in gross income. When the right to receive an amount becomes fixed, the right accrues. When goods are sold, inventory is reduced, and a claim arises for the price of the goods. Gross income means the total sales, minus the cost of goods sold, plus income from investments or other sources. The "total sales" are the account receivable arising from the sales, and these accounts receivable, less the cost of goods sold, figure in the statement of gross income. If the accounts receivable are uncollectible, in whole or in part, the question is one of deduction under the applicable statute. The question is not one of inclusion in gross income because the right to receive income has already accrued and under the accrual method of accounting it is gross income.

Analysis:

Spring (D) was the petitioner in the Supreme Court, which suggests that it appealed a lower court ruling in favor of the Commissioner (P). At the time of the case, there was no provision (as there is now) for a deduction for a partially worthless debt. There was only a provision for a wholly worthless debt, and Spring's (D) bad debt in 1920 was only partially worthless. Spring (D) asserted that (1) there was no income in the first place; and (2) that even if there was income, to the extent it didn't receive payment for the goods, it was a bad debt deduction. Both of Spring's (D) assertions were disallowed by the Commissioner (P) and the Court. Reg. § 1.451–1(a) now sets forth that under the accrual method of accounting, income is includable in gross income when all events have occurred that fix the right to receive such income and the amount thereof can be determined with reasonable accuracy. The language of this regulation is the relevant test for inclusion for an accrual method taxpayer.

■ CASE VOCABULARY

RECEIVER: A court appointed individual who preserves or sells a debtor's assets for the benefit of his creditors.

North American Oil Consolidated v. Burnet

(Company under Receivership) v. *(IRS)*

286 U.S. 417, 52 S.Ct. 613 (1932)

THE CLAIM OF RIGHT DOCTRINE REQUIRES INCLUSION OF INCOME IN THE YEAR THE CLAIM ACCRUES AND NOT NECESSARILY THE YEAR INCOME IS EARNED

■ **INSTANT FACTS** Net profits earned by North American Oil Consolidated (NorthAm) (D) in 1916 while under a (partial) receivership were held not to be income to NorthAm (D) until 1917 when the receivership was vacated and the net profits paid over to the company.

■ **BLACK LETTER RULE** A taxpayer with a claim of right over an amount earned must include that amount in income in the year the claim of right accrues, which is not necessarily the year the amount is earned.

■ **PROCEDURAL BASIS**

On writ of certiorari to the U.S.S.C. affirming the Circuit Court of Appeals decision in favor of the IRS.

■ **FACTS**

Prior to 1916 the Government instituted suit against NorthAm (D) attempting to oust it from possession of a particular section of oil land to which the United States held legal title, and NorthAm (D) operated. The Government also claimed beneficial ownership of the land. On February 2, 1916, a receiver was appointed to operate the property, or supervise its operations, and to hold the net income from the land. In 1916, the land earned a net profit of $171,979.22 and the receiver was paid such amount as was earned. After entry by the District Court in 1917 of the final decree dismissing the bill, the receiver paid to NorthAm (D) the net profit from the prior year. The Government appealed to the Circuit Court of Appeals which affirmed the decision to dismiss the Government's action. An appeal to the U.S.S.C. was dismissed by stipulation. The net profit from 1916 was entered into NorthAm's (D) books as income for 1916, but was not accounted for in that year's return. In 1918, an amended return for 1916 was filed which accounted for the 1916 net profit. The Commissioner (P) audited NorthAm's (D) 1917 return and determined a deficiency based upon other items. NorthAm (D) appealed to the Board of Tax Appeals (Board). In 1927 [ten years later!] the Commissioner (P) asserted that the deficiency should also include a tax on the amount paid by the receiver to NorthAm (D) in 1917. The Board held that the profits were taxable to the receiver as income of 1916. The Board did not make a finding whether NorthAm's (D) accounts were kept on a cash receipts and disbursements basis or on the accrual basis. Upon appeal, the Circuit Court of Appeals held that the profits were taxable to NorthAm (D) as income of 1917, regardless of its method of accounting. It is conceded that the net profits earned during the receivership (1916) constituted income. NorthAm (D) contends that, 1) the net profits should have been reported by the receiver for taxation in 1916; 2) that if not returnable by him, they should have been returned by the company for 1916, because they constitute income accrued in that year; 3) that if not taxable as income for NorthAm (D) in 1916, they were taxable to it as income in 1922, since the litigation was not finally terminated in its favor until 1922.

■ **ISSUE**

Is income which is earned, but to which a taxpayer does not have a claim of right, includable in income in the year earned?

■ DECISION AND RATIONALE

(Brandeis, J.) No. First, the 1916 net profits impounded by the receiver were not taxable to him because he was the receiver of only part of the properties operated by the company. Only in situations where receivers are in control of an entire property or business does the Internal Revenue Act of 1916 as adopted by the Revenue Act of 1918 [I.R.C. § 6012(b)(3)] and as interpreted under the Treasury Regulations require that the receiver make returns in the same manner as if it was the corporation over which it had custody and control. In all other cases, the corporations themselves have to report their income. The language of this section contemplates a complete, not a partial, substitution of the receiver for the company. There is no provision which allows for the consolidation of the receiver's return into the corporate return, nor which allows two separate returns for the same year, each covering only a part of the corporate return. Second, the net profits were not taxable to NorthAm (D) as income of 1916 (the year the profits were earned). NorthAm (D) was not required in 1916 to report as income an amount which it might never receive. There was no constructive receipt of the net profits by NorthAm (D) in 1916, because at no time during the year was there a right in the company to demand that the receiver pay over the money. Throughout the year it was uncertain who would be entitled to the net profits. It was not until 1917, when the District Court entered a final decree vacating the receivership and dismissing the bill, that NorthAm (D) became entitled to receive the money. Whether NorthAm (D) was a cash method or accrual taxpayer, it was not taxable in 1916 on income which it had not yet received and which it might never receive. Third, the net profits from 1916 were not taxable in 1922, the year the litigation was terminated. The net profits became taxable to NorthAm (D) in 1917, when it first became entitled to them and when it actually received them. If a taxpayer receives earnings under a claim of right and without restriction as to its disposition, he has received income which he is required to return, even though it may still be claimed that he is not entitled to retain the money, and even though he may still be held to repay the same amount. [The last sentence is the basic explanation of the "claim of right" doctrine. The idea here is that if a taxpayer has a claim of right in income he has constructively received it regardless of his status as a cash or an accrual taxpayer, and regardless of his possible desire to not claim an amount as income.] If the Government had prevailed in 1922, and NorthAm (D) was obligated to return the net profits, it would have been entitled to a deduction from its profits of 1922, not from those of any earlier year. The Circuit Court of Appeals which held that the profits were taxable to NorthAm (D) as income of 1917, regardless of its method of accounting, is affirmed.

Analysis:

Note that there are two different lawsuits referenced here. The first suit was brought (and lost) by the Government against NorthAm (D) regarding legal and beneficial title to a piece of oil land. The suit at issue here is the tax case against NorthAm (D). The Commissioner (P) argued for inclusion in 1917 of the net profits from 1916. The Commissioner's (P) argument was probably motivated by the fact that he had already determined a deficiency for 1917, and if NorthAm's (D) income was increased for that year, then the amount of the deficiency would likely increase. This means more money for the IRS. One reason NorthAm (D) argued for inclusion in 1916 or 1922 was because it wasn't being audited for those years. The assumption here is that NorthAm (D) would owe less money to the IRS if the net profits were included in a year other than 1917. NorthAm (D), by amended return, included its 1916 net profits in that year's return. The Court held that the amount must be included in NorthAm's (D) 1917 return. This decision indicates the Board of Tax Appeal was incorrect when it found that the net profits were taxable to the receiver, and that NorthAm (D) was incorrect when it included the net profits in its 1916 return.

■ CASE VOCABULARY

BENEFICIAL OWNERSHIP: The equitable ownership of property having all the usual rights associated with ownership, but not the legal title to the property.

BILL: What is now generally referred to as the complaint in a civil action; a bill used to be filed for equitable claims, and complaints for legal claims.

CLAIM OF RIGHT: The unrestricted right to claim income, even though there may be other or later claims regarding the amount received.

DECREE: The final determination of a court of equity, now generally referred to as the judgment of a court.

LEGAL TITLE: The legally enforceable right to hold the title to property (e.g., as a fiduciary), while the equitable or beneficial right to the property is held by another.

STIPULATION: An agreement between opposing parties (particularly in litigation) whereby certain facts, conditions, or issues are accepted to be true or proven.

VACATING: To cancel or void a judgment or entry in the record [think of it as completely erasing the words of a judgment or record]; to leave or empty-out something (to vacate the premises).

New Capital Hotel, Inc. v. Commissioner

(Hotel Owners) v. *(IRS)*

28 T.C. 706 (1957)

AN ADVANCE PAYMENT INTENDED TO BE RENT IS INCLUDED IN GROSS INCOME WHEN RECEIVED; AN ADVANCE PAYMENT INTENDED AS A SECURITY DEPOSIT IS NOT INCLUDED IN GROSS INCOME

■ **INSTANT FACTS** A taxpayer resisted the IRS' decision to declare a receipt of rent for the last year of a multi-year lease as income in the year in which it was received as opposed to the last year of the lease, which is the year when it was earned.

■ **BLACK LETTER RULE** Cash received as an advance payment of rent must be included in income in the year received, even if it is not used until later on when the money is earned.

■ **PROCEDURAL BASIS**

A taxpayer filed an appeal with the Tax Court of an IRS determination that it was deficient for a particular year in the amount of $11,724.50.

■ **FACTS**

New Capital Hotel (P) entered into an agreement under which it would lease certain property, which it owned, to another party for a ten year period (from January 1, 1950 to December 31, 1959). The yearly lease was $30,000, and the lessee agreed to pay the last year's rent in advance. New Capital (P) demanded payment of the last year's rent in the form of a performance bond, but the lessee preferred paying it in cash, which it did. No restrictions were placed on New Capital's (P) use of the money, except that it agreed to refund all or part of the money in the event of the destruction of the property (provided that the rent was not then in arrears). New Capital (P), an accrual basis taxpayer, reflected the advance rent in a liability account entitled "Deposit on lease account" and now argues that it should be reported as income in 1959 (the last year of the lease), the year in which New Capital (P) contends it would be considered earned. The IRS (D) determined that the $30,000 was gross income in 1949, the year in which it was received, under IRC § 22(a). As such, a deficiency of $11,724.50 was assessed against New Capital (P).

■ **ISSUE**

Must cash received as an advance payment of rent be included in income in the year received, even if it is not used until later on when the money is technically earned?

■ **DECISION AND RATIONALE**

(Black, J.) Yes. It is clear from the record that the advance payment made in this case, although securing the lessee's performance of the covenants, was intended to be rent, and was in fact a payment of rent. Since the rent was received in 1949, it would be includable in gross income in that year even though it is to be applied to the rent owed in 1959. This is so regardless of whether the taxpayer keeps his books and computes his income on a cash basis or on an accrual basis. We recognize that the inclusion of prepaid income in gross income in the year of receipt is not in accord with principles of commercial accounting. We have, however, consistently held that the Commissioner (D) has acted within the discretion granted him under IRC § 41 in holding that prepaid income must be returned in the year received in order to clearly reflect income. Under the circumstances of this case, we cannot say that the Commissioner (D) abused the discretion granted him in determining that the $30,000 was includable in New Capital's (P) gross income in 1949. New Capital (P) relies on the case of *John Mantell* [which involved the tax consequences of the receipt of a security deposit]. However, the facts of that case are distinguishable as it involved a security deposit, and not a prepayment of rent. The $30,000 in question was clearly a prepayment of rent, and as such, under established precedent, should be included by New Capital (P) in its gross income in the year of receipt, 1949. Decision so entered.

Analysis:

New Capital addresses the tax consequences of advance payments for the use of property (as opposed to advance payments for goods or services). The rule in this area, as stated by the court, is that income received by a taxpayer as an advance payment for the use of property by another is to be included in the year of receipt. Thus, as in this case, if a ten-year rental agreement specifies a rent of $10,000 per year with the last year's rent due up front, the taxpayer will declare $20,000 of income during the first year of the lease, and $0 in the final year of the lease. Thus, under the rule set out in *New Capital*, an accrual taxpayer who would normally include rent in income at the time it is due (as opposed to the time it is received) must act as a cash method taxpayer when advance payments for the use of property are involved.

■ CASE VOCABULARY

ACCRUAL BASIS TAXPAYER: A taxpayer who pays taxes when money becomes due to him or her, and not when the money is received.

ARREARS: The state of not being up-to-date in the payment of a debt.

CASH BASIS TAXPAYER: A taxpayer who pays taxes upon actual receipt of income, as opposed to paying when money owed to him or her becomes due.

Artnell Co. v. Commissioner

(Baseball Team Owners) v. *(IRS)*
400 F.2d 981 (7th Cir. 1968)

WHEN SERVICES ARE PREPAID, AN ACCRUAL BASIS TAXPAYER MAY DEFER TAXES TO A SUBSE-
QUENT TAX YEAR IF THE SERVICES WILL BE RENDERED AT A FIXED TIME

■ **INSTANT FACTS** The owners of the Chicago White Sox had to pay taxes on all revenues received in a particular year, even if some of those revenues (stemming from the sale of season tickets) would not technically be earned until a subsequent year (when the games paid for were actually paid).

■ **BLACK LETTER RULE** An accrual taxpayer may defer taxes due on prepayments for services until those services are actually rendered so long as the services are to be rendered at a fixed time and in the year following the year of receipt.

■ **PROCEDURAL BASIS**

Certification to the Seventh Circuit Court of Appeals of a Tax Court decision to affirm the IRS' determination of deficiencies on the part of a particular taxpayer.

■ **FACTS**

Early in the 1962 baseball season, the Chicago White Sox, operated by Chicago White Sox, Inc., was operating in its normal manner when it was acquired by Artnell Company (P). In operating in its usual manner, the team sold season tickets and single admissions for future games. It received revenues for broadcasting and televising future games, and it sold season parking books. It also employed the accrual method of accounting for its own and for income tax purposes. Upon the acquisition of the team by Artnell (P), Chicago White Sox, Inc. was liquidated and Artnell (P) became the owner of all the assets and subject to all the liabilities. On May 31, the date of purchase, the balance sheet of White Sox showed as deferred unearned income that part of the amount received for season and advance tickets, radio and television revenues, and parking book sales allocable to games to be played after May 31. As the games were played thereafter, Artnell (P) took into income the amounts of deferred unearned income allocated to each. The White Sox's income tax return for the taxable year ending May 31, 1962 (ending then because of the liquidation) was filed by Artnell (P) as a transferee. The return did not include the deferred unearned income as gross income. The IRS (D) determined that it should have been so included and determined deficiencies accordingly.

■ **ISSUE**

Can an accrual taxpayer defer payment of tax on prepayments for services to be rendered at specified future times until the time that the services are actually rendered?

■ **DECISION AND RATIONALE**

(Fairchild, J.) Yes. When a business receives money in exchange for its obligation to render services in a later accounting period, treatment of the receipt as income tends to reflect an illusory gain for the period of receipt. Accountancy has techniques for achieving a more realistic reflection, such as the deferral of income. The degree to which such techniques are available under the income tax system is a difficult question—one that we are faced with here. The IRS (D) argues that "deferral of income is a matter for Congress to permit and, until Congress acts, deferral must be disallowed." It stands on the established rule that an accrual basis taxpayer must include in gross income in the year of receipt any prepaid items for which services will be performed in a later year. Artnell (P) relies on statutory language which requires computation of taxable income under the accrual method of accounting regularly used by the taxpayer unless such method "does not clearly reflect income." 26 U.S.C. § 446. Artnell (P) contends that the White Sox system does clearly reflect income. One could reason from the statutory language that any deferral of prepaid income which fulfills standards of sound accounting practice could be employed by an accrual basis taxpayer, and the commissioner would not have power to reject it. Three Supreme Court decisions, however, have made it clear that this is not the law: *Automobile Club of Michigan v. Commissioner, American Automobile Association v. United States*, and *Schlude v. Commissioner.* There are two other lines of reasoning, however, reflected in these three decisions. All three held that the IRS did not abuse its discretion in rejecting a deferral of income where the time and extent of performance of future services were uncertain. The uncertainty stressed in those decisions, however, is not present here. The deferred income was allocable to games which were to be played on a fixed schedule. Except for postponement because of rain, there was certainty. We would have no difficulty distinguishing the instant case in this respect. A second consideration is that Congress is aware of the problem and that it is the policy of the Supreme Court to defer, where possible, to congressional procedures in the tax field. Despite this policy of deferral to Congress, there are situations where the deferral of income technique will so clearly reflect income that the Court will find an abuse of discretion if the commissioner rejects it. Prior to 1955, the IRS (D) permitted accrual basis publishers to defer unearned income from magazine subscriptions if they had consistently done so in the past. When it refused to allow others to adopt the method, the Tenth Circuit in *Beacon Publishing Co. v. Commissioner* held that the refusal was an abuse of discretion. While the Supreme Court distinguished *Beacon* in *Automobile Club of Michigan*, it did not express an opinion on its correctness. It is at least arguable that the deferral as income of prepaid admissions to events which will take place on a fixed schedule in a different taxable year is so similar to deferral of prepaid subscriptions that it would be an abuse of discretion to reject similar accounting treatment. In any event, the prepaid admission situation approaches much closer to this certainty than the situations considered by the Supreme Court in its three cases. The instant case was presented to the tax court on a stipulation of facts. The stipulation does not set forth any facts from which it could be determined that all other relevant items, in addition to prepaid game revenue, were so treated in the White Sox method of accounting that the income attributable to the first seven months of its normal fiscal and taxable year was clearly reflected. It is important to have facts carefully developed. As such, we conclude that the tax court erred in deciding that these revenues were income when received regardless of the merits of the method employed. There must be further hearings to determine whether the White Sox method of accounting did clearly reflect its income in its final, seven month taxable year (the taxable year for White Sox was seven months because it ended on the date of liquidation, five months before the end of its traditional tax year). Reversed and remanded.

Analysis:

Artnell went against the traditional rule to hold that taxes due on prepayments for services can potentially be deferred by an accrual taxpayer until the services are rendered, but only when they are to be rendered on a fixed schedule. Thus, in the area of baseball tickets and fixed game schedules, the traditional rule from *North American* was no longer applicable. Following the decision in *Artnell*, the IRS released Rev. Proc. 70–21, which basically adopted the rule in *Artnell.* Rev. Proc. 70–21 provides that in the event that a prepayment for services to be rendered in the current (year one) or immediately subsequent year (year two) is made to an accrual taxpayer, income attributable to services performed in year two need not be included in gross income until that year. Under the rule, however, services must be rendered by the end of year two, and there must be specified future dates for their occurrence (such as the baseball schedule). If that does not occur, then all of the income must be attributed to year two, even though it has not technically been earned. On remand from the Seventh Circuit, the Tax Court found that the accounting system in place in the White Sox organization, though not perfect, did clearly reflect the organization's income, and therefore permitted the deferral of income as set forth by the appellate court.

■ CASE VOCABULARY

DEFERRED UNEARNED INCOME: Income that is received but is not currently recognized as received because it has not been earned.

TRANSFEREE TAXPAYER: A taxpayer who acquires tax liability not originally his own (in this case, Artnell acquired White Sox' tax liability as a result of its purchase of the team).

Schuessler v. Commissioner

(Taxpayer) v. *(IRS)*

230 F.2d 722 (5th Cir. 1956)

RESERVE ACCOUNTING IS A PERMISSIBLE METHOD OF MATCHING ITEMS OF INCOME WITH ANY APPLICABLE COSTS OF PRODUCING THAT INCOME

■ **INSTANT FACTS** The IRS objected to a taxpayer's attempt to take as a future deduction the costs of future expenses, the income for which was maintained in a reserve account.

■ **BLACK LETTER RULE** When the use of a reserve account accurately reflects a taxpayer's income on an annual accounting basis, the tax code permits its use.

■ **PROCEDURAL BASIS**

Certification to the Fifth Circuit Court of Appeals of a Tax Court decision disallowing a taxpayer's current deduction of an amount of income representing the cost of future deductible expenses.

■ **FACTS**

In 1946, Schuessler (P) was in the gas furnace business. For each furnace that he sold, Schuessler (P) provided the buyer with a guarantee that he would turn the furnace on and off each year for five years, a service worth $2 per call. In keeping his books under an accrual method, Schuessler (P) set up a reserve to represent his estimated cost of carrying out the guarantee. Schuessler (P) argues that the only way his income could be accurately reported was by charging the customer the value of the five years of services at the time of purchase. Schuessler (P) sold his furnaces for $20 to $25 more than his competitors, who offered no promise to turn them on and off. In 1946, Schuessler (P) took a deduction in the amount of that $13,300, the value of the reserve.

■ **ISSUE**

Is the use of a reserve account to match items of income with the costs of producing that income permissible under the tax code?

■ **DECISION AND RATIONALE**

(Tuttle, J.) Yes. We think that Schuessler's (P) method of accounting comes much closer to giving a correct picture of his income than would a system in which he sold equipment in one year and received an inflated price because he obligated himself, in effect, to refund part of it in services later, but was required to report the total receipts as income on the high level of the sales year and take deductions on the low level of the service years. We also find that this method of accounting does not offend any statutory requirement, but is actually in accord with the language of the law. Clearly what is sought by the statute is an accounting method that most accurately reflects the taxpayer's income on an annual accounting basis. The decisions of the Tax Court and several Courts of Appeals are not uniform on this subject. Some circuits require a mathematical certainty as to the exact amount of the future expenditures that cannot be satisfied in the usual case. Other circuits, however, seemingly more concerned with the underlying principle of charging to each year's income reasonably ascertainable future expenses necessary to earn or retain the income, have permitted the accrual of restricted items of future expenses. Two such cases are *Harrold v. Commissioner* [taxpayer was permitted to deduct from its gross income in one year the estimated cost of back filling a tract of land which would be done under state law requirements in the following year] and *Pacific Grape Products Co. v. Commissioner* [taxpayer

---

accrued the sales price of canned goods sold on December 31, and at the same time deducted the estimated cost of labeling and preparing the goods for shipping that would actually be paid the following year]. In *Harrold*, the court stated: "[W]hen all the facts have occurred which determined that the taxpayer has incurred a liability in the tax year, and neither the fact nor the amount of the liability is contested, and the amount ... is susceptible of estimate with reasonable accuracy in the tax year, deduction thereof from income may be taken by a taxpayer on an accrual basis." As the Tax Court noted, this case is similar to one decided by the Tenth Circuit, *Beacon Publishing Co. v. Commissioner* [taxpayer deferred prepaid income covering subscriptions to be furnished in subsequent years]. While the Tax Court, though finding this case similar to *Beacon*, declined to follow its reasoning, we prefer to do the opposite. Indeed, we prefer the reasoning as well as the conclusion reached by the court in *Beacon*. In that case the opinion disposed of the "claim of right" theory advanced by the IRS and adopted by the Tax Court in this case. The record amply supports Schuessler's (P) contention that there was a legal liability created in 1946, when the purchase price was paid for the gas furnaces, for the taxpayer to turn them on and off for five years. The cost of such service was reasonably established at a minimum of $2 per visit, and the payment of $20 to $25 extra by the purchasers fully proves their intention to call upon the taxpayer each year for the service. These facts authorized the setting up of a reserve out of the 1946 income to enable the taxpayer to meet these established charges in future years. Reversed.

Analysis:

Under the general rule for prepayment of services, an individual must include the prepayment in gross income in the year it is received, even though it will not technically be earned until a later year. In this case, the taxpayer tried to deal with this rule while still matching income with cost of production by creating a reserve account. Under Schuessler's (P) plan, $20 (the cost of turning the furnace off and on for five years) from each sale was put into the reserve. Then, when the services were rendered in later years, Schuessler (P) compensated himself by taking money out of the fund. The tax issues came into play with respect to Schuessler's (P) deducting the amount of the fund each year. The deduction was technically proper because turning the furnace on and off represented a business expense. The problem was that the deduction was taken before the expense was incurred. It is clear why the IRS would object to Schuessler's (P) method. Income from future services is treated as income in the year received because the government wants to tax the money now, instead of later. As it wants tax revenue now, allowing current deductions for future expenses is very much disadvantageous to the government because such a deduction limits a taxpayer's taxable income in the present (thereby limiting the revenue available now). In *Schuessler*, the Fifth Circuit permitted the deduction and upheld the taxpayer's use of reserve accounting. *Schuessler* was decided in 1956, and since that time the law has changed. Specifically, IRC § 461(h)(5) now precludes the use of reserve accounting except in situations expressly permitted by the Code.

■ CASE VOCABULARY

RESERVE ACCOUNTING: A method of accounting used to match items of income with the costs of later producing that income; this goal is accomplished by placing the cost of performing future services into a reserve account from which money is withdrawn as those services are performed.

CHAPTER TWENTY

How Inelectable Is the Integrity of the Taxable Year?

United States v. Lewis

Instant Facts: A taxpayer who paid income tax on $11,000 of an employee bonus sought to have his taxes refunded to him when he was forced to give the $11,000 back to his employer.

Black Letter Rule: If a taxpayer receives income under a claim of right without any restriction as to how he may dispose of it, he has received income on which he must pay taxes, even though it may still be claimed that he is not entitled to retain the money, and even though he may still be adjudged liable to restore its equivalent.

Van Cleave v. United States

Instant Facts: A taxpayer who received and paid back excessive compensation from his employer corporation filed suit against the IRS when they denied him the use of IRC § 1341 in calculating his post-payback taxes.

Black Letter Rule: Under IRC § 1341, if a taxpayer included an item in gross income in one tax year, and in a subsequent tax year becomes entitled to a deduction because the item or a portion thereof is no longer subject to his unrestricted use, and the amount of the deduction is in excess of $3,000, the tax for the subsequent year is reduced by either the tax attributable to the deduction or the decrease in the tax for the prior year attributable to the removal of the item, whichever is greater.

Alice Phelan Sullivan Corp. v. United States

Instant Facts: When two parcels of land once donated as a charitable contribution were given back to the donor corporation, and the corporation resisted the IRS' determination that it must pay taxes on the land as if the receipt of the parcels was current taxable income, a lawsuit ensued.

Black Letter Rule: When a taxpayer obtains a full tax benefit from earlier deductions, if those deductions are recouped, they constitute income and must be taxed as such at the tax rate which is in effect during the year in which the recovered item is recognized as income.

United States v. Lewis

(IRS) v. *(Taxpayer)*
340 U.S. 590, 71 S.Ct. 522 (1951)

THE "CLAIM OF RIGHT" INTERPRETATION OF THE TAX LAWS IS DEEPLY ROOTED IN THE FEDERAL TAX SYSTEM AND WILL NOT BE SET ASIDE SIMPLY BECAUSE IT DISADVANTAGES SOME TAXPAYERS

■ **INSTANT FACTS** A taxpayer who paid income tax on $11,000 of an employee bonus sought to have his taxes refunded to him when he was forced to give the $11,000 back to his employer.

■ **BLACK LETTER RULE** If a taxpayer receives income under a claim of right without any restriction as to how he may dispose of it, he has received income that must be reported as income and on which taxes must be paid, regardless of whether he later discovers that he did not have an unrestricted right to the income and must return all or part of it.

■ **PROCEDURAL BASIS**

Certification to the United States Supreme Court of a Court of Claims judgment ordering the IRS to refund the tax mistakenly paid by a taxpayer on $11,000.

■ **FACTS**

In his 1944 income tax return, Lewis (P) reported $22,000 which he had received that year as a bonus. In 1946, however, following protracted litigation, Lewis (P) was required to pay back $11,000 of that sum. Until that point, he had claimed and made use of the full amount of the original bonus in the good faith belief that it belonged to him. When he was required to return half of the bonus, Lewis (P) brought suit in the Court of Claims seeking a refund of the overpayment of the 1944 tax. The IRS (D) responded that the tax should not be recomputed, but instead Lewis (P) should claim an $11,000 loss on his 1946 return. The Court of Claims found for Lewis (P), and the IRS (D) appealed.

■ **ISSUE**

When a taxpayer receives income under a mistake of fact which he is later required to pay back after having already reported that income on his taxes, can he have his taxes for the year in which he paid the taxes recomputed and thereafter receive a refund from the IRS?

■ **DECISION AND RATIONALE**

(Black, J.) No. We granted certiorari to this case because the holding of the Court of Claims conflicts with many decisions of the courts of appeals, as well as with the principles that we announced in *North American Oil v. Burnet.* In *North American Oil,* we stated: "If a taxpayer receives earnings under a claim of right and without restriction as to its disposition, he has received income which he is required to report, even though it may still be claimed that he is not entitled to retain the money, and even though he may still be adjudged liable to restore its equivalent." Nothing in this language permits an exception to that rule merely because a taxpayer is "mistaken" as to the validity of his claim to the income. Income taxes must be paid on income received or accrued during an annual accounting period. Further, the claim of right interpretation of the tax laws has long been used to give finality to that period, and is now deeply rooted in the federal tax system. We see no reason to depart from that well-settled interpretation merely because it results in an advantage or disadvantage to a taxpayer. Reversed.

■ DISSENT

(Douglas, J.) Many inequities are inherent in the income tax system, and we only multiply them needlessly by making distinctions which have no place in the practical administration of the law. If the refund were allowed, the integrity of the taxable year would not be violated. The tax would be paid when due; but the Government would not be permitted to maintain the unconscionable position that it can keep the tax after it is shown that payment was made on money which was not income to the taxpayer.

Analysis:

Lewis involves the claim of right doctrine, a doctrine which, in this case, is upheld by the United States Supreme Court. Under that doctrine, any income received during a taxable year that a taxpayer has a claim to, and unrestricted use of, must be reported to the government in that taxable year, even if the taxpayer may later become obligated to return part or all of the income received. The claim of right doctrine works to support the integrity of the tax year system under which we report and pay taxes on a yearly basis. *Lewis* also addresses what happens when a taxpayer receives and claims money as income in a certain year, but sometime later is forced to repay all or part of it. In *Lewis,* the court held that the only way in which relief may be obtained is by permitting the taxpayer to deduct the amount of repayment in the year in which it is repaid. *Lewis,* however, is an early 1950's case, and since that time things have changed. For instance, Internal Revenue Code (IRC) § 1341 now permits the use of a second approach when money previously taxed as income must be repaid. Under IRC § 1341(a)(5), a taxpayer is permitted to reduce her tax due for the year of repayment by the amount of tax for the prior year that is attributable to the specific amount repaid.

■ CASE VOCABULARY

CLAIM OF RIGHT DOCTRINE: A rule of tax law that requires a taxpayer to report on his income tax return any income that is constructively received, regardless of whether or not he holds an unrestricted claim to it.

Van Cleave v. United States

(Taxpayer) v. *(IRS)*

718 F.2d 193 (6th Cir. 1983)

FAILURE TO DISCOVER RESTRICTION ON INCOME REPORTED DOES NOT PREVENT TAXPAYER FROM USING SECTION 1341 TO DEDUCT OVERPAYMENT OF TAXES IN PREVIOUS YEAR

■ **INSTANT FACTS** A taxpayer who received and paid back excessive compensation from his employer corporation filed suit against the IRS when they denied him the use of IRC § 1341 in calculating his post-payback taxes.

■ **BLACK LETTER RULE** Under IRC § 1341, if a taxpayer included an item in gross income in one tax year, and in a subsequent tax year becomes entitled to a deduction because the item or a portion thereof is no longer subject to his unrestricted use, and the amount of the deduction is in excess of $3,000, the tax for the subsequent year is reduced by either the tax attributable to the deduction or the decrease in the tax for the prior year attributable to the removal of the item, whichever is greater.

■ **PROCEDURAL BASIS**

Certification to the Sixth Circuit Court of Appeals of a federal district court judgment denying a taxpayer the benefits of IRC § 1341.

■ **FACTS**

Eugene Van Cleave (P) was the president and majority stockholder of VanMark Corporation. In 1969, the corporation adopted a by-law requiring corporate officers who received income from the corporation that was deemed by the IRS to be excessive had to pay back the excessive amount. This was because anything deemed excessive could not be deducted by the corporation as a business expense. In 1974, Van Cleave (P) received $332,000 from the corporation, $57,500 of which was deemed excessive (and thereby non-deductible by the corporation). Van Cleave (P) paid that amount back to the corporation, thus allowing it to deduct all of his salary as a business expense. As Van Cleave (P) had reported the full $332,000 on his 1974 income tax return, he used IRC § 1341 to calculate his tax due in 1975. The IRS audited the return and disallowed the use of § 1341, resulting in a tax deficiency of $5,987.34. Van Cleave (P) paid the deficiency and sued for a refund. The district court found for the IRS (D) and Van Cleave (P) appealed.

■ **ISSUE**

Are the benefits of IRC § 1341 available to a taxpayer who, in a year subsequent to that in which it is received, paid back excessive compensation to the corporation which employs him?

■ **DECISION AND RATIONALE**

(Brown, J.) Yes. This case turns on the interpretation of Internal Revenue Code (IRC) § 1341. That section was enacted to mitigate the sometimes harsh result of the application of the "claim of right" doctrine. Under that doctrine, a taxpayer had to pay tax on an item in the year in which it was received under a claim of right, even if it was later determined that it had to be returned. The taxpayer is, however, allowed to deduct the amount of the item from his income in the year of repayment. But as the Supreme Court pointed out in *United States v. Skelly Oil Co.,* it is possible for a taxpayer to benefit less from the deduction in the year of repayment than if he had been permitted to deduct the amount repaid from his income in the year of receipt. This occurs when the taxpayer is in a higher tax bracket in the year of receipt than in the year of repayment. IRC § 1341 changes that result, and allows the taxpayer to choose the more favorable of the two alternatives as follows: If a taxpayer included an item in gross income in one tax year, and in a subsequent tax year becomes entitled to a deduction because the item or a portion thereof is no longer subject to his unrestricted use, and the amount of the deduction is in excess of $3,000, the tax for the subsequent year is reduced by either the tax attributable to the deduction or the decrease in the tax for the prior year attributable to the removal of the item, whichever is greater. In denying Van Cleave (P) use of § 1341, the district court seemed persuaded by the IRS' (D) argument that use of § 1341 under these circumstances would open the door to tax avoidance in that taxpayers who controlled corporations could "test the waters" in setting their compensation without risk of an adverse tax result. We believe, however, that such a possibility of tax avoidance is not a proper consideration in applying this statute, and that the consideration is a legislative rather than a judicial consideration. The IRS (D) also argues that § 1341 is not available in the instant case because that section provides for taxpayer relief only if "it appeared that the taxpayer had an unrestricted right" to the excess salary and "it was established after the close of such prior taxable year . . . that the taxpayer did not have an unrestricted right to such item." IRC § 1341(a)(1) and (2). The IRS (D) contends that Van Cleave (P) had more than an appearance of an unrestricted right to the excess compensation in the year in which it was received, and that the right to the compensation became restricted only upon the occurrence of the IRS audit and determination in a subsequent year. The IRS (D) further maintains that since Van Cleave (P) had an unrestricted right to the compensation in the year of receipt, contingent only upon the happening of an event in a subsequent year, § 1341 is not available to him. We reject this argument. The fact that his ultimate right to the compensation was not determined until the occurrence of a subsequent event does not mean that Van Cleave (P) had an unrestricted right to the compensation when he received it. The fact that a restriction on a taxpayer's right to income does not arise until a year subsequent to the time of receipt does not affect the availability of a § 1341 tax adjustment. Therefore, the adjustment is available to a taxpayer in this situation if the other requirements of the section are met. We are aided in this conclusion by examining the cases involving the application of the claim of right doctrine, the effect of which this section was designed to alleviate. Acceptance of the government's (D) reading of the statute would thwart the ameliorative purpose intended by Congress in enacting the section. Accordingly, Van Cleave (P) is entitled to the adjustment under § 1341. Reversed.

Analysis:

Van Cleave deals with IRC § 1341. The benefits of the section are obvious. It permits a taxpayer to reduce his current year's tax by the amount he overpaid in the previous year when the income was reported, or to take a deduction in the current year equal to the amount that was repaid. Which one the taxpayer chooses is totally up to the taxpayer. In order to qualify for § 1341, however, four requirements must be met: (1) it must have appeared in the year the income was included that the taxpayer had an unrestricted right to it; (2) the amount repaid must constitute an allowable deduction and so must fit within the requirements of §§ 152 or 212; (3) it must be established after the close of the prior year in which the income was reported that the taxpayer did not actually have an unrestricted right to that income; and (4) the amount repaid must be over $3,000. Notice that the first and final requirements do not leave much to debate. In this case, these requirements are all satisfied.

Alice Phelan Sullivan Corp. v. United States

(*Corporate Taxpayer*) v. (*IRS*)

381 F.2d 399 (Ct. Cl. 1967)

THE TAX–BENEFIT RULE PERMITS AN EXCLUSION OF RECOVERED PROPERTY FROM CURRENT INCOME SO LONG AS ITS INITIAL USE AS A DEDUCTION DID NOT PROVIDE THE TAXPAYER WITH A TAX SAVINGS

■ **INSTANT FACTS** When two parcels of land once donated as a charitable contribution were given back to the donor corporation, and the corporation resisted the IRS' determination that it must pay taxes on the land as if the receipt of the parcels was current taxable income, a lawsuit ensued.

■ **BLACK LETTER RULE** When a taxpayer obtains a full tax benefit from earlier deductions, if those deductions are recouped, they constitute income and must be taxed as such at the tax rate which is in effect during the year in which the recovered item is recognized as income.

■ **PROCEDURAL BASIS**

A corporation filed suit in the United States Court of Claims when a claim for a refund allegedly due to the corporation on grounds of overpayment of tax was denied by the IRS.

■ **FACTS**

In 1939 and 1940 Alice Phelan Sullivan Corp. (P) donated two parcels of land to charity, for which it took charitable contribution deductions that yielded it an aggregate tax benefit of $1,877.49. Each conveyance was made subject to the condition that the property be used for either educational or religious purposes. When, in 1957, the donee chose to no longer use the land for those purposes, the two parcels were returned to the corporation (P). When an audit of the corporation's (P) income tax return was conducted, the IRS (D) discovered that in the year of recovery the corporation (P) did not claim the return of the property as gross income. (The corporation (P) claimed that the reconveyance was a non-taxable return of capital.) The IRS (D) adjusted the corporation's income for 1957 by adding to it $8,706.93—the total of the charitable contribution deductions taken in the years of donation. Taxed at the 1957 corporate tax rate of 52%, the increased income resulted in a deficiency of $4,527.60. After payment of the deficiency, the corporation (P) filed a claim for a refund of $2,650.11, asserting this amount as overpayment on the theory that a correct assessment could demand no more than the return of the tax benefit originally enjoyed. The IRS (D) denied the claim and the corporation (P) turned to the federal Court of Claims for relief.

■ **ISSUE**

When a taxpayer obtains a full tax benefit from certain deductions in one year, and those deductions are later recouped and treated as income in a later year, should the taxpayer be taxed at the tax rate in effect during the later year in which the recovered item is recognized as income?

■ **DECISION AND RATIONALE**

(Collins, J.) Yes. In *Perry v. United States* we recognized that a return to the donor of a prior charitable contribution gives rise to income to the extent of the deduction previously allowed. At that time we decided that the Government should be entitled to recoup no more than that which it lost, meaning that the tax liability arising upon the return of a charitable gift should equal the tax benefit experienced at the time of donation (i.e., the donor should be taxed at the tax rate applicable at the time of donation). At the request of the government (D), we now reexamine that earlier decision and hold that *Perry* should be reversed. Generally, a transaction which returns to a taxpayer his own property cannot be considered as giving rise to "income"—at least where that term is confined to its traditional sense of "gain derived from capital, from labor, or from both combined." *Eisner v. Macomber.* Yet the principle is well ingrained in our tax law that the return or recovery of property that was once the subject of an income tax deduction must be treated as income in the year of its recovery, the only limitation on that principle being the "tax-benefit rule." This rule permits exclusion of the recovered item from income so long as its initial use as a deduction did not provide a tax saving. But where full tax use of a deduction was made and a tax saving was thereby obtained, then the extent of saving is considered immaterial. The recovery is viewed as income to the full extent of the deduction previously allowed. Once the exclusive province of judge-made law, the tax-benefit rule now finds expression in both the IRC and various Treasury Regulations. Drawing our attention to the language of one regulation, which extends tax-benefit treatment to "all other losses, expenditures, and accruals made the basis of deductions from gross income for prior taxable years," the IRS (D) insists that the present recovery must find its place within the scope of the regulation and, as such, should be taxed in a manner consistent with the treatment provided for like items of recovery. In other words, the government (D) urges that the value of the property returned to the corporation (P) should be taxed at the rate prevailing in the year of recovery, and not the year of donation. While the regulation does not specify which tax rate is to be applied to the recouped deduction, we are compelled to agree with the IRS (D). Ever since the United States Supreme Court decided *Burnet v. Sanford & Brooks Co.,* the concept of accounting for items of income and expense on an annual basis has been accepted as the basic principle upon which our tax laws are structured. "It is the essence of any system of taxation that it should produce revenue ascertainable . . . at regular intervals. Only by such a system is it practicable to produce a regular flow of income and apply methods of accounting, assessment, and collection capable of practical operation." To insure the vitality of the single-year concept, it is essential not only that an annual income be ascertained without reference to losses experienced in an earlier accounting period, but also that income be taxed without reference to earlier tax rates. Since Alice Phelan Sullivan Corp. (P) did obtain a full tax benefit from its earlier deductions, those deductions were properly classified as income upon recoupment and must be taxed as such. This can mean nothing less than the application of that tax rate which is in effect during the year in which the recovered item is recognized as a factor of income. Affirmed.

Analysis:

The tax-benefit rule, simply stated, is a principle of tax law that permits the exclusion of a recovered item from income so long as its initial use as a deduction did not provide the taxpayer with a tax savings. This rule prevents taxpayers from taking advantage of the tax deduction system in ways that might cheat the government out of taxes due. For instance, in *Alice,* the corporation took a charitable contribution deduction in the amount of $8,706.93 for the years 1939 and 1940. If, when the corporation got the land back in 1957, it had been allowed to keep the land without any accompanying tax consequences, it would have received a double benefit: the land in 1957 and tax savings in 1939 and 1940. At the same time, the government would have received a double detriment: a loss of tax revenue in 1939 and 1940 and no aid being given from the corporation to charity from the year 1957 on. The tax-benefit rule, then, is one of fairness and equity, as its application ensures that neither side receives a double benefit or a double detriment. In *Alice,* however, the court recognizes that tax rates may have changed between the year of the donation and the year of recoupment. Despite this problem, however, the rule works as it does because of strict adherence to the single-year tax system, a system that the *Alice* court supports.

■ CASE VOCABULARY

SINGLE–YEAR TAX SYSTEM: The tax accounting system in place in the United States under which taxes are paid and assessed on a regular and periodic (one year) basis.

TAX–BENEFIT RULE: A principle of tax law that permits the exclusion of a recovered item from income so long as its initial use as a deduction did not provide the taxpayer with a tax saving.

CHAPTER TWENTY–ONE

Capital Gains and Losses

Mauldin v. Commissioner

Instant Facts: Taxpayer's deduction of profits from sale of individual lots of property as capital assets challenged by the IRS, which characterized the profits as ordinary income resulting from a business activity.

Black Letter Rule: Property held by taxpayer for sale to customers in the ordinary course of a trade or business is not a capital asset entitled to capital gain or loss treatment, regardless of taxpayer's stated purpose.

Malat v. Riddell

Instant Facts: Taxpayer, a participant in a joint venture that was designed to develop land, sold off all interest in property purchased by the joint venture and treated the profits from the sale as a capital gain.

Black Letter Rule: When determining whether property is held primarily for sale to customers in the course of a trade or business, and thus exempt form capital gain or loss treatment, primarily means of first importance or principally.

Kenan v. Commissioner

Instant Facts: Trustees paid five million dollar specific devise to beneficiary partially out of stock owned by the estate.

Black Letter Rule: Using stock to satisfy a specific monetary gift to a beneficiary results in a capital gain to the estate equal to the amount the stock had appreciated from the time of the decedent's death to the time of transfer.

Hudson v. Commissioner

Instant Facts: Taxpayers who collected money in settlement of a judgment they had purchased reported their profit from the transaction as capital gain.

Black Letter Rule: Collecting money to settle a judgment, even if the judgment was purchased from the original creditor, is not a sale or exchange.

Hort v. Commissioner

Instant Facts: Taxpayer, a landlord, agreed to accept a sum certain in exchange for cancellation of a long-term lease and then claimed the foregone rent payments as a loss and the sum certain paid as a capital gain.

Black Letter Rule: Amounts accepted in exchange for cancellation of a lease constitute ordinary income to the landlord, from which the foregone rent payments cannot be offset as a loss.

Metropolitan Building Co. v. Commissioner

Instant Facts: Sublessee paid tenant a sum certain in exchange for tenant giving up his rights under the lease so Sublessee could enter into transaction directly with the landlord.

Black Letter Rule: When a leasehold interest is forfeited in exchange for a sum certain, the amount paid constitutes a capital gain because the forfeiture of the interest is a sale or exchange of property.

Watkins v. Commissioner

Instant Facts: Watkins (P) won the lottery and elected to take his winnings in twenty-five annual installments, but he sold his interest in the remaining payments after just six years to a third party for a lump sum, and he claimed the payment as a capital gain, but the IRS said it was ordinary income.

Black Letter Rule: Under the substitute-for-ordinary-income doctrine, where a lump sum payment is received in exchange for what would otherwise be received at a future time as ordinary income, capital gains treatment of the lump sum is inappropriate because the consideration was paid for the right to receive future income, not for an increase in value of the income-producing property.

Arrowsmith v. Commissioner

Instant Facts: Taxpayers who paid a judgment on behalf of corporation that had been liquidated and dissolved declared the payment as an ordinary business loss.

Black Letter Rule: Liability for judgment resulting from liquidating and dissolving corporation does not arise from carrying on a business and thus payment of such liability is not an ordinary loss.

United States v. Skelly Oil Co.

Instant Facts: Taxpayer deducted the full amount of money refunded to its customers to settle claims against it, even though the full amount was not previously included in gross income.

Black Letter Rule: A taxpayer may not deduct the full amount of money refunded if the full amount was not previously taxed.

Stephen P. Wasnok v. Commissioner

Instant Facts: The Internal Revenue Service (IRS) brought suit against a taxpayer who claimed a capital loss when he was forced to deed his home back to the mortgage company.

Black Letter Rule: With respect to property used in a trade or business, Internal Revenue Code (IRC) § 1231 provides that while net gains on sales or exchanges of such property shall be treated as capital gains, net losses are not treated as capital losses, but as ordinary losses.

Williams v. McGowan

Instant Facts: A taxpayer sued the IRS to recover taxes which he felt should not have been paid.

Black Letter Rule: When a going business is sold, it should be comminuted into fragments that are matched against the definition in § 117(a)(1) to determine whether gains or losses realized upon sale are to be characterized as capital or ordinary.

Mauldin v. Commissioner

(Taxpayer) v. *(IRS)*

195 F.2d 714 (10th Cir. 1952)

BEWARE OF TAXES WHEN DIVIDING YOUR LAND INTO INDIVIDUAL LOTS FOR SALE

■ **INSTANT FACTS** Taxpayer's deduction of profits from sale of individual lots of property as capital assets challenged by the IRS, which characterized the profits as ordinary income resulting from a business activity.

■ **BLACK LETTER RULE** Property held by taxpayer for sale to customers in the ordinary course of a trade or business is not a capital asset entitled to capital gain or loss treatment, regardless of taxpayer's stated purpose.

■ **PROCEDURAL BASIS**

Appeal to the Tenth Circuit Court of Appeals from the Tax Court's judgment in favor of the IRS' determination that profits from sale of lots was ordinary income derived from a business activity.

■ **FACTS**

Mr. Mauldin (P) began a road construction company in New Mexico in 1916. In 1920, Mr. Mauldin (P) decided to go into the cattle business, and to that end purchased approximately 160 acres of land located one-half mile from the city of Clovis. At the time of purchase, the land was suitable only for cattle feeding and not residential development. Mr. Mauldin (P) did not receive title to the property until June 1921, at which time the country was experiencing a drought, crop and bank failures and a decline in the overall cattle business. As a result, Mr. Mauldin (P) decided to forego going into the cattle business. He tried to sell the property at a loss in 1924, but was unable to do so, in part because a highway had been surveyed diagonally across the center of the tract. A real estate agent advised Mr. Mauldin (P) that he would have a better chance of selling the property if he divided it into smaller lots, and Mr. Mauldin (P) divided the property into 88 lots known as the "Mauldin Addition". By 1939, the 88 lots were incorporated into the city of Clovis. As a result of incorporation, the city began a paving project in the area of the Mauldin Addition and charged Mr. Mauldin (P) $25,000 for their work. Unable to pay this debt, Mr. Mauldin (P) began devoting most of his time to selling off his lots. Mr. Mauldin (P) advertised in newspapers, conducted personal solicitations, and published signs and other advertisements. During 1939 and 1940, Mr. Mauldin (P) was able to sell enough lots to satisfy his obligation to the city. Upon paying off his debt, Mr. Mauldin (P) decided to hold onto the remaining lots for investment purposes. In 1940, Mr. Mauldin (P) began operating a lumber business and devoted full time to it. While working on his lumber business, Mr. Mauldin (P) did not advertise any of his lots for sale, did not hold a real estate license nor retain a real estate agent. From 1940 until 1945, Mr. Mauldin's (P) lots were in great demand due to a population explosion in the city of Clovis. By the end of 1945, Mr. Mauldin (P) had sold all of his lots except 20 acres. In 1940, Mr. Mauldin (P) listed his business as real estate, and showed net income in 1941 and 1944 from the sale of real estate as $3,000. In 1943, he listed his business as lumber. In 1944 he did not designate his business. In 1945, he listed it as lumber and real estate, showing a net income from lumber of $12,339.80 and from the sale of real estate of $20,484.84. For the lots sold during 1944 and 1945, Mr. and Mrs. Mauldin (P) calculated their income as long-time capital assets. The IRS (D) deemed the income from the sale of the lots as ordinary income derived from a business activity, and assessed a deficiency in their taxes. Mr. and Mrs. Mauldin (P) challenged that ruling in the Tax Court, but lost. Mr. and Mrs. Mauldin (P) now appeal to the Tenth Circuit.

■ ISSUE

If a substantial part of a taxpayer's income is derived from the sale of lots, are the profits from those sales entitled to capital gain or loss treatment?

■ DECISION AND RATIONALE

(Murrah, J.) No. The issue here is whether the profits derived from the sale of lots by Mr. and Mrs. Mauldin (P) is entitled to long-time capital asset treatment since they state they held onto the land for investment purposes. Here, if the property was held for investment purposes and not primarily for sale to customers in the ordinary course of a trade or business, then it is entitled to capital gain or loss treatment. [See § 117(a)(1).] There is no rule of thumb by which to determine when property is held primarily for sale to customers in the ordinary course of a trade or business versus when it is held for investment purposes. [Of course not—that would be too easy!] Instead, the determination must be made based on the facts and circumstances of each case. However, prior cases addressing this issue have laid out a number of factors helpful in making this determination. These include the purposes for which the property was acquired, whether the property is for sale or investment and the continuity and frequency of sales as opposed to isolated transactions. Cases that have applied these factors in situations similar to that of Mr. and Mrs. Mauldin (P) are also helpful in determining whether the lots here were held primarily for sale to customers. In *Phipps v. Commissioner,* land purchased and divided into lots held for occasional sale through local brokers was not frequent enough to constitute land primarily held for sale to customers. In *Foran v. Commissioner,* oil producing property purchased and sold within eighteen months, although purchased by a person engaged in the business of selling oil and gas leases, was not, in and of itself, sufficient to constitute holding property primarily for sale to customers in the course of a trade or business. In *Gruver v. Commissioner,* however, the subdividing of land into lots by one engaged in real estate activities for a length of time for the purpose of facilitating their sale constituted holding property primarily for sale to customers in the course of a business. And in *Richards v. Commissioner,* the sale of lots from a tract subdivided when it was too valuable to use solely for farming also constituted holding land for sale to customers and not for investment purposes. As these cases illustrate, while there are numerous factors to consider, the ultimate determination depends on the purpose for which the property was held, and that determination is independent of what the stated purpose is. Here, Mr. and Mrs. Mauldin (P) subdivided their lots and offered them for sale. At that time, Mr. Mauldin (P) was obviously engaged in the business of real estate. While it is possible for someone in the business of real estate to sell off all of their holdings at one time and exit the field, this was not the case here. Rather, although Mr. Mauldin (P) was not actively engaged in trying to sell his lots, the only reason he was not doing so was because they were not in great demand due to economic factors. Additionally, Mr. and Mrs. Mauldin (P) derived a substantial portion of their income from the sale of their lots. In these circumstances, the facts support a finding that the profits from the sale of lots were derived from property held primarily for sale to customers in the course of a business or trade. As such, those profits were not entitled to capital gain treatment. Affirmed.

Analysis:

This case demonstrates how arbitrary the line is between capital assets and non-capital assets. As the court says, each case must be addressed on its own merits. Interestingly, the court agrees with the Tax Court's analysis that Mr. Mauldin (P) was engaged in the business of real estate, even though it acknowledged, as did the Tax Court, that Mr. Mauldin (P) had not actively tried to sell any lots for several years and was engaged full time in the lumber business. Notice how the key fact for both seems to be that Mr. Mauldin (P) made a substantial amount of money from selling his lots. Notice also how neither the Tax Court nor the Tenth Circuit gave any weight to the fact that Mr. Mauldin (P) characterized his property as held for investment purposes. This case is a good example of how courts will not judge a book by its cover, but instead will look inside to see what it is really about. This case is also a good example of how courts apply other cases to a fact situation. This is an important aspect of how the law works. The opinion walks through the cases and then reaches its decision based on those cases and how they are similar or dissimilar to the facts here.

■ **CASE VOCABULARY**

BLOCK: As in city block, a portion of houses enclosed by streets.

LOT: A small area of land suitable for building, usually the land on which an individual home or business sits.

PLATTED: A tract of land is platted when it is divided into separate blocks, individual lots, and streets on a map giving it an urban character.

SUBDIVIDED: Simply refers to sectioning off a tract of land into separate sections, usually in preparation for platting.

TRACT: A piece or parcel of land as a whole.

Malat v. Riddell

(Taxpayer) v. *(IRS Commissioner)*
383 U.S. 569, 86 S.Ct. 1030 (1966)

COURT ISSUES LANDMARK RULING: PRIMARILY MEANS PRIMARILY!

■ **INSTANT FACTS** Taxpayer, a participant in a joint venture that was designed to develop land, sold off all interest in property purchased by the joint venture and treated the profits from the sale as a capital gain.

■ **BLACK LETTER RULE** When determining whether property is held primarily for sale to customers in the course of a trade or business, and thus exempt form capital gain or loss treatment, primarily means of first importance or principally.

■ **PROCEDURAL BASIS**

Appeal to the United States Supreme Court from the judgment of the District Court in favor of the IRS which had been affirmed by the Court of Appeals.

■ **FACTS**

Mr. Malat (P) was a participant in a joint venture that purchased a 45–acre parcel of land to develop and operate as an apartment project. When Mr. Malat (P) and his fellow joint venturers encountered problems obtaining financing for the project, the parcel was subdivided and the interior lots were sold. Mr. Malat (P) reported the income from these sales as ordinary income. Thereafter, the joint venturers encountered further problems with zoning restrictions and, as a result, they sold their remaining interest in the property. Mr. Malat (P) reported the income from this subsequent sale as a capital gain. The IRS (D) denied the capital gain treatment, finding that the property was held primarily for sale to customers of the joint venture in addition to being held for investment purposes. The District Court entered judgment in favor of the IRS (D), and the Court of Appeals affirmed.

■ **ISSUE**

Is the purpose of holding property a primary one if it is a substantial purpose?

■ **DECISION AND RATIONALE**

(Per Curiam) No. It was the opinion of the District Court that Mr. Malat (P) had failed to show that his property was not held primarily for sale to customers in the course of a business or trade. According to the District Court, the joint venturers, Mr. Malat (P) included, knew the purchase of the 45–acre parcel was a good deal and realized that if their plans to operate an apartment complex fell through, they would not lose money because they could still sell the parcel. In ruling in this manner, the District Court adopted the IRS' (D) determination that primarily held for sale meant that the substantial purpose of the property was for sale to customers. In interpreting a statute, such as § 1221(1) [property held primarily for sale to customers in a trade or business is not a capital asset], courts try to use a word's ordinary and everyday meaning, and will often look to the purpose of the statute at issue for guidance. Here, the statute at issue is intended to differentiate between those profits and losses that arise from everyday operation of a business or trade and those realized as a result of the appreciation or depreciation of personal investment property. The literal meaning of the words in this statute thus comport with its purpose. Therefore, primarily should be interpreted as meaning of first importance or principally, rather than substantial. Since the District Court used an incorrect interpretation of the words of the statute at issue insofar as it deemed primarily to equate to substantial, this case must be remanded for further proceedings under the appropriate standard. Reversed and remanded.

Analysis:

The IRS and the lower courts used a less strict standard for determining whether the purpose of property is primarily for sale to customers. For the IRS, where property was held for more than one purpose, if the substantial purpose was for sale to customers, it was not a capital asset. However, under the interpretation given by the Supreme Court here, where dual purposes exist the key is whether the *primary* purpose of the property is for sale to customers, not whether a *substantial* purpose is the sale to customers. While this may seem like hairsplitting, the difference could be important, especially for taxpayers trying to get capital asset treatment. The other lesson to learn from this case is the manner in which the Supreme Court goes about interpreting the statute by looking at the everyday and ordinary meaning of the words, rather than some little-known legal definition.

■ **CASE VOCABULARY**

JOINT VENTURE: A relationship between two or more people who have joined together for a joint business purpose for their mutual benefit.

Kenan v. Commissioner

(Taxpayer/Trustees) v. *(IRS)*
114 F.2d 217 (2d Cir. 1940)

USING STOCK TO SATISFY A DEVISE CONSTITUTES A SALE OR EXCHANGE THAT RESULTS IN CAPITAL GAIN TO THE ESTATE

■ **INSTANT FACTS** Trustees paid five million dollar specific devise to beneficiary partially out of stock owned by the estate.

■ **BLACK LETTER RULE** Using stock to satisfy a specific monetary gift to a beneficiary results in a capital gain to the estate equal to the amount the stock had appreciated from the time of the decedent's death to the time of transfer.

■ **PROCEDURAL BASIS**

Appeal from the Board of Tax Appeals affirming judgment in favor of IRS that transfer of stock resulted in capital gain to the estate.

■ **FACTS**

Mrs. Bingham, the testatrix, died in 1917, leaving a will by which her residuary estate was placed in trust. Her will also provided that upon reaching her fortieth birthday, Mrs. Bingham's niece, Ms. Wise, was to inherit five million dollars. The will further provided that the trustees (P) had the option of substituting marketable securities equal in value to the sum to be paid for the monetary gift. Ms. Wise turned forty in 1935. At that time, the trustees (P) decided to pay her the five million dollars in both cash and securities. The securities transferred to Ms. Wise had all appreciated in value from the time they were held by the trustees (P) to the time of transfer. The IRS (D) determined that the transfer of the stock resulted in a capital gain to the trust and assessed a deficiency of $367,687.12. The Board of Tax Appeals affirmed that determination, but denied an attempt by the IRS (D) to change its determination that the income should be taxed as a capital gain to one that required the gain to be treated as ordinary income.

■ **ISSUE**

Is the transfer of stock to a beneficiary in satisfaction of a monetary devise a sale or exchange of a capital asset?

■ **DECISION AND RATIONALE**

(Hand, J.) Yes. The trustees (P) argue that no tax should be assessed because they neither received income nor realized a gain upon transferring the stock to Ms. Wise. The IRS (D) argues that the trustees (P) did recognize a gain upon transfer and argue that such gain should be taxed as ordinary income to the trust because the gain did not arise out of the sale or exchange of property. § 111 provides that the gain or loss from the sale or other disposition of property is equal to the amount realized less the adjusted basis. The amount realized is defined as the amount of money received plus the fair market value of property, if any, received. § 113 defines basis of property as the cost, but further provides that property transferred at death shall have a basis equal to the fair market value of the property at the time of transfer. The trustees (P) argue that because the will specifically gave them the option of paying the monetary gift out of securities, when they chose to exercise that option, the gift became a specific bequest of property and therefore, no gain was realized upon distribution of that property. Contrary to their argument, however, the transfer at issue here was not a distribution of a bequest of specific property. Unlike a beneficiary of a specific bequest, Ms. Wise did not have a legal right to claim any securities: she had the right to five million dollars, regardless of whether securities held by the estate appreciated or depreciated. Rather, this case is more like the situation in *Suisman v. Eaton*. In *Suisman*, the beneficiary of a will, who was entitled to a specific monetary amount, agreed to take securities in satisfaction thereof. In that case, the Court ruled that the transfer of the stock to the beneficiary resulted in a gain to the estate from the sale or other disposition of property equal to the amount of money it no longer owed to the beneficiary. Here, although the trustees (P) had the choice to use securities and did not need the consent of Ms. Wise to do so, Ms. Wise's claim against the estate is the same as the beneficiary's claim in *Suisman*. What the trustees (P) essentially did here, as in *Suisman,* was elect not to sell stock to satisfy a monetary obligation but to use the stock itself to satisfy the obligation. The fact that the transfer here was authorized by the will makes no difference. The use of "other disposition" in the statute clearly includes an exchange, and when the trustees (P) exercised the option to substitute securities for cash, they exchanged the securities for cash, thereby realizing a gain. Thus, where, as here, a beneficiary does not take specific property, such as securities, under the will, using property to satisfy a claim results in a gain to the estate. This conclusion is not changed by the trustees' (P) argument that double taxation will result. This argument depends on the securities being taxed when sold by Ms. Wise based on the gain realized from such sale less the basis, that basis being the fair market value at the time of transfer since the transfer occurred from a devise or bequest under a will. However, the basis of the securities Ms. Wise received in this transaction is not equal to the fair market value. The securities were not transferred by bequest or devise under a will; rather, they were received via an exchange and thus Ms. Wise's basis in the securities is equal to the amount of the claim she surrendered. Thus, the appreciation of the stock from the time of the decedent's death to the time of transfer will only be taxed once, not twice. The IRS (D) argues that since the trustees (P) upon transfer of the securities to Ms. Wise realized a gain, that gain constitutes ordinary income because it does not constitute a sale or other disposition of property. The reasons for our conclusion that the trustees (P) realized a gain refute this argument, however. Here, the trustees (P) realized a gain when they used securities that were worth more now than when acquired to satisfy a five million dollar obligation. Such an exchange of securities, which are almost always capital assets, should be subject to capital treatment under § 117. Had the trustees (P) sold the securities in order to obtain the cash necessary to satisfy the obligation, the gain realized from the sale would have been taxed under the capital rates. The fact that the trustees (P) exercised their option to use the securities to pay the obligation in lieu of selling them should not change the character of the securities from a capital asset. Affirmed.

Analysis:

Here, since the securities were not actually sold, the trustees (P) did not actually receive any income from the transfer. Nevertheless, income was realized by the trustees (P) upon transfer and that imputed income is taxable. Notice that here, however, as opposed to other situations where income is imputed, it is possible to see where the gain arises. By using the securities that were acquired for substantially less than they were worth at the time Ms. Wise turned forty to pay the five million dollar obligation, the trustees (P) essentially saved themselves a sum certain in cash that they did not have to use to pay Ms. Wise. This is the amount of gain they realized. It is at least worth noting that had the court not found a prior case that seemed substantially the same, *Suisman,* they may not have reached the same conclusion. Notice how much importance the court places on the similarities between this case and *Suisman* in reaching the conclusion that this case also resulted in a capital gain.

■ **CASE VOCABULARY**

LEGATEE: One who takes personal property under a will.

RESIDUARY ESTATE: The portion of a decedent's assets that remain after payment of debts, taxes, expenses associated with administration and specific devises (gifts of certain identifiable property) are made.

TESTATRIX: A woman who makes a will. (The male version is testator.)

Hudson v. Commissioner

(Taxpayer) v. *(Internal Revenue Commissioner)*
20 T.C. 734 (1953)

COLLECTING MONEY TO SETTLE A DEBT IS NOT AN EXCHANGE

■ **INSTANT FACTS** Taxpayers who collected money in settlement of a judgment they had purchased reported their profit from the transaction as capital gain.

■ **BLACK LETTER RULE** Collecting money to settle a judgment, even if the judgment was purchased from the original creditor, is not a sale or exchange.

■ **PROCEDURAL BASIS**

Appeal to the Tax Court of the IRS' determination that profits from settlement of a judgment constitutes ordinary income.

■ **FACTS**

In 1929, Mary Harahan obtained a judgment against Howard Cole in the amount of $75,702.12. In 1943, Mr. Hudson (P) and his partner, Mr. Taylor (P), each purchased fifty percent of that judgment from Ms. Harahan's estate at a total cost of $11,004. In 1945, Mr. Cole paid Mr. Hudson (P) and Mr. Taylor (P) $21,150 in full satisfaction of the total judgment against him. Both Mr. Hudson (P) and Mr. Taylor (P) reported the profit on the judgment as a long-term capital gain. The IRS (D) disallowed capital gain treatment, determining that the profit from the judgment was ordinary income.

■ **ISSUE**

Is the gain realized from a settlement of a judgment purchased from the original creditor capital gain?

■ **DECISION AND RATIONALE**

(Johnson, J.) No. Mr. Hudson (P) and Mr. Taylor (P) argue that the gain they realized on the settlement of the judgment should be treated as capital gain. The IRS (D) disagrees, arguing that the gain is ordinary income. There is no question here that the purchase of the judgment by Mr. Hudson (P) and Mr. Taylor (P) was a bona fide transaction or that the judgment when entered and transferred was a capital asset. The issue here, however, is whether there was a sale or exchange of that capital asset upon collection and settlement. Mr. Hudson (P) and Mr. Taylor (P) argue that sale means "a contract by which one acquires property in the thing sold and the other parts with it for valuable consideration". They also point out that a sale usually means the transfer of property for money or a fixed price. Here, however, it is clear that there was not a transfer of property. When Mr. Cole paid a sum certain to Mr. Hudson (P) and Mr. Taylor (P) in full satisfaction of the judgment against him, all that can be said is that his debt was extinguished. No property changed hands and the judgment creditors, Mr. Hudson (P) and Mr. Taylor (P) did not acquire property in the transaction with Mr. Cole. Neither businessmen nor lawyers would call the settlement of a judgment a sale, and there is no reason to try to make settlement a sale here when the only difference is that the original judgment creditor sold the right to collect the judgment to Mr. Hudson (P) and Mr. Taylor (P). When Mr. Hudson (P) and Mr. Taylor (P) collected money from Mr. Cole, they did not receive income from a sale or exchange. The law is clear that where the gain realized does not result from the sale or exchange of a capital asset, that gain is ordinary income. For instance, in *R.W. Hale,* a compromise of notes for less than face value was deemed a settlement resulting in ordinary income. And in *Pat N. Fahey* a successful settlement of litigation before trial was held to be ordinary income since the gain did not result from a sale or exchange. Likewise, in *Fairbanks v. U.S.,* the redemption of bonds before maturity has also been held not to be a sale or exchange. Finally, in *Bingham v. Commissioner,* the surrender of notes before maturity simply extinguished the right to collect on those notes and thus was not a sale or exchange because the property that was said to be transferred (the notes) simply vanished upon payment. The case at issue here is no different than these cases. When the judgment was deemed satisfied, the property that constituted the capital asset simply disappeared; it was not transferred. Thus, there was no sale or exchange and any gain realized is to be treated as ordinary income and not a capital gain. Affirmed.

Analysis:

A debtor who owes $100 recognizes a gain of $80 if he is able to settle the debt for payment of only $20. Thus, the debtor now has $80 that he would not have had if the debt had not been settled. Viewed this way, it becomes clearer how an exchange takes place upon settlement. When the debtor pays $20 to the creditor, the creditor in turn gives him $80 back (imputed income). When the creditor receives the $20, however, there is no handing back of the debt itself, so no property changes hands when the creditor settles the claim. Interestingly, it could be said that because the creditor is essentially giving back $80 he has a loss equal to what he could have received had he not settled. This is similar to the landlord/tenant situation where the landlord agrees to cancel a lease in exchange for a lesser payment then he is entitled to under the lease. In both cases, because the creditor or landlord has not actually received all that he is entitled to, the relinquishment of the right to receive it is not a loss that the tax code recognizes. The reason behind the disparity in the tax treatment of gain recognized by parties involved in the same transaction can be difficult to understand.

■ CASE VOCABULARY

COOPERAGE: Acting jointly with at least one other person for common benefit.

JUDGMENT: The final decision of a court resolving the rights and claims of all parties and awarding a remedy, usually in the form of money, to the winning party.

JUDGMENT CREDITOR: The person to whom money is owed under a judgment.

JUDGMENT DEBTOR: The person who owes money under a judgment.

Hort v. Commissioner

(*Taxpayer*) v. (*IRS*)

313 U.S. 28, 61 S.Ct. 757 (1941)

CANCELLATION OF LEASE DOES NOT CREATE LOSS FOR LANDLORD

■ **INSTANT FACTS** Taxpayer, a landlord, agreed to accept a sum certain in exchange for cancellation of a long-term lease and then claimed the foregone rent payments as a loss and the sum certain paid as a capital gain.

■ **BLACK LETTER RULE** Amounts accepted in exchange for cancellation of a lease constitute ordinary income to the landlord, from which the foregone rent payments cannot be offset as a loss.

■ FACTS

Mr. Hort (P) inherited property from his father on which a ten-story office building was located. Irving Trust leased the main floor of the building for a fifteen-year term, with yearly rent of $25,000. In 1933, just six years after entering the fifteen-year lease, Irving Trust found it unprofitable to maintain the branch in Mr. Hort's (P) building and negotiated with Mr. Hort (P) for the cancellation of the lease. Mr. Hort (P) agreed to the cancellation upon payment of $140,000. On his tax return for that year, Mr. Hort (P) did not include the $140,000 payment in his ordinary income and declared a loss in the amount of $21,494.75, which was equal to the amount of rent that he had lost due to cancellation of the lease, less the $140,000 payment. The IRS (D) determined that the $140,000 should have been included in Mr. Hort's (P) gross income and denied the loss he claimed entirely. The Board of Tax Appeals and the Circuit Court of Appeals affirmed the IRS' (D) determination.

■ ISSUE

May a taxpayer offset the amount of rental payments that will not be paid when a lease is cancelled?

■ DECISION AND RATIONALE

(Murphy, J.) No. Mr. Hort (P) argues that the amount he received in exchange for cancellation of the lease constituted capital rather than ordinary income. Mr. Hort (P) further argues that if the amount he received must be counted as ordinary income, the amount of rental payments that were "lost" offset the total amount of income. Contrary to his arguments, the entire amount received as compensation for cancellation of the lease must be included in ordinary income. Section 22(a) clearly states that gross income includes rental payments. Had the lease continued, all rental payments would have been included in ordinary income. It is also clear that had Mr. Hort (P) declined to cancel the lease and instead instituted a suit to recover the amount of rental payments that Irving Trust failed to pay, any amount recovered would have been included in ordinary income. The fact that Mr. Hort (P) decided to accept a lump sum payment in exchange for letting Irving Trust out of their lease does not change the character of the payment from rent. The fact that Mr. Hort (P) accepted an amount less than the total amount of rent due under the lease is irrelevant. Clearly, the payment received by Mr. Hort (P) constituted a substitute payment for the rent due under the lease. Additionally, the mere fact that the lease itself constituted "property" does not render the amount paid for cancellation of the lease a return of capital. Not all property is capital. In some cases, like this one, when a right to payment arises from ownership of property, those payments may constitute ordinary income. Regardless of how the payment received by Mr. Hort (P) is classified, there is no doubt that the payment was a substitute for rent. As such, Mr. Hort (P) must include the $140,000 payment as ordinary income. Furthermore, he is not entitled to deduct the foregone rental payments as a loss. To the extent he accepted less than the full amount of rent due under the lease, his gross income was reduced, thereby relieving Mr. Hort (P) of income tax liability for the foregone amount. Moreover, if the cancellation of the lease reduced the value of the property itself, then Mr. Hort (P) will be entitled to claim a loss if and when that loss is realized upon a sale of the property for less than its value with the lease. Affirmed.

Analysis:

Rental payments, although they arise from ownership of property that may be a capital asset, constitute ordinary income under the plain language of § 22(a). Thus, not all income from a capital asset is entitled to capital asset treatment. Notice also that the cancellation of the lease and loss of future rental payments does not equal a loss that is deductible by the landlord. In this case, the inability to deduct the amount of lost rental payments is insignificant in the long run since Mr. Hort (P) received a lump sum payment of $140,000, which was substantially the amount of rent due under the lease. But keep in mind that the general rule is that cancellation of a lease does not entitle a landlord to declare a loss equal to the amount of rent that he loses. The rationale for this rule is that any payment a landlord agrees to accept in exchange for relinquishing his right to sue for breach of the lease and rent is actually a substitute for the rent the landlord could have collected. Looking at it this way, the rule makes perfect sense since what the landlord is receiving is essentially rent and rent is clearly considered ordinary income under § 22(a).

■ CASE VOCABULARY

DEVISE: A gift of specific property in a will.

Metropolitan Building Co. v. Commissioner

(Taxpayer/Tenant) v. *(IRS)*

282 F.2d 592 (9th Cir. 1960)

PAYMENT TO TENANT FOR CANCELLATION OF LEASE RESULTS IN CAPITAL GAIN

■ **INSTANT FACTS** Sublessee paid tenant a sum certain in exchange for tenant giving up his rights under the lease so Sublessee could enter into transaction directly with the landlord.

■ **BLACK LETTER RULE** When a leasehold interest is forfeited in exchange for a sum certain, the amount paid constitutes a capital gain because the forfeiture of the interest is a sale or exchange of property.

■ **PROCEDURAL BASIS**

Taxpayer appeals from the judgment of the Tax Court affirming the IRS' determination that the amount paid to taxpayer in exchange for forfeiture of leasehold interest constituted ordinary income.

■ **FACTS**

In 1907, Metropolitan Building Company (P) acquired a lease of four city blocks in downtown Seattle, owned by the University of Washington. In 1922, Metropolitan Building Company (P) entered into a sublease for a portion of one city block. Under the terms of the sublease, rent was to be paid in the amount of $25,000 a year. The sublease was to end one day shy of the lease Metropolitan Building Company (P) had with the University of Washington. Shortly after the sublease, the Olympic Hotel was constructed upon the property covered by the sublease. In 1936, Olympic, Inc. acquired the sublease. In 1952, two years prior to the end of the original lease, the University of Washington began to negotiate for a long-term disposition of the entire four block area to occur after the lease terminated. To that end, it invited proposals from all interested parties. Among those proposals was one from Olympic, Inc. Olympic, Inc.'s proposal was the most desirable because Olympic, Inc. had current possession of the property under the sublease with Metropolitan Building Company (P). Under Olympic, Inc.'s proposal, Olympic, Inc. would execute a new lease directly with the University of Washington for a higher amount of rent than Metropolitan Building Company (P) was paying, giving rise to a substantial amount of additional income to the University for the period prior to the termination of the lease. To effectuate Olympic, Inc.'s proposal, negotiations were undertaken with Metropolitan Building Company (P) for the cancellation of the lease by the University of Washington. In September 1952, an agreement was reached whereby Olympic, Inc. would pay Metropolitan Building Company (P) $137,000 in exchange for a conveyance of Metropolitan Building Company's (P) entire interest in the lease to the University. The $137,000 amount was equal to ground rent, increased taxes and ad valorem property taxes. Thereafter, the University of Washington entered into a lease directly with Olympic, Inc.. The IRS (D) determined the $137,000 payment was a substitution for rental payments that Metropolitan Building Company (P) would have to make and thus constituted ordinary income. The Tax Court affirmed that determination.

■ **ISSUE**

Is the forfeiture of a leasehold interest a sale or exchange of property?

■ **DECISION AND RATIONALE**

(Merrill, J.) Yes. The IRS (D) argues that the payment is ordinary income, relying on the decision in *Hort v. Commissioner.* [Amounts accepted in exchange for cancellation of a lease constitute ordinary income to the landlord.] In that case, the money that changed hands constituted consideration for the relinquishment of the obligation to pay rent and not for the transfer of any legal interest. Here, however, the money that changed hands was not simply consideration for the relinquishment of the obligation to pay rent but was also compensation for the purchase of Metropolitan Building Company's (P) interest in the lease. In *Hort,* the transaction involved the release of a right to receive future income. Here, the transaction involved the transfer of income-producing property (namely, the hotel). Seen this way, the giving up of the lease is the same as a sale or exchange of property and thus the transaction falls within § 117 and constitutes a capital gain. This is in line with other decisions, like *Commissioner v. Golonsky* [when a tenant in possession of property surrenders that property to the landlord under an agreement reached with the landlord prior to surrender, the proceeds from the transaction received by the tenant constitute a capital gain], involving similar situations. The IRS (D) attempts to distinguish *Golonsky* on the basis that the payment there was made directly by the landlord, whereas here the payment came from a third party, Olympic, Inc. Such a technical distinction is not persuasive. Regardless of where the money came from, it is clear that Metropolitan Building Company (P) profited from the transaction by which it relinquished all rights under the lease with the University of Washington. So long as the transaction is a bona fide transfer for a legitimate business purpose of a leasehold interest in its entirety, it makes no difference who pays the money to the tenant releasing his interest. Therefore, the $137,000 received by Metropolitan Building Company (P) should be taxed as a capital gain. Reversed.

Analysis:

In *Hort,* the payment for cancellation of a lease was ordinary income to the landlord. Here, the payment for cancellation of a lease is capital gain to the tenant. The rule is different for landlords than it is for tenants because in the case of the tenant, a recognized legal interest is being forfeited. Property law acknowledges that a leasehold interest is a property interest just as fee ownership is. In the case of a landlord, however, when the lease is canceled, what the landlord is giving up is the right to future rental payments, but not a legal interest in property. When a tenant cancels a lease at the request of the landlord or another third party, any money the tenant receives is a capital gain, but when a landlord cancels a lease at the request of a tenant, any money the landlord receives is ordinary income. Keep in mind when applying the tenant rule that the transaction must be a legitimate one, and the tenant's entire interest must be transferred.

■ CASE VOCABULARY

AD VALOREM: Literally, according to value; usually refers to a tax assessed on the value of property.

LESSEE: The tenant who leases property directly from the landlord.

SUBLESSEE: Another tenant who leases property from a Lessee for a term less than the original lease held by the lessee.

Watkins v. Commissioner

(Lottery Winner) v. *(IRS Commissioner)*

447 F.3d 1269 (10th Cir. 2006)

THE SALE OF FUTURE LOTTERY–WINNINGS PAYMENTS FOR A LUMP SUM RESULTS IN ORDINARY INCOME

■ **INSTANT FACTS** Watkins (P) won the lottery and elected to take his winnings in twenty-five annual installments, but he sold his interest in the remaining payments after just six years to a third party for a lump sum, and he claimed the payment as a capital gain, but the IRS said it was ordinary income.

■ **BLACK LETTER RULE** Under the substitute-for-ordinary-income doctrine, where a lump sum payment is received in exchange for what would otherwise be received at a future time as ordinary income, capital gains treatment of the lump sum is inappropriate because the consideration was paid for the right to receive future income, not for an increase in value of the income-producing property.

■ **PROCEDURAL BASIS**

Federal appellate court review of a tax court ruling in favor of the IRS.

■ **FACTS**

Watkins (P) won over $12 million from the Colorado State Lottery, and elected to have the winnings distributed to him in twenty-five annual installments. He reported the receipt of the first six annual payments as ordinary income. Watkins's (P) subsequent divorce resulted in splitting the future payments with his wife. He thereafter sold his interest to a third party for the discounted present value of his remaining share. Watkins (P) reported the lump sum payment as the proceeds from the sale of a capital asset. The IRS issued a notice of deficiency, stating that the payment was ordinary income, not a capital gain. The tax court agreed with the IRS, and Watkins (P) appealed.

■ **ISSUE**

Did the proceeds from the sale of the taxpayer's share of his future lottery-winnings payments constitute ordinary income?

■ **DECISION AND RATIONALE**

(Seymour, J.) Yes. Under the substitute-for-ordinary-income doctrine, where a lump sum payment is received in exchange for what would otherwise be received at a future time as ordinary income, capital gains treatment of the lump sum is inappropriate because the consideration was paid for the right to receive future income, not for an increase in value of the income-producing property. That is, when a party exchanges for a lump sum the right to receive, in the future, ordinary income already earned or obtained, the amount received serves as a substitute for the ordinary income the party had the right to receive over time, and the lump sum is accordingly treated as ordinary income for tax purposes. Several other courts have applied this doctrine in lottery sales cases and have consistently held that a lump sum payment in exchange for future installments of lottery winnings is property characterized as ordinary income.

The term "capital asset" is to be construed narrowly in accordance with the purpose of Congress to afford capital gains treatment only in situations typically involving the realization of appreciation in value accrued over a substantial period of time, and thus to ameliorate the hardship of taxation of the entire gain in one year. Here, the substance of what was assigned was the right to receive future income, and the substance of what was received was the present value of income that the recipient would otherwise obtain in the future. Thus, consideration was paid for the right to receive future income, not for an increase in the value of income-producing property. The sale of Watkins's (P) future lottery payments did not represent a capital gain. Affirmed.

Analysis:

As this case demonstrates, capital gain treatment is not available when the substance of what is sold is the right to receive future ordinary income, and the substance of what is received is the present value of that future income. The taxpayer receives ordinary income rather than a capital gain because consideration is paid for the right to receive future income, not for an increase in value of the income-producing property. The Second, Third, Ninth, Tenth, and Eleventh Circuits have all held that a state lottery winner who sells or assigns his right to receive future installments of lottery winnings, in exchange for a lump sum, recognizes ordinary income, not capital gain. This rule has also been applied to bar capital gain treatment for the assignment of oil payment rights.

■ CASE VOCABULARY

CAPITAL GAIN: The profit realized when a capital asset is sold or exchanged.

ORDINARY INCOME: For individual income-tax purposes, income that is derived from sources such as wages, commissions, and interest (as opposed to income from capital gains).

Arrowsmith v. Commissioner

(Taxpayer) v. *(IRS)*

344 U.S. 6, 73 S.Ct. 71 (1952)

PAYMENT OF JUDGMENT AGAINST DISSOLVED CORPORATION NOT ORDINARY BUSINESS LOSS

■ **INSTANT FACTS** Taxpayers who paid a judgment on behalf of corporation that had been liquidated and dissolved declared the payment as an ordinary business loss.

■ **BLACK LETTER RULE** Liability for judgment resulting from liquidating and dissolving corporation does not arise from carrying on a business and is thus payment of such liability is not an ordinary loss.

■ **PROCEDURAL BASIS**

Appeal from the Court of Appeals' reversal of the Tax Court's judgment reversing the IRS (D).

■ **FACTS**

Mr. Arrowsmith (P) and Mr. Bauer (P) were equal owners in a corporation. In 1937, they decided to dissolve the corporation, liquidate and divide the proceeds. Partial distributions of the proceeds were made in 1937, 1938 and 1938, with one final distribution in 1940. Mr. Arrowsmith (P) and Mr. Bauer (P) declared the profits from the distributions as capital gains. In 1944, a judgment was rendered against the corporation and Mr. Bauer (P) individually. Both Mr. Arrowsmith (P) and Mr. Bauer (P) paid the judgment, and each deducted the entire amount paid as an ordinary loss. The IRS (D) disallowed the loss, however, concluding that the loss arose from the liquidation proceeds and should have been treated as a capital loss.

■ **ISSUE**

Is the payment of a judgment against a dissolved corporation that has been liquidated an ordinary loss for the former stockholders?

■ **DECISION AND RATIONALE**

(Black, J.) No. Under § 23(g), losses from the sale or exchange of capital assets are capital losses. Under § 115(c), liquidation distributions constitute an exchange. Under these statutes, the loss at issue here arose from the exchange of capital assets and is thus a capital, not ordinary, loss. The only reason Mr. Arrowsmith (P) and Mr. Bauer (P) were required to pay the judgment was because of the liability they incurred upon receipt of liquidation distributions. This liability in no way arose from their business activities, but arose solely from the liquidation of the corporation. If the judgment had been paid at the time of liquidation, Mr. Arrowsmith (P) and Mr. Bauer (P) concede that the loss would be a capital one. They argue, however, that the loss was converted to an ordinary one because of the well-established principle that each year constitutes a separate unit for tax purposes. Mr. Arrowsmith (P) and Mr. Bauer (P) overlook the fact that this principle is not violated by looking at the overall transactions in prior years to determine the character of the loss sustained here. Looking at the prior transactions is not the same as opening up prior years and changing tax treatment of gains and losses, and as such, the principle is not violated. Mr. Bauer (P) also argues that since the judgment was entered against him personally, his payment of the judgment constitutes an ordinary loss. However, since the entire judgment was entered against Mr. Bauer (P) and he only paid half of it, it is clear that both he and Mr. Arrowsmith (P) were paying the judgment pursuant to their liability arising from the liquidation of the corporation and that Mr.

Bauer (P) did not pay half because of the individual liability attached to him as a result of the judgment. There is no reason to give Mr. Bauer (P) preferential tax treatment simply because the judgment was entered against him individually. Affirmed.

■ DISSENT

(Douglas, J.) Yes. The loss here should be treated as an ordinary one. There were no capital transactions in the year this loss occurred. Since each year is a separate unit for tax purposes, treating this loss as a capital one diminishes gains received and accounted for in earlier years. The principle of annual accounting is violated when such treatment is condoned.

(Jackson, J.) Yes. The only reason this issue has arisen is because the judgment was rendered in a year subsequent to the distributions. Had the judgment arisen in the same year as the distributions, there would be no doubt but that the payment of such judgment would decrease the amount of proceeds available for distribution, decrease the amount of capital gain Mr. Arrowsmith (P) and Mr. Bauer (P) recognized and decrease the income tax liability of the corporation itself. Under a situation such as this, Congress could have allowed the prior tax years to be reopened to adjust the gains as required, as they have in other situations. Since Congress has chosen not to provide this opportunity, however, taxpayers are faced with treating the loss as either capital or ordinary in the year in which the loss occurred. The majority simplifies resolution of this choice by concluding that the loss here fits the statutory definition of a capital loss and should thus be treated as one. The Tax Court and other lower courts have not concluded the same way, however. Resolution of this issue should not be so simple. On the one hand, if the loss is treated as ordinary the taxpayer recognizes a windfall because he may deduct the loss to offset income that could be taxed at a higher rate, while on the other hand, treating this is a capital loss would result in diminishing the capital gains the taxpayer must tax at a lower rate, also resulting in a windfall to the taxpayer [albeit of smaller proportions]. Furthermore, a resolution of this case could have substantial implication in future cases that results in a large loss of revenue to the government. Consider, for example, if instead of paying a judgment Mr. Arrowsmith (P) and Mr. Bauer (P) came into money by virtue of collecting on a judgment in favor of the corporation. Under the majority's rule announced here, the income would be taxed as a capital gain and not ordinary income. Here, where resolution depends on the interpretation of a statute, deference should be paid to the judgment of those dealing with those statutes on a daily basis. Here, the Tax Court determined that this was an ordinary loss. This Court should not be so quick to overrule their determination when it arises from interpretation of statutes with which it is more familiar. The Tax Court is in a better position to recognize the possible loopholes and future consequences a decision like this one may produce.

Analysis:

The majority sees no problem looking at prior years to determine the character of a loss in the current one, while the dissents believe that doing so amounts to reopening the prior years and changing the tax treatment of certain income. Notice also that Justice Jackson's dissent is more concerned with the future implications of this case than with the result itself. Justice Jackson is worried that treating this type of loss as capital because it is related to capital gains that were recognized in prior years may result in the government losing out on revenue when the situation is reversed, and instead of a loss in later years a gain is realized. This case's importance lies in its discussion of the annual accounting principle. The dissents seem to suggest that one reason the majority opinion is wrong is because it pays little respect to this principle. The dissents also seem to argue that this principle means that in computing yearly tax liability, one cannot look to prior years to determine the current year's liability. Notice how this argument is defeated, however, by certain provisions in the tax code that allow a taxpayer to carryover losses and gains from year to year, or that allow a taxpayer to go back and reopen prior years to made adjustments.

■ CASE VOCABULARY

LIQUIDATE: Convert assets to cash.

United States v. Skelly Oil Co.

(IRS) v. (Taxpayer)
394 U.S. 678, 89 S.Ct. 1379 (1969)

ANNUAL ACCOUNTING METHOD DOES NOT PROHIBIT IRS FROM "LOOKING INTO" PRIOR TAX YEARS

■ **INSTANT FACTS** Taxpayer deducted the full amount of money refunded to its customers to settle claims against it, even though the full amount was not previously included in gross income.

■ **BLACK LETTER RULE** A taxpayer may not deduct the full amount of money refunded if the full amount was not previously taxed.

■ **PROCEDURAL BASIS**

Appeal by the IRS (D) from the judgment of the Tenth Circuit Court of Appeals reversing the District Court judgment in its favor.

■ **FACTS**

Skelly Oil Co. (P) is a producer of natural gas. Prior to 1958, Skelly Oil Co. (P) had set its prices based on an order from the Oklahoma Corporation Commission, however, in 1958, that order was vacated and as a result, Skelly Oil Co. (P) had to refund $505,536.54 to two of its customers to settle claims against it for overcharging. During the years that the overcharges were paid, Skelly Oil Co. (P) included the entire amount in gross income, but claimed a percentage depletion deduction equal to 27.5% of the gross income it received. When the overcharges had to be repaid as a result of the 1958 settlement, Skelly Oil Co. (P) deducted the entire $505,536.34 as an ordinary loss. The IRS (D) disallowed the deduction, and Skelly Oil Co. (P) appealed.

■ **ISSUE**

May a taxpayer deduct the full amount of a refund when the entire amount refunded was not previously included in gross income?

■ **DECISION AND RATIONALE**

(Marshall, J.) No. The issue here arises in part out of the claim of right doctrine. Part of the justification for the doctrine is that if it turns out later that all or part of the money previously included in gross income has to be returned, the taxpayer would be entitled to a deduction. Congress approved this approach in its adoption of the annual accounting method. Certain discrepancies arose out of the use of the annual accounting method in connection with the claim of right doctrine, but Congress addressed these by enacting § 1341(a)(5), which allows a taxpayer to reduce taxes in the current year by the amount taxes in previous years were increased because disputed items were included in gross income. § 1341(a)(5) is inapplicable, here, however. Thus, the old rule [the claim of right doctrine] applies here. [See § 1341(a)(4), old rule applies where § 1341(a)(5) does not.] The IRS (D) argues that the decision of the Court of Appeals holding that § 1341 requires that the entire amount refunded by Skelly Oil Co. (P) be deducted is an incorrect interpretation of the statute. We agree. Under § 1341(a)(2), a taxpayer may deduct an amount previously included in gross income if it turns out that he did not have an unrestricted right to that income. However, nowhere in the statute does it require that the deduction be equal to the amount included in gross income. This interpretation is supported by the regulations and the language of the statute that requires that the deduction allowed be determined based on other applicable sections of the code. The parties here dispute whether the refunded payments are deductible as a standard business loss under § 162. Regardless, we believe the tax code should not be interpreted in such a way as to allow Skelly Oil Co. (P) a double deduction. If Skelly Oil Co. (P) is allowed to deduct the full amount refunded, the effect is that it has been able to deduct $505,536.54 when it only included $366,513.99 in gross income due to the percentage depletion deduction. Thus, Skelly Oil Co. (P) would be entitled to deduct $13,9022.55 twice: once as a percentage depletion deduction and once as § 1341 deduction. To avoid this result, the deduction Skelly Oil Co. (P) may claim must be reduced by the deduction previously allowed. While the annual accounting method requires that the amount of a deduction in a current year not be calculated based on gains in prior years, there is no requirement that the prior year not be examined at all to determine whether a loss is capital or ordinary. [Remember *Arrowsmith*?—the case not the band.] Clearly Congress did not intend to give taxpayers a deduction for refunding money that was not previously taxed. This conclusion does not violate the annual accounting principle since the prior year is not being reopened; it is merely being looked at. Moreover, given the unique nature of the percentage depletion deduction, such retrospective analysis is not likely to occur very often. If the approach advanced by Skelly Oil Co. (P) was adopted, the taxpayer would always win and the government would always lose. Surely Congress did not intend to create such a result. Reversed.

Analysis:

The result here makes sense in an economic way. Since Skelly Oil Co. (P) did not include the full amount it refunded in gross income because of a special deduction, the fact that it has to return the money should not mean it should be able to deduct the entire amount refunded. Does this rule make sense in other claim of right situations, however? What if the deduction that was previously taken was not a unique deduction but was a standard one, such as ordinary business losses? Should that deduction offset any subsequent deduction for money that is refunded or returned? According to this opinion, it may not necessarily be that all deductions that reduced the amount of income that is taxed as compared to the amount eventually returned should offset the later deduction. Note the Court's language regarding the unique nature of the percentage depletion deduction. Thus, it would seem that the lesson here is not that money refunded may only be deducted up to the amount it was previously taxed, but rather that money refunded may be deducted in full, unless the specific money refunded was not fully included in gross income because of a deduction applicable to that money. In other words, this case leaves the door open for the IRS to deny full deductions in claim of right cases where the money refunded was subject to a specific deduction that reduced the amount included in gross income when that money was received.

■ CASE VOCABULARY

CLAIM OF RIGHT DOCTRINE: As discussed by Justice Brandeis in *North American Oil Consolidated v. Burnet,* the doctrine means that an amount a taxpayer has an unrestricted claim to must be included in gross income, regardless of whether all or part of it may have to be returned.

PERCENTAGE DEPLETION DEDUCTION: § 613 allows a taxpayer to deduct a certain percentage of income if that income is derived from the depletion of natural resources.

VACATED: Canceled or deleted.

Stephen P. Wasnok v. Commissioner

(Taxpayer) v. *(Internal Revenue Commissioner)*

30 T.C.M. 39 (1971)

RESIDENTIAL PROPERTY RENTED OUT FOR A PERIOD OF YEARS ON WHICH DEDUCTIONS ARE TAKEN IS CONSIDERED TO BE § 1231 PROPERTY FOR TAX PURPOSES

■ **INSTANT FACTS** The Internal Revenue Service (IRS) brought suit against a taxpayer who claimed a capital loss when he was forced to deed his home back to the mortgage company.

■ **BLACK LETTER RULE** With respect to property used in a trade or business, Internal Revenue Code (IRC) § 1231 provides that while net gains on sales or exchanges of such property shall be treated as capital gains, net losses are not treated as capital losses, but as ordinary losses.

■ **PROCEDURAL BASIS**

Certification to the Tax Court of a Small Tax Case Division decision regarding a capital loss claimed by a taxpayer.

■ **FACTS**

Stephen P and Mary Alice Wasnok (D) resided in Cincinnati, Ohio, in 1960. During that year they purchased a home located at 5654 Sagecrest Drive. A substantial portion of the purchase price was borrowed from Spring Grove Avenue Loan and Deposit. The property was set up as security on the loan. In 1961, the Wasnoks (D) decided to move to California. Unable to sell the home on Sagecrest, they were forced to rent it out, which they did between June 1961 and May 1965 for approximately $200 per month. Twice during that time they attempted to sell the property, but both times they were unsuccessful. During those years the Wasnoks (D) also reported rental income on their tax returns and claimed a number of expenses related to the property, including depreciation. In 1965 the Wasnoks (D) were no longer able to afford to make payments on the property, so in lieu of foreclosure they agreed to deed it back to Spring Grove Loan Co., and did so in satisfaction of the then balance due on their note in the amount of $24,421.04. During that year, and the next, the Wasnoks (D) also did not file tax returns because they did not make enough money to do so. Finally, in 1967, the Wasnoks (D) began paying taxes again, and during that year both Stephen and Mary, filing separately, each claimed a capital loss carry-forward deduction in the amount of $1,000 which was predicated upon their disposition in 1965 of the Sagecrest property. An additional capital loss of $389 was carried forward and deducted in 1968. The IRS (P) filed a notice of deficiency on the 1967 and 1968 returns, claiming that the loss on the property was ordinary and should have been claimed in its entirety in 1965.

■ **ISSUE**

Can the disposition of property used in a trade or business at a loss be claimed as a capital loss that is deductible over a period of years?

■ **DECISION AND RATIONALE**

(Sacks, Commissioner) No. Wasnok (D) takes the position that the Sagecrest property was a capital asset and therefore that its disposition at a loss resulted in a capital loss that was properly deferred until 1967 and 1968 when he had sufficient funds to file income tax returns. The IRS (P) contends, however, that the property was not a capital asset, but an asset of the type described in IRC § 1231, losses upon the disposition of which are ordinary in nature and required to be deducted, to the extent that there is gross income, in the year in which it is sustained. Since Wasnok's (D) income in 1965 was more than sufficient to absorb the loss in that year, no deduction of any kind is allowable in the years 1967 and 1968. IRC § 1221 defines the term "capital asset" as any property held by the taxpayer, excluding however "property used in his trade or business, of a character which is subject to the allowance for depreciation ... or real property used in his trade or business." With respect to property used in a trade or business, Internal Revenue Code (IRC) § 1231 provides that while net gains on sales or exchanges of such property shall be treated as capital gains, net losses are not treated as capital losses, but as ordinary losses. In our view, Wasnok's (D) activity in renting out the Sagecrest property for a fairly continuous period of four years between 1961 and 1965, at a substantial rental, together with the concurrent claiming on their income tax returns of the expenses incurred in such rental activity, including depreciation, establishes the use of such property in a "trade or business." We therefore find that the property in question was not a capital asset in Wasnok's (D) hands at the time of its disposition, but an asset of the kind described in § 1231. The loss sustained on the disposition of such an asset is an ordinary loss. Since such loss was sustained in 1965, when Wasnok (D) had gross income sufficient to entirely absorb it, no loss is allowable to them in either 1967 or 1968. Reviewed and adopted.

Analysis:

Section 1231 provides that if, during a taxable year, gains netted from the disposition of certain kinds of property exceed the losses on the disposition of the same kinds of property, all of the gains and losses are treated as long-term capital gains and losses. On the other hand, if the losses on the disposition of § 1231 properties exceed the gains on similar properties, all of the gains and losses are treated as ordinary gains and losses. In the case of Wasnok's property, the Tax Court found that the losses from the property in 1965 exceeded the gains, and therefore they were characterized as ordinary losses (meaning he could not carry them over because only capital losses, and not ordinary losses, can be carried over under the IRC). IRC § 1231 applies specifically to gains and losses recognized in the sale or exchange of depreciable business property and real property used in a trade or business that have, in both cases, been held by the taxpayer for longer than one year. Wasnok's property fell within the purview of § 1231 because he had rented it out for a number of years, deriving income therefrom, and the court considered that to be a trade or business.

■ CASE VOCABULARY

CARRY–FORWARD DEDUCTION: A deduction which cannot be taken in full in a particular year, but which can be reserved in part for a future year and at that time used to offset taxable income.

CHARACTERIZATION: The process of determining whether a particular gain or loss should be taxed as either a capital or ordinary loss or gain.

DEPRECIABLE PROPERTY: Property either used in a trade or business or held for the production of income that is subject to wear and tear (see IRC § 167).

Williams v. McGowan

(Taxpayer) v. *(IRS Representative)*
152 F.2d 570 (2d Cir. 1945)

IRC § 1221 CHARACTERIZES CERTAIN PROPERTY AS CAPITAL ASSETS AND OTHER PROPERTY AS ORDINARY ASSETS

■ **INSTANT FACTS** A taxpayer sued the IRS to recover taxes which he felt should not have been paid.

■ **BLACK LETTER RULE** When a going business is sold, it should be comminuted into fragments that are matched against the definition in § 117(a)(1) to determine whether gains or losses realized upon sale are to be characterized as capital or ordinary.

■ PROCEDURAL BASIS

Certification to the United States Court of Appeals for the Second Circuit of an appeal of a judgment dismissing the complaint in an action by a taxpayer to recover income taxes paid for the year 1940.

■ FACTS

Both Williams (P) and Reynolds were engaged in the hardware business for many years. On January 20, 1926, they entered into a partnership in which Williams (P) was entitled to 2/3 of the profits and Reynolds entitled to 1/3. They agreed that on February 1, 1925, the capital invested in the business had been $118,082.05, of which $29,029.03 was credited to Reynolds. They also agreed that at the end of every business year, Reynolds would pay Williams (P) interest upon the amount of the difference between his share of the capital and 1/3 of the total as shown by the inventory. The business was carried on through the fiscal year ending on January 31, 1940, and ended upon Reynolds' death on July 18th of that same year. At that point, Williams (P) settled with Reynolds' executrix under an agreement by which he would pay her $12,187.90 and would thereby assume all liability of the business. Later that year, Williams (P) sold the business in its entirety for $63,926.28 to the Corning Building Company. This amount was made up of cash of about $8,100, receivables of about $7,000, fixtures of about $800, and a merchandise inventory of about $49,000, less approximately $1,000 for bills payable. To this was added about $6,000 credited to Williams (P) for profits between the beginning of the fiscal year and the ultimate sale. Thus, the total was approximately $70,000. Upon this sale, Williams (P) suffered a loss upon his original 2/3 of the business, but he made a small gain upon the 1/3 which he bought from Reynolds' estate; and in his income tax return he entered both as items of ordinary income, not as transactions in capital assets. The commissioner disallowed such a characterization and recomputed the tax. Williams (P) paid the difference and then sued to recover it.

■ ISSUE

When a business is sold as a going concern, should it be treated as a single piece of property for tax purposes?

■ DECISION AND RATIONALE

(Hand, J.) No. It has been held that a partner's interest in a going firm is regarded as a capital asset for tax purposes. As this is true, it is likely also true that a dead partner's interest is the same. But we need not decide for sure. When Williams (P) bought out Reynolds' interest, he became the sole owner of the business, and the situation for tax purposes was no other than if Reynolds had never been a partner at all, except that to the extent of one-third of the "amount realized" on Williams' sale to the Corning Company, his basis was different. We have to decide only whether upon the sale of a going business it is to be comminuted into its fragments, and these are to be separately matched against the definition in IRC § 117(a)(1) [which characterizes assets as capital or ordinary], or whether the whole business is to be treated as if it were a single piece of property. Even though we might agree that under the influence of the Uniform Partnership Act a partner's interest in the firm should be treated as indivisible, and for that reason a capital asset within § 117(a)(1), we should be wary about extending further so exotic a jural concept. Be that as it may, in this instance the section itself furnishes the answer. It starts in the broadest way by declaring that all property is capital assets, and then makes three exceptions. The first is "stock in trade ... or other property of a kind which would properly be included in the inventory;" next comes "property held ... primarily for sale to customers;" and finally, property "used in the trade or business of a character which is subject to ... allowance for depreciation." In the face of this language, although it may be true that a "stock in trade" taken by itself should be treated as a "universitas facti," by no possibility can a whole business be so treated; and the same is true as to any property within the other exceptions. Congress plainly did mean to comminute the elements of a business; plainly it did not regard the whole as "capital assets." As has already appeared, Williams (P) transferred to the Corning Company "cash," "receivables," "fixtures" and a "merchandise inventory." "Fixtures" are not capital assets because they are subject to a depreciation allowance; the inventory is expressly excluded. There can be no gain or loss in the transfer of cash; and, although Williams (P) does appear to have made a gain of $1,072.71 upon the "receivables," the point has not been argued that they are not subject to a depreciation allowance. That we leave open for decision by the district court, if the parties cannot agree. The gain or loss upon every other item should be computed as an item in ordinary income. Reversed.

■ DISSENT

(Frank, J.) I do not agree that we should ignore what the parties to the sale, Williams (P) and the Corning Company, actually did. They did not arrange for a transfer to the buyer, as if in separate bundles, of the several ingredients of the business. They contracted for the sale of the entire business as a going concern. To carve up the transaction into distinct sales of cash, receivables, fixtures, etc., is to do violence to the realities. I do not think congress intended any such artificial result.

Analysis:

Section 117(a)(1) no longer deals with defining property as a capital asset; the current § 117 deals with qualified scholarships. Today IRC § 1221 provides the definition of a capital asset. That section defines a capital asset, with respect to the facts of this case, as any "property held by the taxpayer (whether or not connected with his trade or business)," not including (1) "stock in trade ... which would properly be included in the inventory of the taxpayer if on hand at the close of the taxable year, or property held by the taxpayer primarily for sale to customers in the ordinary course of [a] trade or business"; or (2) property used in a trade or business that is subject to depreciation, or "real property used in [a] trade or business." *Williams* is instructive because it applies the definition of a capital asset to the sale of a business to determine which parts of the sale result in capital gains and losses and which result in ordinary gains and losses—it demonstrates how IRC § 1221 works in a real-world situation. It also makes it clear that a business sold as a going concern is not to be treated as one piece of property for tax purposes, but should be broken up into smaller fragments. Finally, it is useful to note the procedural history of this case. The IRS did not go after Williams (P) for the taxes, but he paid them and then sought to recover what he felt was the excess. In that way, Williams (P) was still able to seek his money and resolve the dispute with the IRS, without subjecting himself to any criminal liability for avoiding taxes.

■ CASE VOCABULARY

COMMINUTE: To break up into smaller sections.

UNIVERSITAS FACTI: A group of similar items that are treated as a whole (e.g., a group of basketball players is treated as a team).

CHAPTER TWENTY–TWO

Characterization on the Sale of Depreciable Property

United States v. Parker

Instant Facts: A taxpayer brought suit against the IRS seeking to have the sale of certain property that he made to a corporation re-characterized such that his gain was considered capital gain instead of ordinary gain.

Black Letter Rule: IRC § 1239 prevents a sale or exchange of depreciable property to a controlled corporation or a spouse from being characterized as the sale of a capital asset yielding capital gain treatment.

United States v. Parker

(IRS) v. *(Taxpayer)*
376 F.2d 402 (5th Cir. 1967)

IRC § 1239 DEALS WITH THE TAX CONSEQUENCES OF A SALE OF PROPERTY TO A CORPORATION THAT IS THE ALTER EGO OF THE SELLER OF THE PROPERTY

■ **INSTANT FACTS** A taxpayer brought suit against the IRS seeking to have the sale of certain property that he made to a corporation re-characterized such that his gain was considered capital gain instead of ordinary gain.

■ **BLACK LETTER RULE** IRC § 1239 prevents a sale or exchange of depreciable property to a controlled corporation or a spouse from being characterized as the sale of a capital asset yielding capital gain treatment.

■ **PROCEDURAL BASIS**

Certification to the Fifth Circuit Court of Appeals of a district court decision granting summary judgment for a taxpayer in his suit against the IRS to have certain income re-characterized as capital gain income.

■ **FACTS**

On April 1, 1959, Curtis L. Parker (P) and B. K. Eaves, a longtime employee in Parker's (P) oil and gas business, incorporated Parker's (P) business. The corporation had an authorized capital stock of 1,000 shares, 800 of which would belong to Parker (P) and 200 of which belonged to Eaves. The Articles of Incorporation included a provision stating that none of the stock might be transferred unless the stock were first offered to the corporation at the same price offered by the proposed transferee. An agreement was also reached between the two men which provided that whenever Eaves' employment should terminate for any reason, his shares would then be purchased by Parker (P) at a price governed by the fair market value per share of the corporation's assets, specifically excluding good will or any other intangible asset. The face of all stock certificates issued to Parker and Eaves carried notice of the restriction on sale created by the Articles of Incorporation. Only the stock certificates issued to Eaves carried a legend that they were subject to the Eaves–Parker buy-and-sell agreement. At the first meeting of the board of directors, Parker sold to the corporation certain assets which were depreciable property (such as motor vehicles, furniture and fixtures, and other equipment) worth $95,738.70. Parker (P) elected to treat the sale as a capital transaction, and reported the gain from it as long term capital gain under IRC § 1231. The IRS treated the gain as ordinary income under IRC § 1239 based on the contention that Parker (P) owned more than 80% "in value" of all outstanding stock of the corporation at the time of sale. The IRS assessed deficiencies for the years 1959–61. Parker (P) paid them under protest and sued for a refund. The district court granted summary judgment to Parker (P).

■ **ISSUE**

Can income derived from the sale of depreciable property to a corporation by a shareholder who owns more than 80% of the value of the corporation be deemed capital gain income?

■ **DECISION AND RATIONALE**

(Goldberg, J.) No. The IRS (D) argues that even if the full 20% of the shares allotted to Eaves was "outstanding" at the time of the sale, "the restrictions placed upon those shares and their inherent limitations made them worth less per share than Parker's (P)." We agree. IRC § 1239 prevents a sale or exchange of depreciable property to a controlled corporation or a spouse from being characterized as the sale of a capital asset yielding capital gain treatment. Without this section a taxpayer who had property which had been depreciated to a low basis could sell that property to a controlled corporation or spouse and pay only capital gains rates on the gain. The transferee could then re-depreciate the property, using the sale price as a new basis. The depreciation would be deducted from ordinary income. IRC § 1239 renders such a scheme profit less by taxing the gain on the transfer at ordinary rather than capital rates. The issue here is whether Parker's (P) corporation is sufficiently his slave to justify invocation of § 1239. We have concluded that Parker owned exactly 80% of the corporation's outstanding stock. The decisive question now is whether this 80% is, under § 1239, "more than 80 percent *in value* of the outstanding stock." IRC § 1239 does not say 80% of the voting power or number of shares, but "more than 80 percent in value." The words "in value" must have some meaning, and we think that the meaning calls for the process of fair market valuation. Eaves owned 20% of the outstanding stock. Therefore, if any fact can be found which shows that the value per share of Parker's (P) stock exceeded by any amount, no matter how small, the value per share of Eaves', then Parker (P) owned more than 80% in value of the outstanding stock. While it is true that Parker (P) and Eaves owned the same class of stock, Eaves' stock was burdened with impedimenta from which Parker's stock was free. We hold that as a matter of law the impedimenta must have decreased the value per share of Eaves' stock, and as we need only show that this value per share was lower by any indeterminate amount than the value per share of Parker's stock, we are able to render judgment here without remand. The impedimenta which depress the value spring from two sources. A. *The Restrictions on Transfer of Stock.* Eaves' stock was encumbered by two types of restrictions. First, the articles of incorporation stated that the corporation had the right of first refusal If any offer to sell to a third party. Second, Eaves' agreement with Parker (P) stated that if Eaves left the employ of the corporation for any reason, he must sell all of his stock to Parker (P) at a price representing the value per share of the assets, specifically excluding good will. The practical effect of these restrictions was to reduce the number of opportunities for Eaves to sell or give away the stock. "A commodity freely salable is obviously worth more on the market than a precisely similar commodity which cannot be freely sold." *Worcester County Trust Co. v. Commissioner,* 134 F.2d 578, 582 (1st Cir. 1943). Eaves' stock was also burdened by the buy-sell agreement. Even if we consider the Eaves and Parker (P) stock as identically limited by the articles, Parkers' (P) stock was not affected by the buy-sell agreement; Eaves' was. That such a limitation on alienability would depress market value to some greater extent is a well-recognized proposition. B. *The Lack of Control.* Eaves owned only 20% of the stock. This left Parker (P) in sole control of the corporation's affairs. Parker (P) controlled without the possibility of challenge the entire operation from the smallest detail to the largest. He exercised so much power that the corporation was his alter ego, or his slave. This is the situation at which § 1239 aims. Any purchaser of Eaves' stock would not be buying any degree of control over the corporation. The voting power of Eaves' stock was in reality worthless. We hold that this disability which inhered in Eaves' stock reduced its value per share below that of Parker's (P) stock as a matter of law. We reiterate that in the present case it is sufficient for the rendering of judgment to note that the restriction on Eaves' stock and its minority qualities combine to have some depressing effect, no matter how small, on its value per share. We hold, therefore, that Parker (P) owned more than 80% in value of the corporation's stock, and that any gain on the sale of the depreciable property was properly taxed at ordinary rates. Reversed.

Analysis:

IRC § 1239 was enacted to prevent the perpetration of a certain tax fraud upon the government. The court wrote: "IRC § 1239 prevents a sale or exchange of depreciable property to a controlled corporation or a spouse from being characterized as the sale of a capital asset yielding capital gain treatment. Without this section a taxpayer who had property which had been depreciated to a low basis could sell that property to a controlled corporation or spouse and pay only capital gains rates on the gain. The transferee could then re-depreciate the property, using the sale price as a new basis. The depreciation would be deducted from ordinary income. IRC § 1239 renders such a scheme profitless by taxing the gain on the transfer at ordinary rather than capital rates." Such a scheme would be beneficial to both the seller and the buyer of the property. Without § 1239, the seller would recognize capital gain instead of ordinary gain, which would be of benefit because capital gains are taxed at a significantly lower rate than ordinary gains, meaning the seller would pay less in taxes under such a scheme. Further, the buyer (who is the alter ego of the seller) would be purchasing depreciable property that would, under the IRC, reduce ordinary gain income, thus reducing the amount of taxes paid by the corporation. In such a situation, the buyer/seller alter ego combination would realize double tax benefit, and the government would be deprived of income in two instances.

■ CASE VOCABULARY

CLASS OF STOCK: A group of stock that shares similar features (such as voting rights) not shared by other groups of stock issued by the same corporation.

FAIR MARKET VALUATION: A process used to determine the fair market value of a certain security.

OUTSTANDING SHARES: Shares of stock in a corporation that are held by an investor and have not been redeemed by the corporation that issued the stock.

RIGHT OF FIRST REFUSAL: A promise granted by a potential seller of property which guarantees to the promisee the right to meet the terms of an offer of sale made upon the property by a third party, meaning the promisee always has the option to match the terms of sale proposed by another potential buyer.

SALE OR EXCHANGE: A complete transfer of property, whether voluntary or involuntary (such as a sale, gift, deed, casualty loss, condemnation, or foreclosure, but not including an abandonment of property).

CHAPTER TWENTY-THREE

Deductions Affected by Characterization Principles

Howard S. Bugbee v. Commissioner

Instant Facts: A taxpayer who loaned money to a friend which was not repaid disputed the IRS' denial of a bad debt deduction that was claimed on his tax return.

Black Letter Rule: Whether a transfer of money creates a bona fide debt depends on the existence of an intent by both parties, substantially contemporaneous to the time of such transfer, to establish an enforceable obligation of repayment.

Charles J. Haslam v. Commissioner

Instant Facts: The guarantor of a loan made from a bank to his own corporation filed a tax return claiming a business bad debt loss when his company went bankrupt and he was forced to cover the loan with his personal assets.

Black Letter Rule: A debt will only qualify as a business bad debt if it bears a direct relationship to a taxpayer's trade or business.

Pulvers v. Commissioner

Instant Facts: A taxpayer tried to take a casualty deduction when his property value decreased following a landslide in the neighborhood.

Black Letter Rule: The term "other casualty loss" in IRC 165(c)(3) refers to casualty losses involving physical damage or loss of physical property, and not just a decrease in value.

Mary Frances Allen v. Commissioner

Instant Facts: A woman whose brooch disappeared (by either theft or loss) brought an action in court protesting the IRS' decision not to allow her to take a theft deduction for the missing brooch.

Black Letter Rule: If the reasonable inferences from evidence presented regarding the disappearance of a valuable item point to theft, then a taxpayer is justified in taking a § 165 theft deduction.

Howard S. Bugbee v. Commissioner

(Taxpayer) v. *(Internal Revenue Commissioner)*

34 T.C.M. 291 (1975)

TO QUALIFY FOR A BAD DEBT DEDUCTION UNDER IRC § 166 THERE MUST EXIST A BONA FIDE DEBT WHICH ARISES FROM A DEBTOR–CREDITOR RELATIONSHIP BASED ON A VALID AND ENFORCEABLE OBLIGATION TO PAY A FIXED AND DETERMINABLE SUM OF MONEY

■ **INSTANT FACTS** A taxpayer who loaned money to a friend which was not repaid disputed the IRS' denial of a bad debt deduction that was claimed on his tax return.

■ **BLACK LETTER RULE** Whether a transfer of money creates a bona fide debt depends on the existence of an intent by both parties, substantially contemporaneous to the time of such transfer, to establish an enforceable obligation of repayment.

■ **PROCEDURAL BASIS**

Certification to the Tax Court of the United States of a dispute between the IRS and a taxpayer over a bad debt deduction claimed by the taxpayer.

■ **FACTS**

In 1966, Howard S. Bugbee (P) filed a tax return on which he claimed a short-term capital loss in the amount of $19,750. Nine years earlier, in a beer parlor of which Bugbee (P) was a part-owner, he met a man by the name of Paul Billings. The two became friends and, eventually, Bugbee (P) began to lend money to Billings based on the latter's plans to engage in various business ventures which he could not afford to begin on his own. In all, Bugbee (P) advanced $19,750 to Billings, evidenced by unconditional, unsecured demand notes signed by Billings. The notes provided an interest rate of 6%, though no interest was ever paid. No principle was ever repaid either. During the time in which the money was advanced, Billings was unemployed, though Bugbee (P) never investigated nor had any personal knowledge of Billings' financial condition. No business ventures were ever started with the money (much of it went to pay Billings' personal living expenses). When it became clear that repayment was unlikely [it should have been clear from day one], Bugbee (P) claimed a bad debt loss deduction on his taxes. The IRS (D) subsequently disallowed the deduction and found a deficiency in the amount of $7,242.68, at which time the matter went to court.

■ **ISSUE**

Is intent of the parties a key factor in determining whether a debtor-creditor relationship exists for the purposes of a bad debt deduction under IRC § 166?

■ **DECISION AND RATIONALE**

(Sterrett, J.) Yes. The sole issue in this case is whether Bugbee (P) is entitled to claim a short term capital loss under IRC § 166 as a result of Billings' failure to repay the funds Bugbee (P) advanced him. The only factual issue remaining—all others having been disposed of—is whether a debtor-creditor relationship existed between Billings and Bugbee (P) at the time of the advances. To qualify under § 166 there must first exist a bona fide debt which arises from a debtor-creditor relationship based upon a valid and enforceable obligation to pay a fixed and determinable sum of money. "Whether a transfer of money creates a bona fide debt depends on the existence of an intent by both parties, substantially contemporaneous to the time of such transfer, to establish an enforceable obligation of repayment."

Delta Plastics Corp., 54 T.C. 1287, 1291 (1970). This determination then is a question of fact to which the substance of the relationship between Bugbee (P) and Billings must be applied. The IRS (D) has pointed out several factors which it believes amply illustrates its position. The IRS (D) first argues that the advances represented money necessary to investigate prospective business ventures in which both men would share in the potential profits and as such do not represent loans. Billings' stated, however, that the advances were for his personal business ventures and that Bugbee (P) was not involved in them. He also acknowledged liability for them, and there is no indication of an agreement under which Bugbee (P) would be entitled to share in the profits of any of these ventures. We reject this contention. The IRS (D) next argues that bona fide debts never existed since the advances were worthless when made and Bugbee (P) did not have a reasonable expectation that they would be repaid. In support of this proposition, the IRS (D) argues that Billings was unemployed at the time of the loans, they were unsecured, the first interest payment was missed, the ventures were speculative, and repayment was never sought in court. The record in this case does indicate that Billings was in poor financial condition when the advancements were made. However, this Court has said that this factor does not preclude a finding of the existence of a bona fide debt. *Santa Anita Consolidated, Inc.*, 50 T.C. 536, 558 (1968). The use of unsecured notes reflects the nature of the risk involved. Any unsecured debt involves some risk, however this factor is not determinative. *Santa Anita.* This Court has said, "For the advance to be a loan, it is not necessary that there be an unqalified expectation of repayment." *Richard M. Drachman,* 23 T.C. 558 (1954). We have found that Bugbee (P) made the advances because he believed Billings could be successful and that he would be subsequently repaid. We believe his motives were genuine and that they existed throughout the period during which the advances were made. The IRS (D) maintains that, since Billings was in poor financial condition, in reality any repayment was conditioned on his success, and since that condition was never fulfilled, there was never an enforceable repayment obligation. The facts do not reveal that any repayments were conditioned on Billings' ultimate success. Although Bugbee (P) expected to be repaid after one of Billings' ventures was established, we have found that he was to be repaid from any assets that Billings might have. And Billings himself testified that these advances were personal, unconditional loans for which he was liable. The IRS (D) finally argues that, since Bugbee (P) and Billings were close personal friends, these advances might be classified as gifts. The facts simply do not support this contention. [Either Bugbee (P) was a really nice guy, or a really poor businessman.] We believe that Bugbee (P) has established the existence of a debtor-creditor relationship and that the IRS' (D) determination must be denied.

Analysis:

Bugbee deals with IRC § 166, which, in pertinent part, states, "There shall be allowed as a deduction any debt which becomes worthless within the taxable year." IRC § 166(a)(1). *Bugbee* adds to § 166 the requirement that, in order to qualify for a bad debt deduction under IRC § 166, there must exist a bona fide debt which arises from a debtor-creditor relationship based on a valid and enforceable obligation to pay a fixed and determinable sum of money. Thus, as the court points out, a gift is not deductible under this section because a gift does not create a debtor-creditor relationship. *Bugbee* then expounds on the requirement of a debtor-creditor relationship by stating that it is the intent of the parties that controls, meaning whether a debtor-creditor relationship exists (and furthermore, whether a § 166 deduction can subsequently be taken) depends wholly on the intentions of the parties. In sum, then, *Bugbee* teaches that before a bad debt deduction can be taken, one must examine the relationship of the parties and their intentions with respect to money transferred from one to the other to determine whether the deduction is appropriate.

■ CASE VOCABULARY

BAD DEBT: A debt which, because of circumstances, is uncollectible (and therefore, under IRC § 166, tax deductible in the year in which it becomes worthless).

UNSECURED DEMAND NOTE: A demand note (which entitles a creditor to demand payment upon a debt at any time) which is not backed by any pledged collateral, meaning if demand is made and the debtor does not have the money to pay on the note, the creditor will have nothing to fall back on.

Charles J. Haslam v. Commissioner

(Taxpayer) v. *(Internal Revenue Commissioner)*

33 T.C.M. 482 (1974)

A BAD DEBT LOSS, DEDUCTIBLE UNDER IRC § 166, IS CREATED WHEN A TAXPAYER GUARANTEE-ING THE DEBT OF ANOTHER IS FORCED TO SATISFY THAT DEBT AND RECEIVES NOTHING IN RETURN

■ **INSTANT FACTS** The guarantor of a loan made from a bank to his own corporation filed a tax return claiming a business bad debt loss when his company went bankrupt and he was forced to cover the loan with his personal assets.

■ **BLACK LETTER RULE** A debt will only qualify as a business bad debt if it bears a direct relationship to a taxpayer's trade or business.

■ **PROCEDURAL BASIS**

Certification to the Tax Court of the United States of an IRS decision to deny a taxpayer a business bad debt deduction.

■ **FACTS**

In 1954, Charles J. Haslam (P) and Earl Canavan established Northern Explosives, Inc. (Northern), which engaged in the sale and distribution of explosives, Both contributed $10,000.00, each taking 50% of the corporation's stock. Canavan took no active part in Northern's operations, while Haslam (P) worked as an employee. In 1957, Haslam (P) bought out Canavan's interest in Northern. In 1960, Northern encountered financial difficulties and required additional cash to continue its operations. In order to acquire the needed cash, Haslam (P) guaranteed loans in the total amount of $100,000 made to Northern by the National Commercial Bank and Trust Company (Commercial). To secure the guarantees, Haslam (P) pledged certain marketable securities and his personal residence. At the time, stock dividends of about $4,000 to $5,000 per year were Haslam's (P) only income other than what he made working for Northern, which was about $15,000 per year. Despite the loans, Northern went bankrupt and was unable to pay the loans, thus requiring Haslam (P) to pay them. To do so, Commercial sold the securities pledged by Haslam for $70,464.58, $55,956 of which was applied to the Northern debt. Following the bankruptcy, Haslam (P) took another job which paid him approximately $10,000 per year. Haslam (P) and his wife filed a joint tax return for the year 1967 on which they claimed a business bad debt in the amount of $55,956. The IRS [not believing it was truly a business debt, but rather a bad investment] denied the deduction, thereafter finding a deficiency on the part of Haslam (P) in the amount of $979.01.

■ **ISSUE**

Can a taxpayer who sustains a loss on a guarantee to a corporation in which he has both an employee and stockholder interest claim a business bad debt deduction when his dominant motivation in entering into the guarantees was to protect his investment interest?

■ **DECISION AND RATIONALE**

(Forrester, J.) No. A bad debt loss, deductible under IRC § 166, is created where a taxpayer sustains a loss upon payment on the guarantee of a debt, and the debtor is unable to satisfy the guarantor. Thus, Haslam (P) sustained a bad debt loss upon payment of his guarantee of Northern debts subsequent to its bankruptcy. Under § 166, business bad debt losses are deductible against ordinary income, while nonbusiness bad debt losses are deductible only as short-term capital losses. Haslam (P) argues that his losses are business bad debt losses. The IRS (D) disagrees. The character of a bad debt loss is determined by the relationship it bears to the taxpayer's trade or business. A debt will only qualify as a business bad debt if it bears a direct relationship to the taxpayer's trade or business. In this case, Haslam (P) argues that his guarantee to Northern bears such a relationship to his trade or business as an employee of that corporation. It is clear that being an employee may constitute a trade or business for the purpose of § 166. It is also clear that the debt obligations in this case were directly related to Haslam's (P) trade or business as an employee. The determination of whether the guarantees were proximately related to Haslam's (P) trade or business as an employee, however, presents a more difficult question, in that Haslam (P) also had an interest in Northern as its sole shareholder. Being an investor in a corporation does not constitute a trade or business, and losses resulting from guarantees made to protect a taxpayer's investment are not deductible as a business bad debt. [Investors, beware of the debts you guarantee!] Where a taxpayer sustains a loss on a guarantee to a corporation in which he has both an employee and stockholder interest, a proximate relationship between the taxpayer's trade or business as an employee and his loss is established only if the taxpayer's dominant motivation in entering into the guarantees was to protect the employee interest. *United States v. Generes,* 405 U.S. 93 (1972) [holding that no such motivation existed]. Haslam (P) must therefore prove that his dominant motivation in guaranteeing the loans to Northern was to protect his employment in order to establish the requisite proximate relationship. The determination of a taxpayer's dominant motivation is a factual question on which the taxpayer bears the burden of proof. In this case, Haslam (P) testified that his dominant motivation in guaranteeing loans to Northern was to protect his employment. It is our conclusion that the facts support his testimony, and accordingly we hold that his loss is deductible as a business bad debt. Unlike the taxpayer in *Generes,* Haslam (P) was a full-time employee of his corporation and he had no other employment or major source of income. From his position as an investor, it is clear that the preservation of the corporation would at best afford him some prospect of saving the $20,000 he had invested in the corporation. From his position as an employee, however, such preservation would assure his continued employment at an annual salary of approximately $15,000. In our opinion, his interest in the salary was greater than his interest in the investment. We thus decide that his dominant motivation was in retaining his employment. We decide for Haslam (P).

Analysis:

The important distinction addressed in *Haslam* is that between business and nonbusiness bad debts. The most significant difference between the two types of losses is the way in which deductions are treated. Under the statute, business bad-debt losses are deductible as ordinary losses. Nonbusiness bad debt losses, as the court points out, are treated as short-term capital losses. IRC § 166(d)(1)(B). Since ordinary income is usually taxed at a much higher rate than capital gains income, a deduction measured against ordinary income is worth more in tax savings than a similar deduction measured against capital gains income. A second difference in treatment between the two types of debts is that business debt can generate deductions upon becoming partially worthless (i.e., at least part of it is wholly uncollectible). IRC § 166(a)(2). The same is not true of nonbusiness bad debt losses—with nonbusiness bad debts, it is all or nothing. IRC § 166(d)(1)(A).

■ CASE VOCABULARY

BUSINESS BAD DEBT: A debt acquired in connection with a trade or business (investment debts are excluded).

NONBUSINESS BAD DEBT: A debt not acquired in connection with a trade or business; a personal debt or one acquired in connection with an investment.

PARTIAL WORTHLESSNESS: In the context of IRC § 166, a debt which is "recoverable only in part." There is no deduction permitted for partially worthless nonbusiness bad debts.

TOTAL WORTHLESSNESS: In the context of IRC § 166, a debt is totally worthless when there is no hope or possibility of any recovery on the debt.

Pulvers v. Commissioner

(Taxpayer Whose Property Went Down in Value) v. *(Internal Revenue Service)*
407 F.2d 838 (9th Cir. 1969)

IRC § 165(c)(3) PERMITS A DEDUCTION TO BE TAKEN IN THE EVENT OF A CASUALTY LOSS CAUSED BY FIRE, STORM, SHIPWRECK, OR OTHER CASUALTY OR THEFT

■ **INSTANT FACTS** A taxpayer tried to take a casualty deduction when his property value decreased following a landslide in the neighborhood.

■ **BLACK LETTER RULE** The term "other casualty loss" in IRC 165(c)(3) refers to casualty losses involving physical damage or loss of physical property, and not just a decrease in value.

■ **PROCEDURAL BASIS**

Certification to the Ninth Circuit Court of Appeals of a Tax Court decision denying a casualty loss deduction where the taxpayers suffered no actual loss, but simply a decrease in the value of their property.

■ **FACTS**

A landslide carried away three homes in Pulvers' (D) neighborhood, but it did not touch his home. There was no substantial impairment of ingress or egress on the street serving his home. Pulvers (D) sought to take a casualty loss deduction because the landslide decreased the value of his home (owing to the possibility that it might happen again).

■ **ISSUE**

Can a casualty loss deduction be taken when a natural disaster results in no physical damage to a piece of property, but does result in a decrease in its value?

■ **DECISION AND RATIONALE**

(Chambers, J.) No. Pulvers' (D) property value certainly went down, but we think his loss is one that Congress could not have intended to include in IRC § 165(c)(3). The specific losses named are fire, storm, shipwreck, "other casualty" and theft. Each of those surely involves physical damage or loss of the physical property. Thus, we read "other casualty," in para materia, to mean "something like those specifically mentioned." The first things that one thinks of as "other casualty losses" are earthquakes and automobile collision losses, both involving physical damage. One trouble with Pulvers' (D) construction of the statute is that the consequences of such an interpretation would be limitless. Anything depreciating the value of property would result in a deduction. [Like the neighbor's barking dog.] We will not imply that Congress intended such a thing. Pulvers' (D) argument is appealing—the ingenuity is admirable—but the language is such that we do not think Congress intended such a construction. Affirmed.

Analysis:

Pulvers serves to interpret the meaning, at least in part, of IRC § 165(c)(3), which provides that a tax deduction is allowed for "losses of property not connected with a trade or business or a transaction entered into for profit, if such losses arise from fire, storm, shipwreck, or *other casualty,* or from theft"

Pulvers v. Commissioner (Continued)

(emphasis added). In interpreting this section of the Code, *Pulvers* makes it clear that the phrase "other casualty" means something such as an earthquake or a car accident that results in physical damage or loss of property. A mere decrease in value resulting from a natural disaster or other casualty loss is not enough to allow for a § 165(c)(3) deduction.

■ **CASE VOCABULARY**

CASUALTY LOSS: In the tax arena, a loss or damaging of physical property arising from an unexpected event, such as a hurricane, flood, or tornado.

EGRESS: To exit, or a place of exit.

INGRESS: To enter, or a place of entrance.

IN PARA MATERIA: Latin phrase meaning "in the same matter," or something relating to a similar subject.

Mary Frances Allen v. Commissioner

(Taxpayer) v. *(Internal Revenue Commissioner)*
16 T.C. 163, 1951 WL 73 (1951)

THE BURDEN OF PROOF IS ON THE TAXPAYER TO SHOW THAT A § 165(c)(3) LOSS HAS OCCURRED AND THAT A DEDUCTION IS THEREFORE APPROPRIATE

■ **INSTANT FACTS** A woman whose brooch disappeared (by either theft or loss) brought an action in court protesting the IRS's decision not to allow her to take a theft deduction for the missing brooch.

■ **BLACK LETTER RULE** If the reasonable inferences from evidence presented regarding the disappearance of a valuable item point to theft, then a taxpayer is justified in taking a § 165 theft deduction.

■ **PROCEDURAL BASIS**

A taxpayer brought a claim in Tax Court contesting the IRS's decision to deny her a § 165(c) deduction.

■ **FACTS**

Allen (P) owned a brooch which disappeared while she was visiting the Metropolitan Museum of Art in New York. She has no proof of theft [but there are probabilities of theft], but only that the brooch disappeared and was never found by or returned to Allen (P). Allen (P) took a tax deduction under IRC § 165(c)(3), which the IRS (D) subsequently disallowed (causing a $1,800.16 tax deficiency).

■ **ISSUE**

Does the taxpayer bear the burden of proving a § 165(c) theft when a deduction under that code section is contested by the IRS?

■ **DECISION AND RATIONALE**

(Van Fossan, J.) Yes. Allen (P) has the burden of proof. This includes presentation of proof which reasonably leads us to conclude that the article was stolen. If the reasonable inferences from the evidence point to theft, Allen (P) is entitled to prevail. If the contrary is true, or the evidence is in "equipoise," Allen's (P) claim must fail. In this case, we cannot find as a fact that a theft occurred; in fact, the reasonable inferences from the evidence point otherwise. [Not according to the dissent.] There is no evidence as to the nature of the clasp by which Allen's (P) pin was fastened to her dress. Nor is there any evidence that she was jostled in the crowd (the usual occurrence when a theft from the person is attempted). Also, there was no testimony as to damage to her dress, which would have occurred had the brooch been properly fastened and was subsequently stolen. The inference that the brooch was merely lost is more readily drawn. However, we need not go so far. We need only hold that Allen (P), who had the burden of proof, has not established theft, a *sine qua non* to a decision in her favor. The IRS's (D) determination is sustained.

■ **DISSENT**

(Opper, J.) Based on the evidence, I would find for Allen (P) because of all the possibilities, the most probable is a loss by theft. If the evidence is believed, Allen (P) had the brooch pinned on her dress at about 4:30 in the afternoon. She was present only in well-lighted rooms so constructed that no article could reasonably be lost—especially in view of the subsequent search. At 5:00 she discovered that the brooch was missing, having in the meantime mingled with a crowd of 5,000 people preparing to leave the museum. Absolute proof by an eye witness is so improbable that the burden being imposed on taxpayers by this decision virtually repeals *pro tanto* section 23(e)(3). Ever since Appeal of Howard J. Simons, in 1 B.T.A. 351, the rule has been otherwise. The probabilities of theft have been demonstrated as completely as such circumstances could ever permit.

Analysis:

Allen stands for the proposition that, in order to take a deduction under IRC § 165(c)(3) for theft of valuable property, a taxpayer must be able to produce evidence that, according to the majority, "reasonably leads us to conclude that the article was stolen." In this case, the majority found no such evidence, while the dissent did. The dissent attacks the standard used by the majority, implying that by saying the words "reasonably leads us to conclude that the article was stolen," the majority actually means that an eyewitness is necessary. The majority never actually states that an eyewitness should be produced, however, and the tone and language of the majority opinion do not suggest that an eyewitness is required.

■ CASE VOCABULARY

EQUIPOISE: A state of equality or equilibrium.

PRO TANTO: Latin phrase meaning "as far as it goes."

CHAPTER TWENTY–FOUR

The Interrelationship of Timing and Characterization

Burnet v. Logan

Instant Facts: A taxpayer received various payments as a stockholder from her stock holdings but did not include them in her income tax reports because she claimed she had not recovered her capital investment yet.

Black Letter Rule: When the value of an installment obligation is impossible to determine, the transaction will be treated as open by the IRS and payments thereunder will be free from income tax until the owner has recouped his capital investment.

Burnet v. Logan

(Commissioner) v. *(Taxpayer)*

283 U.S. 404, 51 S.Ct. 550 (1931)

A TRANSACTION WILL BE TREATED AS "OPEN" IF IT IS IMPOSSIBLE TO DETERMINE THE FAIR MARKET VALUE OF AN INSTALLMENT OBLIGATION

■ **INSTANT FACTS** A taxpayer received various payments as a stockholder from her stock holdings but did not include them in her income tax reports because she claimed she had not recovered her capital investment yet.

■ **BLACK LETTER RULE** When the value of an installment obligation is impossible to determine, the transaction will be treated as open by the IRS and payments thereunder will be free from income tax until the owner has recouped his capital investment.

■ **PROCEDURAL BASIS**

Appeal to United States Supreme Court of a Appeals Court reversal of the Commissioner's deficiency assessment.

■ **FACTS**

From March 1, 1913 to March 11, 1916, Mrs. Logan (D) owned 250 of the 4000 shares of stock in Andrews and Hitchcock Iron Company ("Andrews"). Andrews, in turn, held 12% of the stock in Mahoning Ore and Steel Co. ("Mahoning"). Mahoning regularly mined ore from a mine and distributed it among its shareholders according to their holdings. Andrews received 12% of the ore from Mahoning. On March 11, 1916, the shareholders of Andrews sold all of their shares to Youngstown Sheet and Tube Co ("Youngstown"). Youngstown thereby became entitled to the same 12% of ore from Mahoning to which Andrews had previously been entitled. Youngstown agreed to pay a total of $2,200,000 to the shareholders and further agreed to make annual payments of $.60 for each ton of ore apportioned to it into a fund that was divided up amongst the former shareholders. The former shareholders would receive distributions of the annual payment by Youngstown according to their former stock holdings. As a result of this deal, Mrs. Logan (D) got $137,000 for her stock and became entitled to receive 250/4000th of the annual payment from Youngstown. In 1917, Mrs. Logan's (D) mother died. Her mother had owned 1,100 shares of the same stock and left ½ of her interest in the annual payments from Youngstown to Mrs. Logan (D). For estate taxation purposes, this interest was valued at $277,164.50. During the years 1917, 1918, 1919, and 1920, Mrs. Logan (D) received large annual payments for both her interest and the interest left to her by her mother. Over that period, the total amount received by Mrs. Logan (D) was $173,089.80 ($137,500.00 in cash for her stock plus $35,598.80 in annual payments). She also received sizable amounts from the interest left to her by her mother. She reported none of the payments as income. Mrs. Logan (D) claimed that her shares on March 1, 1913 were valued at more than the amount she received from the total payments. She claimed that no taxable income could be reported until the payments received equaled or exceeded the value of her shares in 1913. In 1913, her shares were worth more than the $173,089.80 she had received up until that point. Additionally, she said the payments she'd received for the interests left to her by her mother had not exceeded the valuation given them for estate taxation purposes. She claimed that she would have no income until the payments equaled or exceeded the valuation for estate taxation. Until the payments equaled the value of the interests, Mrs. Logan (D) contended that they were the recoupment of her capital investment and not taxable income. The Commissioner (P), using complicated estimates and assumptions, ruled that the obligatory annual payments from Youngstown had an ascertainable fair market value of $1,942,111.46 on March 16, 1916—the day of the sale of Andrews to Youngstown. Mrs. Logan (D) contended that the value of these payments was too speculative at the time to determine. The Commissioner (P), believing that the value of Mrs. Logan's (D) interests could be readily ascertained, assessed tax deficiencies. The Board of Tax Appeals approved the assessment. The Circuit Court of Appeals reversed, stating that it was impossible to accurately estimate the fair market value of Youngstown's agreement to pay annually $60 per ton of ore received by it. Therefore, according to the Circuit Court of Appeals, Mrs. Logan (D) was entitled to a return of her capital before having to declare the payments as income. Because the facts indicated that Mrs. Logan (D) had not yet recouped her capital, there was no taxable income to report. The Commissioner (P) appealed.

■ ISSUE

Does a promise to pay indeterminate sums of money in the future have a readily determinable fair market value?

■ DECISION AND RATIONALE

(McReynolds, J.) No. The 1916 transaction was a sale of stock. There is no need to resort to speculation, guesses or estimates to put a value on the promise to pay conditional amounts in the future. There may have been a need for valuation with respect to the mother's estate, but the same need does not arise under the tax laws. As annual payments were actually made by Youngstown, the payments could be apportioned between the return of capital and profit. The promises to pay money were totally contingent upon several facts and circumstances, and there was no way in 1916 to foretell whether those circumstances would indeed arise. The promise to pay was not capable of being valued with any certainty and was not equivalent to cash. The transaction was not a closed one. Mrs. Logan (D) might never recoup her capital from payments only conditionally promised. If and when she does recoup her capital investment, she will be accountable for any taxable income in the form of profits thereafter. She properly demanded the return of her capital investment before declaring any taxable income. The rule is that, in determining the amount of loss or gain from a transaction, there has to be subtracted from the gross proceeds the amount of the capital investment. With regard to the interest received from her mother's estate, it was valued for estate taxation purposes at $277,164.50 and was properly taxed under the estate taxation provisions. Until the payments received by Mrs. Logan (D) exceed this valuation, there will be no taxable income. Affirmed.

Analysis:

Mrs. Logan was arguing here that she shouldn't have to pay income tax on any payments she received until the payments exceeded her capital investment. That is, she wanted to break even first, and only then would she start having to declare additional payments as income. The only way she was going to be allowed to do this was if the transaction was considered open. The only way the transaction would be considered open was if it was impossible to accurately determine how much those future promised payments from Youngstown would be. If it was impossible to determine the value of those payments, then it was also impossible to say *exactly how much Mrs. Logan sold the stocks for in 1916.* Without a definite amount received as payment in the sale, the IRS couldn't figure out how much gain or loss she had. The Commissioner was arguing that it was possible to estimate the value of the future payments and get a good idea of the total amount Mrs. Logan received in the sale of her stocks. If the Court had agreed with the Commissioner, the transaction would have been considered closed and she would have been taxed accordingly on her gain. But the Court said that there were too many contingencies associated with the payments from Youngstown. There was no guarantee in 1916 that Mrs. Logan would ever receive another dime from Youngstown. For the Court, those future payments were too dependent upon other factors and too speculative to give them a firm value. It agreed with Mrs. Logan and allowed her to treat the transaction as open. The effect was that Mrs. Logan could collect payments until the sum she received equaled her capital investment, and only after that point would she have to report further payments as income.

■ CASE VOCABULARY

OPEN TRANSACTION: A type of installment sale in which payments under the sale are contingent on other factors, making it impossible to determine exactly how much the installment obligations are worth at the time of the sale.

VALUATION: A procedure by which the value of property is estimated or ascertained with certainty.

CHAPTER TWENTY–FIVE

Disallowance of Losses

McWilliams v. Commissioner

Instant Facts: A taxpayer who managed his wife's holdings and his own created tax losses by having his broker sell his wife's stocks on the open market, only to then repurchase the same amount of stocks in his name and vice versa.

Black Letter Rule: The tax code disallows losses generated by intra-family sales.

McWilliams v. Commissioner

(*Taxpayer*) v. (*IRS*)

331 U.S. 694, 67 S.Ct. 1477 (1947)

§ 267 DISALLOWS LOSSES RESULTING FROM DIRECT OR INDIRECT INTRA–FAMILY SALES

■ **INSTANT FACTS** A taxpayer who managed his wife's holdings and his own created tax losses by having his broker sell his wife's stocks on the open market, only to then repurchase the same amount of stocks in his name and vice versa.

■ **BLACK LETTER RULE** The tax code disallows losses generated by intra-family sales.

PROCEDURAL BASIS

Appeal to the Supreme Court of an Appellate Court reversal of a tax court finding of non-delinquency.

FACTS

John P. McWilliams ("McWilliams") (D) managed the independent estate of his wife and his own holdings. On several occasions in 1941, he ordered his broker to sell certain stock from one account and to buy the same number of shares of the same stock from the open market for the other. He told his broker he was trying to establish tax losses. On each occasion, the sales and purchases were accomplished through the Stock Exchange on the open market. McWilliams (D) did not know the identity of the persons buying from the accounts or selling to the accounts. The buying spouse would receive different stock certificates from those that the selling spouse had sold. However, on each occasion the buying spouse bought the same number of shares the selling spouse sold, in practically simultaneous transactions. The spouses filed separate income tax returns for these years and each claimed the losses that he or she sustained as a result of the sales at issue. The Commissioner (P) disallowed these deductions under § 24 [now § 267], which prohibits deductions for losses from sales or exchanges between family members, directly or indirectly. McWilliams (D) applied to the tax court, which held § 24 inapplicable to the situation. The Circuit Court of Appeals reversed the tax court. The Supreme Court granted certiorari due to a conflict amongst the Circuits.

ISSUE

Do reciprocal sales and purchases of stock on the open market between husband and wife fit within the § 24 (b) [§ 267] prohibition against allowance of intra-family losses?

DECISION AND RATIONALE

(Vinson, C.J.) Yes. McWilliams (D) contends that Congress did not intend § 24's prohibitions to extend to the kinds of transactions that took place here—bona fide sales made through a public market. McWilliams (D) also contends that to subject taxpayers to such a prohibition in these circumstances would be to treat husband and wife as a single individual for tax purposes. McWilliams (D) relies on the pre–1934 rule that made the deductibility of a loss turn on the good faith of the sale. Additionally, McWilliams contends that § 24 was enacted to deal with those situations where the closeness of the family relationship made it difficult to obtain the evidence necessary to show bad faith. He claims that, in the instant situation, the evidence showing good faith is easily gathered. He points out that these were bona fide sales for value on a public market, in which title was actually transferred. He also contends that § 24 applies only to sales made immediately between family members, or immediately through a controlled entity. We do not believe that Congress took so limited a view of this type of tax avoidance problem. We find that Congress enacted § 24 to overcome the difficulties of determining the validity and finality of intra-family transfers. Securities transfers have been the most common vehicle for the creation of intra-family losses. It matters not whether one spouse is purchasing the property directly from another, or by prearrangement, one spouse is selling fungible property and the other is buying the same amount of the fungible property. The problems created are the same. There are certainly evidentiary problems with regard to these transactions, but we do not believe the evidentiary problems were the only ones Congress intended to rectify by the enactment of § 24 [§ 267]. § 24 [§ 267] absolutely prohibits the allowance of losses on *any* sales between family members (as defined in the statute). The rationale behind the section is that the family members, although distinct legal entities, have common economic interests. The section prohibits loss recognition from even legally genuine intra-family transactions because of the familial relationship. It is thought that such transactions do not really result in economically genuine realizations of loss as within the family group. Congress did not deem these sorts of losses to be appropriate occasions for deductibility. The legislative history supports this conclusion. Congress apparently intended to curtail the "practice of creating losses through transactions between members of a family and close corporations" because such practices were "frequently utilized for avoiding the income tax." We conclude that § 24 [§ 267] was enacted to put an end to the artificial creation of losses by means of intra-family transfers regardless of the manner in which these transfers were accomplished. We do not find McWilliams' (D) contentions to be viable. McWilliams (D) urges us to find that § 24 [§ 267] was not intended to apply to open market transfers made via the Exchanges. Despite issues of timing, we find that § 24 [§ 267] was intended to apply absolutely to intra-family transfers. McWilliams (D) also contends that the prohibition of recognition of losses from sales "between" family members does not apply to the instant fact situation, where he and his wife both bought from and sold to unknown members of the public. We believe the statute encompasses both direct sales and indirect sales of the character involved here. To find otherwise would be to put a crippling exception into the statute that is not apparent from its wording. Affirmed.

Analysis:

McWilliams (D) was hoping the Court would give him some wiggle room under the portion of the statute that prohibits losses from "direct or indirect" intra-family transfers. He would have had to concede liability if he sold the stock directly to his wife or vice versa. He would also have been liable if he sold the stock first to an intermediary, who then sold the same stock to his wife. He was trying to claim, though, that because he sold his stock on the public market to unknown people, and his wife bought stocks on the open market from unknown people, the section did not apply to his situation. The Court, using the familiar substance over form analysis, refused to recognize a distinction. Stripped of the public market fluff, the fact is that McWilliams (D) sold three shares of X Company stock and his wife simultaneously bought three shares of X Company stock. This was the kind of "indirect" sales transaction contemplated by the statute. It was this kind of tax avoidance scheme that Congress sought to prohibit by the enactment of § 24 (b) (now § 267).

■ CASE VOCABULARY

BONA–FIDE SALES: Sales made to a good faith purchaser and for value, where title is effectively transferred.

PUBLIC MARKET: In terms of securities, generally the national and international stock markets.

CHAPTER TWENTY–SIX

Nonrecognition Provisions

Commissioner v. Crichton

Instant Facts: A woman exchanged her interest in a tract of unimproved land in the country for her children's interest in improved land in the city.

Black Letter Rule: An exchange is a "like-kind" exchange if the character of the property given and received is the same.

Leslie Co. v. Commissioner

Instant Facts: A company bought ground and built a facility on it, then sold the land and building and leased the building back for a term of 30 years plus options to renew. The company claimed a loss on the sale and the IRS disallowed the loss, calling the transaction a like kind exchange.

Black Letter Rule: A sale and leaseback arrangement for a 30–year + term is not necessarily a like kind exchange.

Harry G. Masser v. Commissioner

Instant Facts: An owner of an interstate trucking business sold the land he used for loading and unloading his trucks when the city condemned the parking lot he used to store his trucks.

Black Letter Rule: If two parcels of land make up one economic unit, the involuntary conversion of one will be an involuntary conversion of the other.

Clifton Inv. Co. v. Commissioner

Instant Facts: A real estate investment corporation involuntarily converted a six story office building and bought 80% of the Times Square Hotel as replacement property. It sought § 1033 nonrecognition of gain and the IRS balked.

Black Letter Rule: § 1033 only applies to replacement property that is similar or related in service or use.

Commissioner v. Crichton

(IRS) v. (Taxpayer)
122 F.2d 181 (5th Cir. 1941)

THE TERM "LIKE–KIND" REFERS TO THE CHARACTER OR NATURE OF THE PROPERTY AND NOT TO DIFFERENCES IN GRADE OR QUALITY

■ **INSTANT FACTS** A woman exchanged her interest in a tract of unimproved land in the country for her children's interest in improved land in the city.

■ **BLACK LETTER RULE** An exchange is a "like-kind" exchange if the character of the property given and received is the same.

■ **PROCEDURAL BASIS**

After the Commissioner assessed a deficiency, the Board disagreed and the Commissioner appealed.

■ **FACTS**

In 1936, Mrs. Crichton (D) and her children owned a tract of unimproved country land and an improved city lot. Mrs. Crichton (D) transferred to her children a 3/12 interest in the mineral rights of the country land and her children transferred to her a ½ interest in the city lot. The ½ interest in the city lot had a value of $15,357.77. The interest conveyed to the children had a cost basis of zero. Mrs. Crichton (D) treated the exchange as one of property for property under then § 112 (b) [now § 1031 (a)—like-kind exchanges]. Consequently, Mrs. Crichton (D) did not report any gain from the transaction. The Commissioner (P) determined that the exchange did not fall within § 112(b) [§ 1031(a)], found a gain of $15,357.77 to Mrs. Crichton (D) and assessed a deficiency of $628.66. The Board disagreed with the Commissioner's (P) findings. The Board thought that the exchange was "solely in kind" and redetermined the deficiency to be $86.46. The Commissioner (P) appealed, insisting that the Board wrongfully decided the question.

■ **ISSUE**

Is an exchange of unimproved land for improved land considered a "like-kind" exchange?

■ **DECISION AND RATIONALE**

(Hutcheson, Cir. J.) Yes. We agree with the Board that the exchange here was a "like-kind" exchange under the statute and Treasury Regulation 94. We believe that this is a situation where the language of the code section is "so general in its terms as to render an interpretive regulation appropriate." Indeed, the IRS has provided us with Treasury Regulation 94 to aid us in determining what types of transfers fit within § 112(b) [§ 1031(a)]. The regulation provides that no gain or loss is realized by one, other than a dealer, from an exchange of real estate for other real estate. The statute distinguishes between categories of property, i.e. real and personal. It was not intended to distinguish between parcels of real property, no matter how dissimilar. The Commissioner (P) concedes that, under Louisiana law, interests in mineral rights are real rather than personal property. As such, the exchange was an exchange of real interests in property. The Board was correct in its determination. Affirmed.

Analysis:

The non-recognition provisions of § 1031 apply only to *like-kind* exchanges. As can be seen from the instant case, the term "like-kind" has been interpreted broadly in real estate transactions. Any parcel of real estate, no matter how improved or productive, can be exchanged for another parcel of real estate. Although the IRS doesn't like it too much, dissimilarity in the grade and quality of the real estate being exchanged is not enough to take the exchange out of § 1031. However, the section does have some limitations, even with respect to real estate. For example, real estate located inside the United States is not of a like kind with real estate located outside of the United States.

■ CASE VOCABULARY

IMPROVED REAL ESTATE: Real property to which additions have been added, i.e. sewers, buildings, landscaping, etc. for the purpose of increasing its value.

LIKE KIND EXCHANGE: An exchange of property held for investment or for use in business for similar property, also to be held for investment or for use in business.

UNIMPROVED REAL ESTATE: Real property, either in its natural state or formerly improved but allowed to revert to its natural state.

Leslie Co. v. Commissioner

(Taxpayer) v. *(IRS)*

539 F.2d 943 (3d Cir. 1976)

A SALE–LEASEBACK ARRANGEMENT DOES NOT CONSTITUTE A LIKE–KIND EXCHANGE

■ **INSTANT FACTS** A company bought ground and built a facility on it, then sold the land and building and leased the building back for a term of 30 years plus options to renew. The company claimed a loss on the sale and the IRS disallowed the loss, calling the transaction a like-kind exchange.

■ **BLACK LETTER RULE** A sale and leaseback arrangement for a 30–year + term is not necessarily a like-kind exchange.

■ **PROCEDURAL BASIS**

Appeal to the United States Court of Appeals for the Third Circuit by the Commissioner of a Tax Court allowance of loss from a sale-leaseback arrangement.

■ **FACTS**

Leslie Company ("Leslie") (P) was engaged in manufacturing and distributing pressure and temperature regulators and various other parts of hot water heaters. Leslie (D) found that its facilities were lacking and determined to construct a new manufacturing plant. In March of 1967, Leslie (P) purchased land in Parsippany, on which it planned to construct the new plant. Leslie (P) was unable to procure financing to build the plant, so it entered into an agreement with Prudential Life Insurance Company ("Prudential") to build the plant, then sell the plant and land to Prudential for $2,400,000. Prudential would then lease the plant back to Leslie for a term of 30 years with two 10–year options to renew. Additionally, the lease provided that after 15 years, Leslie (P) could offer to repurchase the plant and land at five year intervals. The lease specified the purchase price at each of these intervals. [If you're just burning to know the prices—read the case!] The lease entitled Prudential to all condemnation proceeds and structural improvements, without any deduction for Leslie's (P) leasehold interest. Construction of the plant was completed in 1968 at a total cost to Leslie (P) of $3,187,414. Leslie unconditionally conveyed the plant and land to Prudential for $2,400,000, according to the terms of the agreement. On its 1968 corporate tax return, Leslie (P) claimed a loss on the sale of $787,414. The Commissioner (D) denied the loss, claiming that the sale-leaseback arrangement constituted a like-kind exchange under § 1031, and therefore the parties could recognize no loss or gain. The Commissioner (D) treated the $787,414 essentially as an expense incurred in obtaining the lease, and said that the sum had to be amortized over the term of the 30–year lease. Accordingly, the Commissioner (D) assessed corporate tax deficiencies for the years 1965, 1966 and 1968. Leslie (P) petitioned the Tax Court for a redetermination of the deficiencies assessed against it. Leslie (P) contended that the transaction was a sale, on which loss can be recognized, rather than a like-kind exchange. The Tax Court agreed with Leslie (P), holding that, to be considered an exchange, the transaction must have encompassed a reciprocal transfer of properties rather than a transfer of property for money. Because Leslie (P) received $2,400,000 as the sole consideration from Prudential for the property, the transaction was not a like-kind exchange as contemplated under § 1031. The transaction was a sale rather than a like-kind exchange and the provisions of § 1002 [allowing the recognition of loss on sales] applied. Six judges of the Tax Court dissented. The gist of both dissenting opinions was that regardless of the characterization of the transaction i.e. sale or exchange, the loss was attributable to the acquisition of the leasehold and should have been amortized over the 30–year lease term. The Commissioner (D) appealed.

■ ISSUE

Is a sale-leaseback arrangement with a lease term of 30 or more years always considered a like-kind exchange?

■ DECISION AND RATIONALE

(Garth, Cir. J.) No. The threshold question is whether this transaction constituted a sale of property or an exchange. Only if we find that the transaction was an exchange do we have to consider whether it was also a like-kind exchange. Leslie contends that the transaction was a sale. If it was a sale, then § 1031 is inapplicable and Leslie could have properly recognized the loss in the year of sale. The Tax Court's determination that the transaction was a sale was dependent upon its interpretation of applicable Treasury Regulations. Treasury Regulation § 1.1002–1(d) defines exchange as follows: "(d) Exchange. Ordinarily, to constitute an exchange, the transaction must be a reciprocal transfer of property as distinguished from a transfer of property for a money consideration only." The Tax Court found that Leslie's leasehold interest had no capital value, and consequently found that the only consideration received by Leslie for the transaction was money. Therefore, the Tax Court found that the transaction was a sale. It cited *Jordan Marsh Co. v. Commissioner* [finding that a sale-leaseback transaction similar to the instant one constituted a sale] in support of its result. The Tax Court specifically declined to consider any possible conflict between the result it reached and the Eighth Circuit decision in *Century Electric Co. v. Commissioner* [reaching the opposite conclusion and finding a sale-leaseback arrangement with a long term lease to be an exchange.] The Commissioner (D) argues that *Century Electric* should control. He contends that the only appropriate consideration is whether the conveyance of the fee title and the conveyance of the long-term leasehold were reciprocal. If so, then the transaction was a like-kind exchange. Leslie (P) urges us to adopt the reasoning of the *Jordan Marsh* court. The Eighth Circuit held in *Century Electric* that a sale-leaseback of the type here involved constituted a like-kind exchange and was governed by the nonrecognition provisions of § 1031. It based its holding solely on the finding that the sale and leaseback were reciprocal. The Eighth Circuit did not consider the value of the two interests, because it found that the Congress was uninterested in the relative values of the properties involved. By contrast, the Second Circuit, in *Jordan Marsh,* held that a similar sale-leaseback arrangement resulted in a sale on which a loss was recognized. The *Jordan Marsh* court found that the leasehold interest had no separate capital value. The court noted that, in its opinion, Congress was concerned about the inequity of forcing a taxpayer to recognize a paper gain in cases where the money was tied up in a continuing investment. The essential difference between the *Century Electric* holding and the *Jordan Marsh* holding is their respective views of the need to value the property involved in a sale-leaseback transaction. We find the reasoning of the *Jordan Marsh* court more persuasive. First, it is supported by the Commissioner's own definition of exchange under the Treasury Regulations. That definition distinguishes an exchange from a transfer of property for money. Second, we believe that, in determining whether an exchange has occurred, the fair market value of the properties involved must be ascertained. We cannot determine if a transfer was for money consideration only without first determining the fair market value of the interests involved. Here, the Tax Court found that Leslie's (P) leasehold interest had *no capital value.* In contrast, the plant and property sold had a fair market value of at least $2,400,000. Leslie (P) transferred the property to Prudential for money consideration only. The transaction was therefore a sale, and Leslie (P) was entitled to claim the loss on its tax return. Affirmed.

Analysis:

The IRS has taken the position in Treas. Reg. § 1.1031(a)–1(b), (c) that fee title to real estate is of a like-kind to a leasehold interest in real estate for a term of thirty years or more. As you can see from the instant case, some circuits have agreed with the IRS position and some have not. The IRS, for its part, has indicated that it will not follow the *Jordan Marsh* ruling when confronted with sale-leaseback transactions. Again, the IRS sometimes falls back on the "substance over form" argument to support its finding that the transactions involved really constitute an exchange. Understand that in the instant case, if the Third Circuit had agreed with the IRS, Leslie would have suffered some pretty steep conse-quences. Leslie would have had to amortize the $787,414 loss over a period of thirty years. Effectively, that would have resulted in a very small deduction for the company on its corporate tax return every year for thirty years. Instead, because the court disagreed with the IRS and found the transaction to be a *sale*, Leslie got a whopping $787,414 deduction that first year.

■ CASE VOCABULARY

AMORTIZATION: A method of spreading the relative cost of an asset over the period of its useful life, or over some other statutorily defined period.

NONRECOGNITION: A tax term providing that not all gains or losses have to be considered immediate-ly upon their occurrence, but may in some cases be deferred until a later time.

Harry G. Masser v. Commissioner

(Taxpayer/Business Owner) v. *(Internal Revenue Commissioner)*

30 T.C. 741 (1958)

WHEN TWO PARCELS OF LAND CONSTITUTE ONE ECONOMIC UNIT, THE INVOLUNTARY CONVERSION OF ONE PARCEL REPRESENTS THE INVOLUNTARY CONVERSION OF THE WHOLE ECONOMIC UNIT

■ **INSTANT FACTS** An owner of an interstate trucking business sold the land he used for loading and unloading his trucks when the city condemned the parking lot he used to store his trucks.

■ **BLACK LETTER RULE** If two parcels of land make up one economic unit, the involuntary conversion of one will be an involuntary conversion of the other.

■ **PROCEDURAL BASIS**

Petition to the Tax Court to determine whether a nonrecognition section of the code applied to this factual situation.

■ **FACTS**

Masser (P) owned an interstate trucking business. He owned two parcels of land, located across the street from one another, both of which he used to operate his business. One parcel was improved—it contained a building with offices and a bunkhouse and was the area where the trucks were loaded and unloaded. The other parcel, immediately across the street, was unimproved. Masser (P) used the unimproved lot to store and park his trucks pending loading and unloading. It was conceded that the parking area was "involuntarily converted" by Masser as a result of the threat or imminence of condemnation. Masser (P) could have retained the improved land, but the closest available replacement property for the parking area was located at least 1 and ½ miles away from the improved land. Although it was theoretically and physically possible for Masser (P) to run his operation with a parking lot located some distance away, it was economically impractical. Masser (P) would have incurred additional expenses due to the excess labor required, and it would have to manage complicated traffic problems inherent in the New York Metropolitan Area. Additionally, Masser (P) was concerned about the increased possibility of traffic accidents and cargo thefts resulting from the parking lot being a distance away from the operation. After the involuntary sale of the parking lot, Masser (P) decided in good faith and in the exercise of prudent business judgment to sell the improved land too and to use the proceeds of both sales to purchase similar property in the same locality for use as a truck terminal.

■ **ISSUE**

Does the involuntary conversion of one parcel of property justify the sale of another parcel as an involuntary conversion when both parcels together make up one economic unit?

■ **DECISION AND RATIONALE**

(Kern, J.) Yes. Although we are not aware of any authorities directly on point, we are guided by two basic principles of tax law in our decision. First, tax law is eminently practical, and second, relief provisions under the Code should be liberally construed to effectuate their purposes. The question here is whether the sale of the improved property qualified under § 1033 for nonrecognition of gain. We conclude that in these circumstances, the sale of the improved property constitutes an involuntary

---

conversion under that section. It was conceded that the parking lot was involuntarily converted due to the threat or imminence of condemnation. It is also true that the two parcels effectively constituted one economic unit. They were necessarily used together in the operation of Masser's (P) business. We believe that the section should be liberally construed to allow nonrecognition in such cases. Here, one parcel of the business was involuntarily sold and the owner, in a prudent business move, decided to sell the other and use the proceeds from both sales to obtain suitable replacement property. We think the transaction, considered as a whole, constitutes an involuntary conversion of one economic property unit within the meaning of § 1033.

Analysis:

IRC § 1033 governs when there has been a compulsory or involuntary conversion of property. A compulsory or involuntary conversion occurs if the property is stolen, totally destroyed, seized or condemned, or if it is sold under the threat of imminent seizure or condemnation. The rationale of the section is that a taxpayer should not be forced to recognize gain if he or she is forced, involuntarily, to sell the property at issue. There are prerequisites to the application of the section, however. First, gain is not recognized if the taxpayer goes out and purchases replacement property that is "similar or related in service or use." Second, if the cost of the replacement property is *less* than the proceeds received, gain is recognized to the extent of the difference. The replacement property must be purchased within the time limits contemplated by the statute (usually about two years from the involuntary conversion). Lastly, the taxpayer must elect § 1033 nonrecognition treatment.

■ CASE VOCABULARY

CONDEMNATION: A governmental taking of private property for public use, with the payment of just compensation to the owner of the property.

INVOLUNTARY CONVERSION: The total destruction, theft or seizure of property, or a sale of property under threat of seizure, reclamation or condemnation (usually by a government entity).

Clifton Inv. Co. v. Commissioner

(Nonrecognition Seeking Taxpayer) v. *(IRS)*

312 F.2d 719 (6th Cir. 1963) cert. denied 373 U.S. 921, 83 S.Ct. 1524 (1963)

TO QUALIFY FOR § 1033 TREATMENT, THE PROPERTIES INVOLVED MUST BE "REASONABLY SIMILAR IN THEIR RELATION TO THE TAXPAYER"

■ **INSTANT FACTS** A real estate investment corporation involuntarily converted a six story office building and bought 80% of the Times Square Hotel as replacement property. It sought § 1033 nonrecognition of gain and the IRS balked.

■ **BLACK LETTER RULE** § 1033 only applies to replacement property that is similar or related in service or use.

■ **PROCEDURAL BASIS**

Appeal of a Tax Court decision upholding deficiencies assessed by the Commissioner.

■ **FACTS**

Clifton Investment Company ("Clifton") (D) was a real estate investment corporation. In 1956, Clifton sold a six-story office building in Cincinnati to the City because the City was threatening to exercise its power of eminent domain. Clifton (D) held the office building for the collection of rental income from commercial tenants. Clifton (D) used the proceeds from the sale of the office building to purchase an 80% interest in a corporation that was planning to buy the Times Square Hotel in New York The purchase of the hotel was effectuated. Clifton (D) contended that the purchase of the controlling stock in the hotel corporation was an investment in property "similar or related in service or use" to the office building. Consequently, Clifton sought to elect § 1033 nonrecognition of gain in the transaction. Specifically, Clifton contended that both properties were used for investment purposes and were productive of rental incomes. The Commissioner (P) disagreed with the characterization of the transaction and held that any gain from the sale of the office building had to be recognized. The Commissioner assessed a deficiency of $19,057.09 in 1958. The Tax Court agreed with the Commissioner (P) that the properties were not "similar or related in service or use." Clifton (D) appealed.

■ **ISSUE**

Does property acquired after involuntary conversion qualify as replacement property if the relation of the taxpayer to the new property has substantially changed?

■ **DECISION AND RATIONALE**

(Boyd, D.J.) No. In order to qualify for § 1033 nonrecognition of gain, the properties must be reasonably similar in their relation to the taxpayer. The Tax Court applied the so-called "functional test" to the factual situation herein to determine the similarity of the properties. This approach takes into account only the actual end use to which the properties are put, without regard to the relation to the taxpayer. We reject the functional test as the applicable test to determine the requisite similarity necessary under § 1033. We believe that the soundest approach to this situation is the one advanced by the Second Circuit in the *Liant* decision. That is, in order for a taxpayer to obtain the benefits of § 1033 he must have a continuity of interest as to the original property and the replacement property. To determine whether this continuity exists, a court must examine a number of factors to decide if the relation of the taxpayer to the property has been changed. Factors to be considered include the extent and type of the taxpayer's management activities, the amount and kinds of services rendered by him to tenants, and the nature of the business risks associated with ownership of the properties. Each case, then is dependent on its particular facts. The ultimate use to which the properties are put does not end the inquiry. Despite the fact that the Tax Court applied the wrong test, we agree with its holdings. The record indicates that both the office building and the Times Square Hotel provided rental income to Clifton (D). However, an examination of the services required to be rendered and the managerial obligations reveals an alteration in the nature of Clifton's (D) interests. Clifton (D) itself managed the office building, but Clifton (D) procured a professional management company for management of the Times Square Hotel. The office building required only two employees while the hotel requires in excess of 130. The bulk of the rental income from the office building came from long term commercial tenants, while 96% of the rental income from the hotel came from daily guests. The services Clifton (D) is required to provide to the hotel's daily guests are vastly different from those it was required to provide to its commercial tenants. Additionally, there are significant restrictions on the types of commercial tenants the hotel will accept as compared to the relatively restriction free environment of the office building. For these reasons and more, we conclude that there is a material variance between the uses of the office building and the hotel. It is true that both properties produced rental incomes for Clifton (D). However, in making the determination of the similarity of service or use required for nonrecognition under § 1033, both that which the taxpayer receives from the property and that which the property demands from the taxpayer must be evaluated. In this case, the properties are not "similar or related in service or use" as is required under the statute. Affirmed.

■ CONCURRENCE

(Shackelford Miller, Jr., Cir. J.) Although I concur in the result reached by the majority, I believe that more emphasis should be placed upon the investment character of the properties involved. While I do not think that investment characteristics alone are sufficient to satisfy the provisions of § 1033, I note that the statute was enacted to protect persons whose property was involuntarily converted rather than to penalize them. Accordingly, I believe the provision should be construed liberally. Nevertheless, I do not think the instant situation requires reversal.

Analysis:

When property is involuntarily converted into money, as happened in the instant case, § 1033 allows an electing taxpayer nonrecognition of gain if he purchases similar property or purchases a controlling interest of qualifying corporate stock in a corporation that owns similar property. It is the latter situation that occurred in *Clifton*. "Control" implies that the taxpayer has acquired at least 80% of the total voting power or 80% of the total number of shares of all classes of stock in the corporation. As noted in the facts above, Clifton acquired 80% of the stock of the hotel corporation, thus it passed the 80% test mandated by the statute. Additionally, however, the taxpayer has to show that the replacement property is "similar or related in service or use" to the original property. It is this test that Clifton failed. Generally, the requisite similarity is determined by looking at the relationship between the taxpayer and the original property and comparing it to the relationship of the taxpayer to the replacement property. Different standards apply to those using the property for business reasons and those using the property for investment purposes only.

■ CASE VOCABULARY

EMINENT DOMAIN: A power possessed by government bodies and some private individuals or corporations with characteristics of government bodies to seize private property for public use, with the payment of just compensation. (Similar to condemnation).

QUALIFYING CORPORATE STOCK: In tax terms, the acquisition of at least 80% of a corporation's outstanding stock or 80% of the total voting power in a corporation.

CHAPTER TWENTY–SEVEN

Computations

Klaasen v. Commissioner

Instant Facts: A taxpayer with a large family brought suit against the IRS, resisting the IRS' decision that they must pay the alternative minimum tax instead of the regular tax.

Black Letter Rule: The alternative minimum tax serves to impose a tax whenever the sum of specified percentages of the excess of alternative minimum taxable income over the applicable exemption amount exceeds the regular tax for the taxable year.

Klaasen v. Commissioner

(Protesting Taxpayer) v. *(IRS Representative)*

T.C.M. (RIA) 98,241, 1998 WL 352260 (1998)

THE ALTERNATIVE MINIMUM TAX IS THE DIFFERENCE BETWEEN THE TENTATIVE MINIMUM TAX AND THE REGULAR TAX

■ **INSTANT FACTS** A taxpayer with a large family brought suit against the IRS, resisting the IRS' decision that they must pay the alternative minimum tax instead of the regular tax.

■ **BLACK LETTER RULE** The alternative minimum tax serves to impose a tax whenever the sum of specified percentages of the excess of alternative minimum taxable income over the applicable exemption amount exceeds the regular tax for the taxable year.

■ **PROCEDURAL BASIS**

Certification to the tax court of a taxpayer's disagreement with the IRS' imposition of the alternative minimum tax.

■ **FACTS**

Klaasen (P) and his wife are members of the Reformed Presbyterian Church of North America. As members of that church, Klaasen (P) and his wife have been taught that it is a great blessing to have many children. In 1994, the Klaasens (P) had ten children (they had 13 by 1998), all of whom qualified as dependents under IRC § 151(c). In 1994, Klaasen (P) properly filed an income tax return claiming 12 personal exemptions, one for each person in the family. Doing so reduced Klaasen's (P) taxable income by $29,400. In that same year, Klaasen (P) also took deductions for medical and dental expenses and for state and local taxes. Klaasen (P) did not attach Form 6251 (Alternative Minimum Tax (AMT)—Individuals), nor did he report any liability for the AMT in his Form 1040. In March of 1997, the IRS issued a notice of deficiency to Klaasen (P) for the taxable year 1994. The notice stated that Klaasen (P) was liable for the AMT. Klaasen (P) appealed the deficiency notice to the Tax Court.

■ **ISSUE**

Does the alternative minimum tax apply to large families?

■ **DECISION AND RATIONALE**

(Authoring Judge Not Indicated) Yes. IRC § 55 imposes the alternative minimum tax (AMT) which, when applicable, supersedes the regular tax. In this case, Klaasen's (P) regular tax was $5,111. Pursuant to § 55(a), the AMT is the difference between the tentative minimum tax and the regular tax. The tentative minimum tax is 26% of the excess of a taxpayer's alternative minimum taxable income (AMTI) over an exemption amount of $45,000. IRC § 55(b)(2) defines the term AMTI as the taxpayer's taxable income for the taxable year determined with the adjustments provided in § 56 and increased by the amount of items of tax preference described in § 57. Klaasen (P) had no items of tax preference in 1994. Accordingly, AMTI means Klaasen's (P) taxable income determined with the adjustments provided in § 56. Klaasen's (P) taxable income for 1994 was $34,092.47. In this case, the adjustments provided in § 56(b) are threefold. First, § 56(b)(1)(A)(ii) states that no itemized deduction for State and local taxes is allowed when computing AMT income. Second, § 56(b)(1)(B) states that in determining the amount allowable as a deduction for medical expenses, a floor of 10% applies in lieu of the regular 7.5% floor. And third, § 56(b)(1)(E) states that no personal exemptions shall be allowed in computing AMTI. The effect of these sections is to increase Klaasen's (P) taxable income by a total of $34,739.97. After taking into account these adjustments, Klaasen's (P) AMTI for 1994 equals $68,832.44. AMTI exceeds the applicable exemption amount of $45,000 by $23,832.44. Klaasen's (P) tentative minimum tax is therefore 26% of that excess, or $6,196.43. Because this amount exceeds Klaasen's (P) regular tax of $5,111, Klaasen (P) is liable for the AMT in the amount of the excess, or $1,085.43. Klaasen (P) does not challenge the mechanics of this computation. Rather, he contends that he is not liable for the AMT for two reasons. First, Klaasen (P) contends that the elimination of personal exemptions under the AMT adversely affects large families and results in an application of the AMT that is contrary to congressional intent. Second, Klaasen (P) argues that the AMT violates various constitutional rights, including the right to freedom of religion. A. Congressional Intent. We begin with Klaasen's (P) contention that he is not liable for the AMT because it was not intended to apply to his family. In this regard, Klaasen (P) emphasizes that he did not have a single item of tax preference, and that he is being unfairly saddled with the AMT simply because of the size of his family. The clearest expression of legislative intent is found in the actual language used in the statute. As the Supreme Court has stated, "There is ... no more persuasive evidence of the purpose of a statute than the words by which the legislature undertook to give expression to its wishes." *United States v. American Trucking Associations, Inc.*, 310 U.S. 534, 543 (1940). Accordingly, where, as here, a statute is clear on its face, unequivocal evidence of a contrary purpose must be demonstrable if we are to construe the statute so as to override the plain meaning of the words used therein. "The statutory scheme governing the imposition and computation of the alternative minimum tax is clear and precise, and leaves ... no room for interpretation." Okin v. Commissioner, T.C. Memo. 1985–199. Thus, there is no justification to ignore the plain language of the statute. The AMT serves to impose a tax whenever the sum of specified percentages of the excess of AMTI over the applicable exemption amount exceeds the regular tax for the taxable year. AMTI essentially means the taxpayer's taxable income for the taxable year determined with the adjustments provided in § 56 and increased by the amount of items of tax preference described in § 57. If Congress had intended to tax only tax preferences, it would have defined AMTI differently. Instead, Congress provided for a tax measured by a broader base, namely, AMTI, in which tax preferences are merely included as potential components. The foregoing analysis leads to the conclusion that the AMT is triggered by a number of factors, including the value of personal exemptions claimed on a return, and that the IRS correctly determined such tax on the facts of this case. Accordingly, because we can understand and apply the plain meaning of unambiguous statutory text, we need not defer to the legislative history. Klaasen (P) is liable for the AMT. The IRS' (D) determination of deficiency is sustained.

Analysis:

In order to prevent certain taxpayers from taking advantage of various deduction and credit provisions of the tax code that allowed them to almost wholly avoid tax, Congress enacted the Alternative Minimum Tax (AMT) in 1969. Under the law, taxpayers must pay the higher of the regular tax (computed in the regular way) and the AMT. To compute AMT liability, a taxpayer will first determine his or her alternative minimum taxable income (AMTI), which is the taxpayer's normal taxable income with certain modifications contained in IRC §§ 56 and 58 and the addition of certain "tax preference" items listed in IRC § 57. Once the AMTI is computed, it is reduced by a statutory exemption and the remainder is then taxed at a rate of either twenty-six or twenty-eight percent, which results in what is called the tentative minimum tax. When the tentative minimum tax is larger than a taxpayer's regular tax for a particular tax year, it essentially becomes the tax due for that taxpayer for that year.

■ **CASE VOCABULARY**

ALTERNATIVE MINIMUM TAX (AMT): A flat tax, usually imposed on high-income individuals and corporations, to ensure that income tax liability is not avoided by means of exclusions, deductions, and credits. The AMT is the difference between the tentative minimum tax and the regular tax when the former is higher than the later.

ALTERNATIVE MINIMUM TAXABLE INCOME (AMTI): A taxpayer's taxable income determined with the adjustments provided in IRC §§ 56 and 58, increased by the amount of those items of tax preference described in IRC § 57.

REGULAR TAX: Income tax computed on taxable income by reference to the pertinent tax table in IRC § 1.

TENTATIVE MINIMUM TAX: The amount of tax arrived at when a taxpayer's AMTI is taxed at the statutory rate of either 26 or 28 percent. When the tentative minimum tax is larger than a taxpayer's regular tax, it essentially becomes the tax due for that taxpayer for that year.